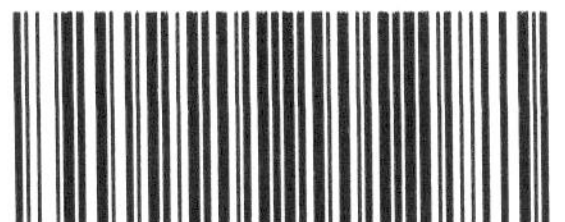

PRACTICAL ILLUSTRATIONS

Galatians - Colossians

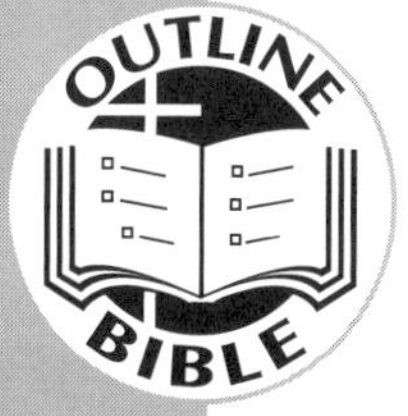

Indexed and Keyed to the Preacher's Outline and Bible®

Practical Illustrations has been compiled for God's people to use both in their personal lives and in their teaching. Leadership Ministries Worldwide wants God's people to use *Practical Illustrations.* The purpose of the copyright is to prevent the reproduction, misuse, and abuse of the material.

May our Lord bless us all as we live, preach, teach, and write for Him, fulfilling His great commission to live righteous and godly lives and to make disciples of all nations.

Please address all requests for information or permission to:
Leadership Ministries Worldwide
PO Box 21310
Chattanooga, TN 37424-0310
Ph.# (423) 855-2181 FAX (423) 855-8616 E-Mail info@outlinebible.org
http://www.outlinebible.org

Library of Congress Catalog Card Number: 2001 135014
International Standard Book Number: 1-57407-161-0

PRINTED IN THE U.S.A.

PUBLISHED BY LEADERSHIP MINISTRIES WORLDWIDE

1 2 3 4 5 01 02 03 04

LEADERSHIP MINISTRIES WORLDWIDE

DEDICATED

To all the men and women of the world who preach and teach the Gospel of our Lord Jesus Christ and to the Mercy and Grace of God

- Demonstrated to us in Christ Jesus our Lord.

"In whom we have redemption through His blood, the forgiveness of sins, according to the riches of His grace." (Eph. 1:7)

- Out of the mercy and Grace of God His Word has flowed. Let every person know that God will have mercy upon him, forgiving and using him to fulfill His glorious plan of salvation.

"For God so loved the world, that he gave His only begotten Son, that whosoever believeth in Him should not perish, but have everlasting life. For God sent not his son into the world to condemn the world, but that the world through him might be saved." (Jn. 3:16-17)

"For this is good and acceptable in the sight of God our Saviour; who will have all men to be saved, and to come unto the knowledge of the truth." (1 Tim. 2:3-4)

Practical Illustrations has been compiled for God's servants to use in their study, teaching, and preaching of God's Holy Word.

- To share the Word of God with the world.
- To help the believer, both minster and layman alike, in his understanding, preaching and teaching of God's Word
- To do everything we possibly can to lead men, women, boys and girls to give their hearts and lives to Jesus Christ and to secure the eternal life which He offers.
- To do all we can to minister to the needy of the world.
- To give Jesus Christ His proper place, the place the Word gives Him. Therefore, no work of Leadership Ministries Worldwide will ever be personalized.

7/00

About Practical Illustrations

This volume of *Practical Illustrations* covers Galatians, Ephesians, Philippians, and Colossians. You can use it alone or as a companion to other Outline Bible Resource Materials. This book is cross-indexed several ways to make it easy to find the illustrations you need. The following information is provided to help you use the book more effectively:

Each illustration includes the following elements to aid in your study and in locating the approprate illustration, whether by topic or Scripture reference:

Key Number: Each illustration is numbered. The first digit indicates the *Practical Illustrations* volume number (which is the same as the corresponding volume of *Preacher's Outline and Sermon Bible®*). The second digit indicates the order in which the illustration appears in *Practical Illustrations.*

Subject Heading: Each illustration is categorized by topic.

Scripture Reference: Each illustration is keyed to the Scripture passage it illustrates.

POSB Reference: This indicates where additional information can be found in the *Preacher's Outline and Sermon Bible®*.

Illustration Title: Each illustration is given an appropriate title.

Scripture Index **145**

Use this index if you want to find illustratons for a particular passage of Scripture.

Topical Index **159**

Use this index if you want to find illustratons on a particular topic.

PRACTICAL ILLUSTRATIONS

Galatians
Ephesians
Colossians
Philippians

9-101

Abortion

Ephesians 2:19-22

(POSB, note 4.)

Satan's Attempt to Destroy the Church

The church of Jesus Christ has a destiny to grow. Satan has opposed this growth throughout the ages. History has proven that he will stop at nothing to achieve his goal (which will ultimately fail).

Anyone who has seen a picture produced by a *fetal* ultrasound has seen one of God's greatest miracles: a growing organism; a little child who has hands and feet and a heart that beats. Today, there is a literal war that rages around the world, and the innocent children in their mothers' wombs are caught in the crossfire. There are many who desire to solve the problem of pregnancy by claiming that life begins after the fetus is born. But the fetal ultrasound allows us to see for ourselves that life begins before birth.

Throughout the history of the church, Satan has also tried to abort or destroy the body of Christ, the church. He has, in a sense, seen God's *spiritual* ultrasound and fears a church that is a growing organism. In spite of his opposition, the church will be triumphant. Jesus reminded us of this when He said **"...upon this rock I will build my church; and the gates of hell shall not prevail against it" (Mt. 16:18b).**

Look closely at the ultrasound and rejoice. The church is alive and growing!

9-102

Access to God

Ephesians 2:11-18

(POSB, note 5.)

Access to God: Through Christ Alone

Do you picture your heavenly Father as too busy running His Kingdom for you to interrupt Him? Do your needs really matter to Him?

Kay Arthur, the founder of Precept Ministries, shared this insight with a group of Bible college students concerning access to God by the believer.

A little boy bruised his knee and needed his Daddy to fix it up. With tears streaming down his face, he ran to see his Daddy. Seeing him coming, the [secretary] quickly opened the massive doors and let him into his Daddy's office.

His father was busy managing his business and was surrounded by his assistants. But in the midst of all of this, the little boy ran up to his father and climbed onto his waiting lap.

What do you think his Daddy did? Push his son aside and have him removed from the room? No! Daddy's first response was "where does it hurt and how can I make it better?"

And so it is with our Heavenly Father and us, His children. When we need our Father, we have direct access to Him through Jesus Christ. And in the middle of His managing the Kingdom, He invites us to sit in His lap to tell Him where it hurts.

9-103

Access to God

Ephesians 3:1-13

(POSB, note 3, point 3.)

The Folly of False Gods

The Christian has the great blessing of being able to approach God through Jesus Christ. Those who serve other gods do not have it so good.

Oswana lives with her tribe in Africa. Her god is not approachable at all. Being an animist (one who believes that god is in everything), she spends the majority of her time appeasing the good and bad spirits. She fails most of the time.

Prima is a good Hindu. Her access to her god is framed by three ways to salvation: 1) the way of works, 2) the way of knowledge, and 3) the way of devotion. Just in case one god is unapproachable, there are a million others from which to choose. And if she does not like the way this life is going, she can always come back as a cow.

If you are a Buddhist, your goal is not access to god but to a place called Nirvana to become a god. Your goal of life is the end of existence. The only "catch" to Nirvana is that it is impossible to get there from here. Ask Dali. He was convinced that "the eightfold path" would get him to Nirvana: simple for a god; impossible for a mortal man. In order to get to Nirvana and have access to the gods and become a god, he had to: 1) have right views, 2) have right aspirations, 3) have right speech, 4) have right conduct, 5) have the right livelihood, 6) have the right effort or endeavor, 7) have the right mindfulness, and 8) have the right meditation or concentration.

What a glorious privilege Christians have, for our goal in life is to live in the presence of our Heavenly Father both now and forever! That guarantee does not depend on how effectively we can work out the details, nor does it depend upon our becoming gods. We have access to the Father as a result of one thing and one thing only: the shed blood of Jesus Christ.

9-104

Access to God

Colossians 2:20-23

(POSB, Introduction)

Man Has No Power by Himself

Most of us are familiar with the children's story about the three little pigs and the big bad wolf. The first little pig's house was built with straw. After huffing and puffing, the big bad wolf blew it down. He then moved on to the second little pig's house which was built out of wood. As before, the wolf huffed and puffed and blew this house down also.

By this time, the big bad wolf was feeling pretty confident. Filled with pride, he approached the next house—the one made of bricks. Once again, he huffed and he puffed but nothing happened. So he huffed and he puffed and he huffed and he puffed and . . . he failed to blow down this house. He had been deceived by his previous experiences.

In the same way, man often acts like the big, bad wolf. He deceives himself into thinking he can tear down the walls that keep him from approaching God. But Scripture declares that man has no power to approach God.

"But doesn't my life count for something?" you might ask. "I go to church; I'm a good person; I do good things for people. Isn't that the basis for approaching God?" No! Man-made approaches are totally inadequate. The only way to approach God is through Jesus Christ.

9-105

ACCESS TO GOD

Galatians 1:17-24

Practicing the Presence of God

(POSB, note 1, point 2.)

It is during some of the loneliest times of our lives that we find ourselves with God. This seems to be a paradox, but it is true. For when we are truly alone, we can clearly listen to Him. And as Brother Lawrence, a humble Frenchman of the 17th century, stated so well, we can "practice the presence of God." How is that done in a practical sense?

Jeremiah Denton was a prisoner of war in North Vietnam for seven horrendous years. As one of the highest ranking American captives, he was subjected to particularly grueling torture, spending almost his entire incarceration in solitary confinement. In such a barren, brutal situation, it would be hard not to focus on the pain and [monotony]. Yet, Denton not only survived but also came back and was elected a United States senator from Alabama.

How did he survive? He stated on many occasions that an essential survival skill was quoting passages from the Bible. Internalized Scripture became the unseen sword that enabled him to fend off the cruelest weapons of the enemy. By inwardly focusing on the power of God to sustain and strengthen him, he was able to rise above the squalor of his lonely existence.[1]

9-106

ADOPTION

Ephesians 1:3-7

Adoption by God

(POSB, note 3, point 4.)

Have you ever known children who were orphans? They did not have a family, a home? In most cases, they are destined to a childhood without loving parents to care for them and to love them. It surely has to be one of the most lonely feelings known to man.

How many of us had our hearts broken for the orphans of a foreign country in misery? Some adults have been so moved by the need that they have packed suitcases and flown to other nations seeking to adopt a needy child. What kind of child did they adopt? A child who was not in their normal circle of influence. A child who could not care for himself. A child who was drained of love. A child who had no hope at all.

1 Charles Stanley. *How to Listen to God.* (Nashville, TN: Oliver-Nelson Books, 1985), p.97.

And yet, these adults wanted to make a difference and share their love with children who did not even speak the same language. These loving adults took the initiative and gave, and they continue to give to these children whom they have now legally adopted.

And so it is with our heavenly Father. When we were separated from Him due to our sin, separated because we were out of His will, we became orphans with eternal needs. We were drained of love until we met Love. And we were orphaned children with no hope until we met God the Father. But He sent us His Son to care for our every need.

God, our Father, took the initiative and came to us and adopted us just because He loved us and because He wanted to "according to the good pleasure of His will." (Eph. 1:5)

9-107

Adoption

Galatians 4:1-7

(POSB, Deeper Study: Adoption)

The Security of Being Adopted into God's Family

The single red rose placed at the front of the church was there to honor the newest member of the church family. A little boy had been born, and he would be reared by parents in a loving, Christian home.

But this little boy was fortunate in even more ways, for he had almost been aborted. The nine months in his mother's womb were spent in great uncertainty. He was conceived in sin and his mother did not want to care for him. Her options ranged from abortion to adoption. Thankfully, she chose to give the gift of life to this little baby boy.

While she was waiting to deliver, adoptive parents were sought out and secured. These willing parents *wanted* this little boy to become their own. He would be given their name. He would become their heir. He would become a legal member of their family—and would not be given away to anyone else ever again.

Our heavenly Father did the same thing for us. He has given each Christian believer His name. We have become joint-heirs with Jesus. We are in the family of God—and He will never give us away again.

Have you been adopted into His family?

9-108

Anger

Ephesians 4:25-32

(POSB, note 2, point 2.)

The Consequence of Anger

Do you know any angry people? You know, those people who are volcanoes just waiting to erupt on anyone who happens to be near. Everyone around them walks on eggshells. Practically everything that is said to them is taken personally. Take a look at such a man probably familiar to many of us.

Rusty was an angry man. The son of a stern military father, he grew up being yelled at most of the time. There was never any physical abuse, but there was verbal and emotional abuse aplenty. Rusty lived for the day when he would be old enough to leave home.

Well, he finally left home and got married while in college. He had grown up with one agenda only: never to be controlled again by anyone. His father had taught him the secret of gaining control: yell and yell a lot. All his associates kept out of his way. His new wife learned quickly never to cross him. A son was born a few years later and become a mirror-image of his father and his father before him. Another generation was being formed into the shape of anger.

How do you channel your anger? Rest assured you are making an impact on someone—either good or bad.

9-109

BACKSLIDING

Galatians 5:7-12

(POSB, Introduction)

Freedom from Worldly Attachments

A constant frustration for sailboat owners is barnacles. These tiny sea creatures attach themselves to the hull of the boat. For the sailor who wants to keep his boat in ship-shape condition, the barnacles must be removed.

If the Christian believer wants to be in the best shape, he too must be free of worldly attachments. How is this done? He must stop backsliding by scraping away the barnacles of sin until he sees the surface of the truth.

9-110

BACKSLIDING

Galatians 4:8-11

(POSB, note 3, point 2.b.)

Critical Need to Set Up Familiar Spiritual Landmarks

What things would cause a Christian believer to backslide? Perhaps some illumination will come through this story.

The boy scout was really excited about going on the annual winter camperee. With a couple feet of snow on the ground, the setting was perfect for a great weekend.

His was one of the first troops to hike in and set up camp. The boy scout, along with his troop, forged into the wilderness. Upon arrival, they set up camp and prepared for their weekend adventure.

After pitching his tent, the boy scout realized that he had left something in the bus. So, he proceeded to take the long walk back to the bus which was a few miles away. Feeling confident in his "retriever skills," he did not take care to look for the important landmarks which would show him the way back to camp.

Coming back from the bus proved to be an unplanned adventure. The confusion from other scouts setting up their own camps caused him to question which paths to take. After awhile, every path looked the same. To say that he was getting worried would be an obvious observation. "How could I have missed it? If only I could find something (or someone) familiar."

Backsliders are a lot like this confused boy scout. They forget to set familiar landmarks in place to keep themselves on track. What are those landmarks? Regular time in God's Word, frequent prayer, and accountable fellowship with other believers.

Whatever happened to that backslidden boy scout you might be wondering? Every approach to his camp ended in failure. Hours later, his scoutmaster found him and brought him back to camp. That is exactly what the Great Scoutmaster, the Good Shepherd, does for His wayward sheep. He finds them and brings them home to Himself.

9-111

BACKSLIDING
Colossians 4:7-18
(POSB, note 8.)

Warning: Backsliding Does Not Happen Suddenly

What goes through the mind of a professing believer when he turns away from Christ? How can a person who shows excitement for the things of the Lord suddenly act like none of that means anything at all? Well, backsliding does not happen suddenly.

Mike Yaconelli writes in *The Wittenburg Door*:

I live in a small, rural community. There are lots of cattle ranches around here, and every once in a while a cow wanders off and gets lost....Ask a rancher how a cow gets lost, and chances are he will reply, "Well, the cow starts nibbling on a tuft of green grass, and when it finishes, it looks ahead to the next tuft of green grass and starts nibbling on that one, and then it nibbles on a tuft of green grass right next to a hole in the fence, so it nibbles on that one and then goes on to the next tuft. The next thing you know the cow has nibbled itself into being lost."

...[Backsliders] keep moving from one tuft of activity to another, never noticing how far we have gone from home or how far away from the truth we have managed to end up.[2]

2 Craig B. Larson, Editor. *Illustrations for Preaching and Teaching.* (Grand Rapids, MI: Baker Books, 1993), p.230.

9-112

Bondage

Galatians 4:1-7

(POSB, note 1.)

Allowing the Power of the Cross to Set You Free

How often have you heard someone in your church say this: "We've always done it this way before"? People tend to be creatures of habit. Often, to our own detriment, we voluntarily give ourselves over to bondage. Instead of depending on God's divine creativity (the power of the cross), there is the tendency to get stuck on what is familiar, on whawe can create. Listen to this scenario:

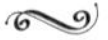

The school's talent show was filled with young children who were more than willing to dazzle the proud parents in the audience. Of all the talent on display that night, one 1st grader had the most unique talent. Standing on the stage, he held his accordion and played one note. After a few seconds, he played the same note again. For his big finish, he played that same note a third time. With his shoulders held erect and his head held high, he stated to the amused audience that he had written that song—"all by myself!"

Like this little boy, there are many Christians who get stuck on one note—and then brag about how wonderful they are doing. But it takes more than one note to make up a song. And it takes more than your best efforts to become free from the bondage of your fallen nature. It took Jesus Christ, the New Song, and His completed work on the cross to release believers from the power and bondage of the law.

Are you stuck on one note or has Christ freed you and added spiritual harmony to your life?

9-113

Bondage

Galatians 5:16-21

(POSB, Introduction)

Forced to Surrender Unconditionally

Do you experience the victorious Christian life? Or would you compare your life to that of a prisoner of war? Can your life be described by this graphic testimony?

I lost my freedom while fighting in this spiritual war. Years ago, the enemy surrounded me and forced me to surrender unconditionally. And now, I stare through the fence of bondage and long for the freedom that was once mine. Every day I listen to propaganda from the enemy. Its message is pounded into my mind that there is no hope for escape.

Often we forget how to escape from the clutches of the flesh and its lusts. But God is always faithful to remind us how to escape as well as how to *stay free*—**by walking in the Spirit of God!**

9-114

Burdens

Colossians 1:1-2

(POSB, note 5, point 2.)

Carrying Burdens in Your Own Strength

How many of us take on heavy burdens that weigh us down? Somehow, a warped sense of personal strength or obligation makes us turn away from God's grace. Instead, we try to work things out ourselves. In carrying around all these burdens, is it any wonder we get frustrated and crabby?

The little red-headed girl's attention was fixed on the hermit crab. She noticed that when he wanted to move, his shell went along for the ride. Her conclusion expressed the frustration that many Christians face: "Daddy, every time that crab moved, he had to carry his house with him."

Just imagine if we had to lift our house whenever we wanted to move! It would be impossibly heavy to bear!

Doing things in our own strength will crush us and make us crabby to everyone we know. Are you like the hermit crab: carrying the weight of the world on your back? Why not turn it over to the Lord? He alone can bear it.

9-115

Burnout

Philippians 1:1-2

(POSB, note 2.)

Serving for the Right Reasons

How many of you have ever burned out on serving? If you have, you might be able to relate to this story. Listen closely:

Burnout. Was this my reward for giving so much to so many people? I volunteered for every committee duty. "Teach a Sunday school class? Sure, and I'll help with vacation Bible school as well."

I thought that serving in a civic club would relieve me of the guilt I felt for not caring for the poor as I should. I was sure that my efforts would be praised by many. "We can change the hearts of men if we work hard and get the right politicians in office." Or so I thought. I worked hard for those people and only got a generic post-card thanking me for my vote!

Well, I've had it! From now on, I'm going to do my own thing and forget about serving other people. So many of them are ungrateful anyway, no matter how much I do.

Oswald Chambers has some words of wisdom for those who relate to this story:

If we are devoted to the cause of humanity, we shall soon be crushed and broken-hearted...but if our motive is love for God, no ingratitude can hinder us from serving our fellow men."[3]

[3] Oswald Chambers. Quoted in *The Speaker's Sourcebook* by Eleanor Doan. (Grand Rapids, MI: Zondervan Publishing Company, 1971), p.224.

9-116

Call

Ephesians 1:1-2

(POSB, note 1, point 4.)

I Surrender All

How many of you know the story behind the hymn, *I Surrender All*? All of us can relate to this story as it was told by composers J.W. Van DeVenter and W.S. Weeden.

For many years I had been studying art. My whole life was wrapped up in its pursuit and the farthest thing from my mind was active Christian service,...My dream was to become an outstanding and famous artist.... The Spirit of God was strongly urging me to give up teaching and to enter the evangelistic field but I would not yield. I still had the burning desire to be an artist. This battle raged for five years. At last the time came when I could hold out no longer and I surrendered my all—my time and my talents. It was then that a new day was ushered into my life. I became an Evangelist and discovered that deep down in my soul was hidden a talent hitherto unknown to me. God had hidden a song in my heart and touching a tender chord He caused me to sing songs I had never sung before.

I wrote "I Surrender All" in memory of the time when, after the long struggle, I had surrendered and dedicated my life to active Christian service for the Lord.

All to Jesus I surrender, All to Him I freely give;
I will ever love and trust Him, In His presence daily live.
I surrender all, I surrender all,
All to Thee, my blessed Savior, I surrender all.[4]

9-117

Changed Life

Galatians 1:10-16

(POSB, Introduction)

A Changed Life in the Political Arena

One of the greatest political minds in America in the twentieth century belonged to that of Lee Atwater. He was known for his keen political insight and for his questionable political techniques that would help his candidate win the election. Atwater considered politics to be war. Obviously, this kind of life was meant to please only his candidate. His gospel was to win at any cost, and enemies made along the way were considered to be trophies collected during the political war.

One day, his world came to a screeching halt. Atwater discovered that he had a malignant brain tumor. All of a sudden he saw life in a different light. In the remaining months of his life, he gave his heart to Christ. Lee Atwater began to share the gospel of Jesus Christ with whomever would listen (and a lot did). He also made it a point to repent for his political sins and went to each of his self-made enemies to ask for their forgiveness. It was not long after Atwater became a Christian that he left this world for a land where the only politician is the Lord Himself, the Lord Jesus Christ.

---

4 Alfred B. Smith. *Al Smith's Treasury of Hymn Histories.* (Greenville, SC: Better Music Publications, Inc., 1985), p.53.

What lessons can we draw from this example? It is a very easy thing for us to want to please men instead of God. The gospel we proclaim can become tainted with our own personal agenda. And our lifestyle can offend unless we...

- set our hearts to please God.
- proclaim the gospel of Christ.
- show that we are different by the example of our lives.

9-118

CHANGED LIFE
Galatians 2:1-10
(POSB, note 1.)

Only the Gospel Can Make a Difference

Does the gospel make a difference? To put it simply, yes, without a doubt!

A well-known preacher of the United States was asked to say a few words to a gathering in an open air meeting. At the close of his address an atheist stepped up to him and challenged him to a debate, assuring him that he would bear all the expense of renting the hall and advertising.

I accept on one condition: "When you bring with you fifty people who have been helped by your philosophy, I am ready. I will bring you hundreds who will testify to the transformation this Gospel has wrought in their lives."

Needless to say the challenger departed somewhat chagrined.[5]

Only the true gospel can produce the fruit of changed lives. No false religion or false god can bring about the love, peace, security, and salvation that the gospel can and does produce.

9-119

CHRIST, JESUS
Colossians 1:16-17
(POSB, note 4.)

Christ Holds Everything Together

Do you realize the power that Christ has at His disposal? He holds *everything* together. For example:

A guide took a group of people through an atomic laboratory and explained how all matter was composed of rapidly moving electric particles. The tourists studied models of molecules and were amazed to learn that matter is made up primarily of space. During the question period, one visitor asked, "If this is the way matter works, what holds it all together?" For that, the guide had no answer.

But the Christian has an answer: Jesus Christ! [6]

---

5 *Gospel Herald.* Walter B. Knight. *Three Thousand Illustrations for Christian Service.* (Grand Rapids, MI: Eerdmans Publishing Company, 1971), p.317.

6 Warren W. Wiersbe. *The Bible Exposition Commentary*, Vol.2. (Wheaton, IL: Victor Books, 1989), p.116.

9-120

Christ, Jesus

Colossians 1:12-14

(POSB, Introduction)

Count Your Blessings

Have you ever attempted to count the stars on a clear night? Or have you tried to count the number of waves that roll in from the sea? On that same sea shore, how long would it take you to count the grains of sand that lie before you? Obviously, an attempt to try any of these tasks would frustrate you to no end. In the same sense, when we attempt to count the total number of God's blessings, we discover there is no end. But what a wonderful frustration! Go ahead and try to count all of His blessings. You will discover what King David did:

> **"Many, O Lord my God, are the wonders which Thou hast done, and Thy thoughts toward us; there is none to compare with Thee; if I would declare and speak of them, they would be too numerous (many) to count" (Ps. 40:5, NASB).**

9-121

Christ, Jesus

Colossians 1:15

(POSB, note 1, point 3.b.)

Christ, the Express Image of God

Jesus Christ is the express image of God. Imagine if you will the excitement of a news editor who might have been living at the time of Christ.

Bernie Newsome, the religion editor, glanced at a memo on his desk from one of his investigative reporters. It read "Bernie...Rumor has it that God's Son has come in the flesh..Looks like a breaking story...Send me an artist...I think a Pulitzer Prize is ours...Please advise soon. An informer told me that God's Son would be betrayed and would not be available for any interviews." Signed, I.B. Wright.

Bernie took out his pen and wrote these instructions:

"Good work I.B. Forget the interview...Just get me his picture!" As Bernie thought about what his reporter was working on, he wondered out loud, "I wonder what God's Son is going to look like? Will He resemble His Father?" Then a thought shot through Bernie's mind—"What does His Father look like?"

Remember: Jesus Christ is the exact image of God. He shows us exactly what God looks like. If you have seen the Son, you have seen the Father. If you know the Father, then you know the Son. You cannot know one without knowing the other.

9-122

CHRIST, JESUS

Colossians 1:20-23

(POSB, Introduction)

Christ: The Reconciler of All Things

All over the world men are seeking peace. They are seeking peace with family members, neighbors, co-workers, employers, governments, and races of people. Solution after solution will be tried over and over again, but man-made solutions to peace only serve as temporary Band-Aids to terminal problems. The only lasting solution to peace is for man to find peace with God.

But what is the secret to peace with God? The secret to peace and reconciliation with God is the cross. But not an ordinary cross. Many men have died through the ages on crosses for many causes. True and lasting peace comes to men because of the *blood of the cross, because of Jesus Christ.* The blood which Jesus Christ shed upon the cross is the only thing that can bring permanent peace to the heart of man.

9-123

CHRIST, JESUS

Galatians 5:1-6

(POSB, note 1, point 2.)

Christ Has Freed the Believer from the Law's Power

Christ has freed the Christian believer from the power of the law. With that truth stated, keep yourself free. In *Who Will Deliver Us?*, Paul F.M. Zahl writes:

A duck hunter was with a friend in the wide-open land of southeastern Georgia. Far away on the horizon he noticed a cloud of smoke. Soon he could hear cracking as the wind shifted. He realized the terrible truth: a brushfire was advancing, so fast they couldn't outrun it.

Rifling through his pockets, he soon found what he was looking for—a book of matches. He lit a small fire around the two of them. Soon they were standing in a circle of blackened earth, waiting for the fire to come.

They didn't have to wait long. They covered their mouths with handkerchiefs and braced themselves. The fire came near—and swept over them. But they were completely unhurt, untouched. Fire would not pass where fire had already passed.

The law is like a brushfire. I cannot escape it. But if I stand in the burned-over place, not a hair of my head will be singed. Christ's death is the burned-over place. There I huddle, hardly believing yet relieved. The law is powerful, yet powerless: Christ's death has disarmed it.[7]

[7] Craig B. Larson, Editor. *Illustrations for Preaching and Teaching,* p.127.

9-124

CHRIST, JESUS

Galatians 4:1-7

(POSB, Introduction)

Christ Was Right on Time

Have you ever watched and waited for a pot of water to boil? It seems to take forever! In the same sense, we sometimes look at God and wonder *when is He going to do this or do that?* No matter how impatient we get, God will do things in His time—the right time.

Just as water boils at the right temperature, God sent His Son into the world at the right time. God was not early. God was not late. He was right on time...just in time!

9-125

CHRIST, JESUS

Colossians 3:1-4

(POSB, note 2, point 2.b.)

Hidden with Christ

An excellent illustration of what it means to be "hid with Christ" is this: take the index finger of your right hand and wrap your left hand around it. Say that the index finger represents you and the left hand represents Christ. Where are you (the index finger)? *In Christ.* You are hidden in Christ. When God looks at you, He sees you *hidden in Christ!*

9-126

CHRIST, JESUS

Galatians 1:1-5

(POSB, note 4, point 4.)

Christ's Work on the Cross

Have you ever given quality time to meditate on Christ's work on the cross? Take a moment now to fix your attention on Calvary...to a time...to a Savior...to *your* involvement in His crucifixion.

Rembrandt, the famous Dutch artist, painted a picture of the crucifixion. Vividly he portrayed Christ writhing in...agony on the cruel cross. Vividly he depicted the various attitudes of those about the cross toward the suffering Saviour by their facial expressions. Apart from the Saviour's death, the most significant thing about the painting is the artist's painting of himself, standing in the shadows on the edge of the onlookers. This was Rembrandt's way of saying, "I was there, too! I helped to crucify Jesus!" We, too, were there, standing with Rembrandt in the shadows![8]

We were there—standing in the shadows of our sin. Christ was there—standing in our sin, dissolving the shadows with His great love for us!

8 Walter B. Knight. *Knight's Treasury of 2,000 Illustrations.* (Grand Rapids, MI: Eerdman's Publishing Company, 1992), p.96.

9-127

Christ, Jesus
Colossians 1:15
(POSB, note 2.)

Keeping Our Focus on Christ

If we do not take great care, our focus will subtly shift away from the Lord Jesus.

Leonardo da Vinci took a friend to criticize his masterpiece of the "Last Supper," and the remark of the friend was, "The most striking thing in the picture is the cup!" The artist took his brush and wiped out the cup as he said, "Nothing in my painting shall attract more attention than the face of my Master!"[9]

How we all need to be careful of distractions! Our focus should be upon Jesus Christ, first and foremost.

9-128

Christ, Jesus
Colossians 1:18-19
(POSB, note 1, point 3.)

Christ Must Be the Head of the Church

When Jesus Christ is removed as the Head of the local church, that body will eventually die.

I heard of a poor half-witted fellow whose companion, working beside him, dropped dead. He was found trying to hold up the dead man, trying to make him stand and sit upright. Finding his effort without avail, he was saying to himself, "He needs something inside him." I suspect that is the reason we live at a poor dying rate. We need a living Spirit within to control and uphold us.[10]

How are your vital signs? Only the Head can give you a pulse. Only His Spirit will hold you up.

9-129

Christ, Jesus
Colossians 1:16-17
(POSB, note 1, point 4.)

Christ's Perfection Is All We Need

Just think for a moment: man's best attempts at perfection are *always* a dismal failure. But Christ provides all of the perfection we need.

In the town hall in Copenhagen stands the world's most complicated clock. It took forty years to build at a cost of more than a million dollars. That clock has ten faces, fifteen thousand parts, and is accurate to two-fifths of a second every three hundred years. The clock computes the time of the day, the days of the week, the months and years, and the movements of the planets for twenty-five hundred years. Some parts of that clock will not move until twenty-five centuries have passed.

---

[9] Walter B. Knight. *Three Thousand Illustrations for Christian Service*, p.379.

[10] Walter B. Knight. *Knight's Master Book of 4,000 Illustrations.* (Grand Rapids, MI: Eerdmans Publishing Company, 1956), p.289.

What is intriguing about that clock is that it is not accurate. It loses two-fifths of a second every three hundred years. Like all clocks, that timepiece in Copenhagen must be regulated by a more precise clock, the universe itself. That mighty astronomical clock with its billions of moving parts, from atoms to stars, rolls on century after century with movements so reliable that all time on earth can be measured against it.[11]

9-130

CHRIST, JESUS

Colossians 2:20-23

(POSB, Summary)

Christ Will Stand in for the Believer

Without God's involvement in our lives, we will ultimately fail every test that comes our way. His challenge to us is to *pass the test* on His terms.

Steve Winger...writes about his last college test—a final in a logic class known for its difficult exams:

> To help us on our test, the professor told us we could bring as much information to the exam as we could fit on a piece of notebook paper. Most students crammed as many facts as possible on their 8-1/2 x 11 inch sheet of paper.
>
> But one student walked into class, put a piece of paper on the floor, and had an advanced logic student stand on the paper. The advanced logic student told him everything he needed to know. He was the only student to receive an "A."

The ultimate final exam will come when we stand before God and He asks, "Why should I let you in [into heaven]?" On our own we cannot pass that exam. Our creative attempts to earn eternal life fall far short. But we have Someone who will stand in for us.[12]

9-131

CHRIST, JESUS

Galatians 3:6-14

(POSB, note 4, point 2.)

Christ: The Curse-Breaker

It took a *curse-breaker* to set us free from the guilt of sin. Jesus Christ took our place and took the curse upon Himself when He shed His blood for our sins.

In his book Written in Blood, Robert Coleman tells the story of a little boy whose sister needed a blood transfusion. The doctor had explained that she had the same disease the boy had recovered from two years earlier. Her only chance for recovery was a transfusion from someone who had previously conquered the disease. Since the two children had the same rare blood type, the boy was the ideal donor.

"Would you give your blood to Mary?" the doctor asked.

---

11 Craig B. Larson, Editor. *Illustrations for Preaching & Teaching*, p.45.

12 Selected from *Leadership Journal.* (Carol Stream, IL: Christianity Today Inc., 1994), Fall 1994, Vol.XV, #4, p.43.

Johnny hesitated. His lower lip started to tremble. Then he smiled and said, "Sure, for my sister."

Soon the two children were wheeled into the hospital room—Mary, pale and thin; Johnny, robust and healthy. Neither spoke, but when their eyes met, Johnny grinned.

As the nurse inserted the needle into his arm, Johnny's smile faded. He watched the blood flow through the tube. With the ordeal almost over, his voice, slightly shaky, broke the silence. "Doctor, when do I die?"

Only then did the doctor realize why Johnny had hesitated, why his lip had trembled when he'd agreed to donate his blood. He'd thought giving his blood to his sister meant giving up his life. In that brief moment, he'd made his great decision.

Johnny, fortunately, didn't have to die to save his sister. Each of us, however, has a condition more serious than Mary's, and it required Jesus to give not just His blood, but His life.[13]

9-132

CHRIST, JESUS

Ephesians 3:1-13

(POSB, Introduction)

The Great Mystery of Christ

Prejudice, bitterness, segregation, hatred, disturbance, hurt, anger, and division rage between people. They rage in the hearts of husbands and wives, children and parents, students and teachers, neighbors and workmen, races and religions, denominations and organizations, neighborhoods and nations. Division in all its various forms is one of the greatest problems confronting the world. It is the most serious problem confronting men, for as long as men are divided from God and from each other, there is no hope of man's ever being reconciled to God. God's eternal purpose has been to create a new body of people, a people who will love Him and each other supremely. Note that this is what is known as the great mystery of Christ.

9-133

CHRIST, JESUS

Galatians 4:1-7

(POSB, note 2, point 6.c.)

Why Christ Had to Come

There is an old missionary tale that describes in a simple fashion why Jesus Christ's coming was so important.

The missionary was becoming frustrated over his inability to communicate the gospel to his lost friend. There was a very real mental and spiritual block. One day while walking in a field they came upon an ant hill. The missionary and his friend were struck by how hard these ants were working. As they were observing this wonder of nature, they suddenly looked up to see an anteater lumbering toward them.

---

13 Craig B. Larson, Editor. *Illustrations for Preaching and Teaching,* p.25.

"Well, this looks like the end of this ant hill," remarked the missionary in a casual tone. Sorry that their study of this ant hill was coming to a close he said, "I wish I could warn them about the anteater."

"That's it!" said the missionary. "My friend, God saw man as ants who were working as hard as they knew how to. But sin was killing them. The only way to warn them was to become one of them. Then they would understand and take action to save themselves."

God sent His Son into the world as a man to save you from destruction. The choice is yours: listen to Christ and be saved, or shut your ears to Christ and be doomed to death!

9-134

CHRISTIAN EXAMPLE

Galatians 1:17-24

(POSB, note 5, point 2.)

Becoming a Living Example of Faith

There is a bottom line when a Christian believer has placed God in the center of his life. Word does get out when God blesses and people want to see living examples of faith. In the book, *Everyday Discipleship for Ordinary People*, Stuart Briscoe wrote:

One of my young colleagues was officiating at the funeral of a war veteran. The dead man's military friends wished to have a part in the service at the funeral home, so they requested the pastor to lead them down to the casket, stand with them for a solemn moment of remembrance, and then lead them out through the side door.

This he proceeded to do, but unfortunately the effect was somewhat marred when he picked the wrong door. The result was that they marched with military precision into a broom closet, in full view of the mourners, and had to beat a hasty retreat covered with confusion.

This true story illustrates a cardinal rule or two. First, if you're going to lead, make sure you know where you are going. Second, if you're going to follow, make sure that you are following someone who knows what he is doing![14]

Your testimony is either for God or against God. Will your testimony lead others to Christ and stir believers to honor Christ? Or will it lead some innocent souls down the wrong path of life and doom them for eternity?

---

[14] Stuart Briscoe. *Everyday Discipleship for Ordinary People.* (Wheaton, IL: Harold Shaw Publishers, 1988), p.25.

9-135

CHRISTIAN LIFE
Colossians 1:3-8
(POSB, Introduction)

Being Identified as a Follower of Christ

A Hindu student said to Billy Graham in Madras, "I would become a Christian if I could see one!" Said Graham, "And when he said that, he was looking at me! That was one of the greatest sermons ever preached to me!"[15]

When we claim to be a follower of Christ, we must assume that our lives will be closely examined by the lost. People will inspect our lives for any flaws and failures. How then can we be strong in the Lord? How can we keep from collapsing and from being a poor testimony before the world? By placing our faith, love, and hope in Christ and Christ alone.

9-136

CHRISTIAN LIFE
Galatians 5:13-15
(POSB, note 4.)

How to Win the Vicious Battle Within

There is an old Indian story told about two wolves, one black and one white. As the story is told, a man was describing to his chief the vicious battle that was taking place inside of him:

"Old and wise chief, help me to understand those things which trouble me." Taking a deep breath, the chief shared his insightful wisdom. "My son, inside each man are two wolves: one good and one bad. They will be in continual conflict for as long as you live. Your responsibility in this inner-struggle is to feed the good one and to starve the bad one. Your life will become an open record based upon your ability to do this."

How about you? Everyone faces an internal war between the good and the bad. Which one do you tend to feed the most? Are gossiping, criticizing, accusing, hurting, and so on a part of your daily diet? If so, then the bad in you will continue to win the battle. It is only as you starve the bad and overcome it with good (love, care, concern) that the good will take over!

9-137

CHRISTIAN LIFE
Galatians 2:1-10
(POSB, Introduction)

The Christian Life: Your Best Defense

Perry Mason, a fictional but masterful television lawyer, set the standard for every successful trial attorney. In the world of television entertainment, Perry Mason was employed to defend those who had been falsely accused.

---

15 Walter B. Knight. *Knight's Treasury of 2,000 Illustrations,* p.34.

In the course of each trial, he would carefully investigate each fiber of evidence. His search for clues enhanced his client's defense. No evidence was overlooked. When the case came to trial, Mason had to present the evidence and defend his client before a prosecutor, jury, and judge. And in the end, after the truth became known, his client would be set free.

The Apostle Paul found himself in the position of being put on trial, of having to defend both himself and the gospel. In the context of the trial, he presented every shred of evidence in defending the gospel and his part in it. In his closing arguments, he challenged each man to proclaim the gospel to men who are guilty of sin so they too might be set free.

9-138

CHRISTIAN LIFE
Ephesians 4:25-32
(POSB, Introduction)

Put Off the Garments of the Old Man

Have you heard the phrase: "Clothes make the man"? A lot of money is spent on clothes throughout the world. The right combination of clothes can enhance a person's appearance. The right color and style go a long way toward the process of dressing up properly.

Of course, the reverse is true as well. The wrong combinations, colors, and styles will be offensive to many who have different tastes.

Therefore, when a person clothes himself, he wants to be sure to put on the right clothes. If he *dresses improperly*, putting on clothes that clash or are unsuitable, he is frequently unacceptable and shunned. Most people avoid the person who is improperly dressed, for he embarrasses them. So it is with God. There are things that we are to put on and things that we are not to put on, things that are to clothe our lives and things that are not to clothe our lives. The believer's duty is to discover those things that are to be stripped off, allowing the Lord to cleanse Him through and through. The believer is to put off the garments of the old man.

9-139

CHRISTIAN LIFE
Colossians 3:1-4
(POSB, note 1.)

Risen with Christ

What does it mean to be risen with Christ? It means to be alive! Author and pastor Warren W. Wiersbe shares a graphic story from World War II.

It is possible to be alive and still live in the grave. During World War II, several Jewish refugees hid in a cemetery, and a baby was actually born in one of the graves. However, when Jesus gave us His life, He lifted us out of the grave and set us on the throne in heaven! Christ is seated at the right hand of God, and we are seated there "in Christ."[16]

Because of Christ, up from the grave *we* arose!

---

[16] Warren W. Wiersbe. *The Bible Exposition Commentary*, Vol.2, p.133.

9-140

Christian Life

Philippians 2:12-18

(POSB, note 1.)

The Need to Persevere

Have you ever felt weary and worn, as though you were being stretched and pulled in every direction at once, like you were going to snap? Listen to this man's story...

Jimmy was ready for the race of his life. His day had finally arrived. He was ready to compete at the peak of his ability and performance. As with any qualified athlete, his training had not begun on race day. It had started years ago when he committed his body to undergo a strenuous training program. Daily, he had stretched and lifted weights. He had spent hours running and running. He had disciplined his mind to eat only the right food. Many times during the process, he had wished for an easier, less painful training session and program.

Had he wanted to quit? Almost always. Was it easy? Never. Then why did he do it? As Sherlock Holmes would say: "Elementary dear Watson. He did it because he wanted to win the race!"

Are you properly preparing for the race of your life? Are you training and working out your salvation day by day with fear and trembling? Are you even in the race? God wants you to be in His training program. It worked for Paul—and it will work for you.

> **"I have fought a good fight, I have finished my course, I have kept the faith" (2 Tim. 4:7).**

Christian believer, this is a race that you have to win!

9-141

Christian Life

Galatians 5:16-21

(POSB, note 1, point 4.)

Tug of War: The Struggle Between the Flesh and the Spirit

With a little imagination, we can take a peek into our hearts and see the struggle between the flesh and the Spirit being acted out:

The scene is a field with two opposing teams tightly gripping a rope. On one side is a team that could pass for gladiators or professional football players. On the other end of the rope is you, yes, just you. In the middle of the rope is a smelly pit of slime. As you survey the situation, it doesn't take long to reach this conclusion: you will not be able to avoid the pit that lies before you. The opposing team is ready to pull you in. You need help and you need it now. "Holy Spirit! Fill me now. Hold this rope with me as I hold onto You!"

Put a real face on what we have just seen. Fred was a fine Christian man. He had a wife and a child who were gifts from God. In a weak moment, Fred was tempted to break his word to his wife and child. A woman where he worked "needed" him. Fred was such a good listener, so every time she got a chance, the woman filled his ear with her problems. The more Fred listened, the more dangerous the situation became. Before he knew what was happening, the snares were set and every step Fred took presented a threatening temptation, a temptation that could devastate him and his dear family.

Fred felt trapped! The more he struggled with this, the deeper he sank in despair. "Lord, I feel so weak. Please help me to resist—for the sake of my family. For Your sake, give me the strength to resist." At that very moment, a vibrant light entered Fred's heart and a strength that was not his own took over. In a very dramatic moment, Fred jerked the rope in his heart and pulled temptation into the pit and walked away a free man—a man who walked away in the Spirit.

Don't be left holding your rope alone. Walk in the Spirit...and pull!

9-142

Christian Life

Philippians 2:12-18

(POSB, Introduction)

Working Out Your Own Salvation

There are some Christians whose lives are like a parked car—if God wants them to move down the road of life, He will have to push them Himself.

Others live the Christian life by keeping their car washed and polished—looking good on the outside—but they fail to give proper attention to the engine that supplies the power.

Still others live the Christian life by holding the steering wheel and patiently waiting for instructions on where and when to go. Their car has been gassed up by the presence of the Holy Spirit who freely gives His power and counsel for the journey ahead: a lifetime of adventure in the Spirit!

Are you like that parked car? Waiting for a push? Or can your life be described as one that looks good on the outside but lacks power on the inside?

Your most powerful force will be to learn how to sit in God's presence and use His power and counsel to work out your salvation. The only thing the Lord will not provide is the decision to sit behind the wheel and drive. This is a choice of the will that each one of us must make.

9-143

Church

Ephesians 2:19-22

(POSB, Introduction)

God: The Light of the Church

Have you ever wondered how the film in your camera is developed into pictures? The principle is very simple: point your camera at your subject, press the shutter button, and the light will burn an impression of your subject on the film. After your film is processed by a lab, pictures appear. If everything worked (such as adjusting all the settings, holding the camera still, using the proper lighting), you have in your possession a record of your memories.

God has pointed His camera at the church, pressed the shutter, and His light has burned an impression on the film. The fruit of His labor is a photo album of six pictures of the church: a new nation, God's family, God's building, a growing organism, a worldwide temple, the local church

9-144

CHURCH

Colossians 1:18-19

(POSB, Introduction)

Keeping Chirst as the Head of the Church

When the head of a human body is removed, the conclusion is obvious: the body dies. The same is true of the church. When the true Head, Jesus Christ, is removed, the church body dies. And when a foreign head is placed on the body of Christ, a monster is created. In far too many cases, Jesus Christ has been pushed aside and removed as the Head of the church. Who has replaced Him—the pastor, the board of directors, the richest families, the denomination itself? All of these have become the head in far too many churches.

We must give Jesus Christ His proper place at the head of the church, lest we forget and create a monster.

9-145

CHURCH

Philippians 1:27-30

(POSB, Introduction)

The Marks of a Great Christian Church

Think for a moment. What is the mission of the church? The *mission* of the church is the *Great Commission.* Any church that is structured with the Great Commission in mind will become a great church.

But listen to this brief quote:

We have structured too many churches for the sake and comfort of those who already are Christians and are attending them, rather than for the sake of those people who are unchurched....Church members without question assume that the church exists to meet their needs, and they therefore structure their programs and build their facility with that in mind.[17]

Is this true? Are we missing the mark in our churches? What makes a Christian church great?

- not a large physical building, but Christian conduct
- not hi-tech programs for every age group, but honoring the gospel
- not a leader with a charismatic personality, but standing fast with courage and fearlessness...

...proclaiming the gospel to all!

[17] Robert Logan. *Beyond Church Growth.* (Grand Rapids, MI: Fleming H. Revell, 1989), p.63.

9-146

CHURCH

Philippians 1:1-2

(POSB, Introduction)

The Marks of a Healthy Church

When you take a picture with most cameras, it takes time for the film to develop. But if you have a camera that produces a picture instantly, you can see the picture develop right before your very eyes. At first glance, that picture looks pretty unimpressive—just a white square. But in a matter of moments, form and color begin to appear. Shapes become more distinctive and the color sharpens. In a few minutes, the subject of your attention has been captured on film, an eyewitness record of what has been seen.

In the same sense, every church needs time to develop into a healthy church. Some churches develop faster than others for a variety of reasons. As you look at your own church, do not become discouraged if it appears to be unimpressive and incomplete in the beginning. Christ has made an eternal commitment to the church until it becomes fully mature. Look closely, and you will begin to see Him bring shape and color—a glorious maturity—to the church.

9-147

CITIZENSHIP

Ephesians 2:19-22

(POSB, note 1, point 2.)

Citizenship in the Kingdom of Heaven

Have you ever wondered what emotions entered the mind of Columbus when he discovered a new world? After finally finding land (the island of San Salvador), we pick up his story:

They reached the southern tip of the island, just as the sun rose above the blue horizon on their larboard beam. A new day was dawning, a new era for mankind. The fears and aches of weeks at sea seemed like nothing at all now. In every heart was dawning an awareness of the enormity of what they had accomplished—and the awe of it was overwhelming! Whereas, at the time of the first sighting, there had been laughing and dancing, now they were silent, as every eye followed the coastline slowly unfolding before them, glowing in the morning sun...Columbus was the first to set foot on dry land...Their eyes filled with tears, as they knelt and bowed their heads... Columbus prayed: "O Lord, Almighty and everlasting God, by Thy holy Word Thou hast created the heaven and the earth, and the sea; blessed and glorified be Thy Name, and praised be Thy Majesty, which hath deigned to use us, Thy humble servants, that Thy holy Name may be proclaimed in this second part of the earth."[18]

Historians have called the United States a "melting pot." Ever since there has been an America to come to, people from all over the world have come to this land looking for a new start in a new land. Many families came to America with only the clothes upon their backs. Others came to America bringing with them great wealth. But no matter what their economic status or what part of the world they came from, once in America, they

[18] Peter Marshall & David Manuel. *The Light and the Glory.* (Old Tappan, NJ: Fleming H. Revell Company, 1977), p.41.

became part of a new nation. America became a picture of men, women, boys, and girls from every part of the earth—a spectacular blending of cultures and races.

There was a time when we were as strangers and foreigners to God, when we were not citizens of God's kingdom. We had no relationship and no fellowship with God and no home and no rights to citizenship in His kingdom.

But note the glorious news: we are no longer strangers and foreigners to God. Jesus Christ has brought us to God. We are now fellowcitizens with all of God's people. We now have a home and all the rights of citizenship in God's kingdom.

9-148

COMMITMENT

Philippians 1:20-26

(POSB, Introduction)

The Marks of a Great Christian Believer

There are two kinds of Christian believers: those who *marvel* and those who are *marveled at.* Greatness comes to the Christian when he becomes committed to the cause of Christ.

Athletes become great when they make a total commitment to their sport. They fully understand the need to do what is best for their bodies. Their commitments become a matter of life and death. The committed athlete enjoys a challenge but is always pressing for even greater challenges. Greatness comes to an athlete who is willing to sacrifice everything.

It is easy to settle for a marginal life. Most people do. But God has a better plan for His people: greatness—the kind that comes only through a life of commitment!

9-149

COMMITMENT

Philippians 2:25-30

(POSB, note 2.)

Signs of Reduced Committment

Today, we are living in a culture that shrinks back from commitments. Most people (by far most) are noncommittal. George Barna points this out in eight striking facts. These are...

*** Signs of Reduced Commitments In Life ***
(America, 1990)

1. The divorce rate is climbing: half of all new marriages will end in divorce.
2. Adults feel they have fewer close friends than did adults in past decades.
3. Brand loyalty in consumer purchasing studies has dropped in most product categories, and by as much as 60% in some categories.
4. The proportion of people willing to join an organization is declining in relation to churches, labor unions, political parties, clubs, and community associations.
5. Book clubs and record clubs are less likely to attract new members when multiple-year or multi-product commitments were required.

6. The percentage of adults who sense a duty to fight for their country, regardless of the cause, has dropped.
7. The percentage of people who commit to attend events but fail to show is on the rise.
8. Today's parents are less likely to believe that it is important to remain in an unhappy marriage for the sake of the children than they were 20 years ago. [19]

9-150

COMMITMENT

Philippians 2:25-30

(POSB, note 3.)

Trusting God in Difficult Circumstances

Oftentimes it is little children who come up with profound thoughts that few adults would dare express. Here is one such example:

The lawyer made it a habit to put his little girl to bed at night by reading her a Bible story. This particular night he read her the story of Job.

Her eyes lit up as she heard the story of the man who lost his wife, cattle, and children. His body was racked with sores and his friends forsook him. The little girl's summary of the events compelled her to ask her father this probing question:

"Daddy, why didn't Job sue God?"

We can curse God, blame God, abandon God, and, yes, even *try* to sue God—but a true Christian believer clings to God in time of trouble; he doesn't forsake God.

9-151

COMMUNICATION

Colossians 1:15

(POSB, Introduction.)

Duty: Do Not Guess About the Truth—Know It

A married couple can live together for years but fail to really know each other. An example: for many years a wife made her husband beets for supper because she thought he liked them. One day, the husband could take it no more and told her:

"I do not like beets; I never have liked beets; I never will like beets! Why are you fixing me beets?" Her reply, "You never told me!"

Obviously, they had failed to communicate. An assumption here, a guess there—and the truth was never known! There are many Christians whose experience with Jesus Christ is based on the "best guess" method. How are we to know the "real Jesus"? By communicating—through Scripture, through prayer, through a personal relationship with the Lord.

---

[19] George Barna. *The Frog In The Kettle.* (Venture, CA: Regal Books, 1990), p.34.

9-152

Communication

Colossians 3:1-4

(POSB, note 2, point 3.)

Duty: Know the Language of Heaven

Are you bilingual (having the ability to speak more than one language)? Have you ever thought about what language is spoken in heaven? Will you know how to communicate when you get there?

"There...is a man who tells you he intends to be in Heaven some day; but he has no wish whatever to talk on Heavenly subjects. He enjoys the world and the things of the world. His heart is set upon earthly things. Yet he tells you he has a hope of Heaven. Vain, delusive hope! They that are on their way to Heaven are cultivating an experimental acquaintance with the language and ways of a Heavenly people. Let me ask, is this the case with you?"[20]

9-153

Communication

Ephesians 5:1-7

(POSB, note 6.)

Warning: Do Not Tune Out God's Message

We cannot follow God and walk closely with Him if we are not tuned in to what He is telling us. Listen to this story.

A former park ranger at Yellowstone National Park tells the story of a ranger leading a group of hikers to a fire lookout. The ranger was so intent on telling the hikers about the flowers and animals that he considered the messages on his two-way radio distracting, so he switched it off. Nearing the tower, the ranger was met by a nearly breathless lookout, who asked why he hadn't responded to the messages on his radio. A grizzly bear had been stalking the group, and the authorities were trying to warn them of the danger.

Any time we tune out the messages God has sent us, we put at peril not only ourselves, but also those around us. How important it is that we never turn off God's saving communication! [21]

9-154

Compassion

Philippians 2:1-4

(POSB, note 4.)

The Need for Compassion

It has been said that the church is not a club for saints but a hospital for sinners who have been wounded by the scars of sin.

Look around at the people you go to church with every week. Chances are that, looking at outward appearances, all is well: the forced smile has been pasted on; the deep pain of life has been pushed temporarily aside; the convenient cliché (I'm fine! How are you? Fine. That's fine...) comes to mind.

---

20 Walter B. Knight. *Three Thousand Illustrations for Christian Service*, p.338.

21 Craig B. Larson, Editor. *Illustrations for Preaching and Teaching*, p.238.

A church that has unity is unified *because* they have compassion for people. They have made a decision to become real and vulnerable. They have discovered by their own experience that the church should be a place for compassion. It is not a place for pretending.

9-155

Cornerstone

Ephesians 2:19-22

(POSB, note 3, point 2.)

Jesus Christ, the Sure Foundation

How many of us would hire a contractor to build our dream house if he did not use *blueprints*? If he used *your* money to build *your* house without instructions? You can imagine the results: he poured the foundation in the wrong place. He put the electrical wires where the hot water pipes should go. He made your bedroom the size of a phone booth and your fireplace wound up in a closet!

You would never entrust your house to a contractor without some plan or blueprint. In the same sense, God would not build His church without a *blueprint.* Unlike the contractor above, God made certain that His foundation was sure by making Jesus Christ the chief cornerstone. Because the Cornerstone is in place, every other stone will be in line, and the church will be built the right way. This is one building project that is very important to God. His investment cost Him a lot—His own Son, the Lord Jesus Christ.

9-156

Corruption

Fighting Off Corruption with the Truth

Galatians 5:7-12

(POSB, note 3.)

Is there any way you can avoid the corruption that falsehood brings to your culture?

There once was an old fashioned prophet who came to a large city. His agenda was pretty simple, "Repent or perish!" At first glance, many of the city's residents listened to his sermons. But after a few days, they went back to doing what they wanted to do. Listening to this prophet was not on their list of things to do.

The prophet did not stop preaching. Every day he would stand in the marketplace and preach to those within the sound of his voice. A shopkeeper approached the prophet and asked, "Why are you still preaching? No one is paying any attention to you." The prophet narrowed his eyes and responded, "I'm preaching so their hardness to the gospel will not change me!"

Are you allowing a little evil into your life each day? Or do you bind yourself to God so closely that it has no room to get in? Don't compromise and allow the leaven of the world to water down the gospel. Keep on living and teaching the truth. The more you speak it and hear it, the less likely you are to be corrupted by the world.

9-157

COURAGE

Philippians 2:25-30

(POSB, Introduction)

A Man Who Was Not a Quitter

Have things ever gotten so bad that you just wanted to quit? If we are truthful, all of us would admit to having these kind of thoughts at some point in our lives. Listen to this lesson from history:

"Never, never, never give up," Winston Churchill shouted before the parliament of England. After repeating these passionate words to a post-World War II college graduating class, Churchill, the great British leader, returned to his seat and sat down.

Churchill could speak from personal experience, for he was the great prime minister of England when England was at the mercy of Hitler's German war machine. Facing seemingly insurmountable odds, he rallied his fellow countrymen to be courageous and fight for the cause of freedom.

Under Churchill's leadership, the flow of history was changed. England, with her allies, was able to overcome and defeat the Axis powers. Many historians credit Churchill's leadership as a key to victory. He refused to lose. He refused to quit. And his courage was contagious.

If you are on the edge of despair and ready to quit, remember: never, never, never give up!

9-158

COVENANT

Galatians 3:15-18

(POSB, note 4.)

God's Unchanging Promise

We should be thankful that God kept His promise after the law came to Moses. Can you imagine what life would be like if our justification came as a result of our ability to keep all of the rules—perfectly?

Booker T. Washington describes meeting an ex-slave from Virginia in his book *Up from Slavery*:

I found that this man had made a contract with his master, two or three years previous to the Emancipation Proclamation, to the effect that the slave was to be permitted to buy himself, by paying so much per year for his body; and while he was paying for himself, he was to be permitted to labor where and for whom he pleased.

Finding that he could secure better wages in Ohio, he went there. When freedom came, he was still in debt to his master some 300 hundred dollars. Notwithstanding that the Emancipation Proclamation freed him from any obligation to his master, this black man walked the greater portion of the distance back to where his old master lived in Virginia, and placed the last dollar, with interest, in his hands.

In talking to me about this, the man told me that he knew that he did not have to pay his debt, but that he had given his word to his master, and his word he had never broken. He felt that he could not enjoy his freedom till he had fulfilled his promise.[22]

[22] Craig B. Larson, Editor. *Illustrations for Preaching and Teaching*, p.190.

The law did not change this man's commitment to keep his promise. Even more so, the law did not change God's plan for man. As Malachi 3:6 says: **"I am the LORD, I change not."**

9-159

COVENANT

Galatians 3:15-18

(POSB, note 1.)

The Integrity of Keeping a Promise

We live in a society where promises are expected to be broken. Are you a man or woman of your word? Or are your commitments made or broken as a matter of convenience.

Years ago, Harry, a department manager in a retail store, seemed bound for a rise up the corporate ladder. He worked faithfully and kept his witness for Christ before all the employees. One day he was offered a position as a youth leader in a local church. With great excitement, he accepted the offer and turned in his notice to his manager, asking only for permission to select and train his replacement.

Tim was a non-Christian friend who had been an end-of-Christmas-layoff casualty. Harry had befriended Tim and had shared Christ with him. Sensing an opportunity to reach out in a practical way, Harry chose Tim to be his replacement. Harry had it all figured out: train Tim for a month and then start at the church the following day.

Either Harry was a good trainer or Tim was a fast learner or both, but somehow Tim learned the job in two weeks, not four. Observing this, the store manager called Harry into his office and said, "Harry, I can't afford to pay two men to do the same job. Are you sure this church job is a guaranteed position? If not, I'll keep you and release Tim."

There was no struggle for an answer in Harry's heart. It did not matter if the church position fell through. He had given both his job and his word to Tim. He quickly remembered the words of King David, "He swears to his own hurt, and does not change" (Ps. 15:4b, NASB). God would honor Harry's integrity. God always takes care of those who are promise-keepers. But did it make a difference to Tim? Absolutely! Years later, he is a better employee and a better Christian because of what Harry did for him.

9-160

CREATION

Galatians 3:23-29

(POSB, note 2, point 2.b.)

God Takes Delight in His Creation: The Believer

How much do you value your relationship as a child of God? Sometimes, we might be tempted to doubt God's love. We fail time and again and come up ever so short. Some of us even commit terrible sin. We wonder, "How could God forgive me? How could He love me after I've failed so much and so terribly?" Jim Adams shares this eye-opening story with us:

Perhaps no composer has captured the musical heart and soul of America as did Irving Berlin. In addition to familiar favorites such as "God Bless America" and "Easter Parade," he wrote, "I'm Dreaming of a White Christmas," which still ranks as the all-time best-selling musical score.

In an interview for the San Diego Union, Don Freeman asked Berlin, "Is there any question you've never been asked that you would like someone to ask you?" "Well, yes, there is one," he replied. "What do you think of the many songs you've written that didn't become hits? My reply would be that I still think they are wonderful."

God, too, has an unshakable delight in what—and whom—He has made. He thinks each of His children is wonderful, and whether they're a "hit" in the eyes of others or not, He will always think they're wonderful.[23]

9-161

CREATION

Colossians 1:16-17

(POSB, Introduction)

Creation: Not an Accident

The probability of life originating [by] accident is comparable to the probability of the...dictionary resulting from an explosion in a printing shop.[24]

9-162

CROSS

Galatians 1:10-16

(POSB, note 3, point 1.b.)

The Cross Keeps Us on Course

Before his conversion, Paul had done all the right things except for one: in spite of all his zeal, he was missing the mark and heading in the wrong direction. Listen to this account:

The space ship Mariner II made big headlines when it completed its thirty-six-million-mile trip towards Venus. Until then, we did not know very much about our closest neighbor.

Most of us have forgotten that Mariner II had a forerunner. Mariner I, which attempted the same journey through space...What happened that time?

Well, there was nothing wrong with Mariner I. It was just as close to perfect as the scientists could make it. But when it was launched, it went off course and missed Venus by tens of thousands of miles. Why?

It seems that in typing out the electronic instructions to the missile, someone left out a hyphen. That meant that the signals were off by one electronic impulse. And, of course, the missile behaved—or misbehaved—in accordance with the faulty instructions.

Damage? The project was held up for two years—and eighteen million taxpayer's dollars were wasted. That's what a hyphen can cost!" [25]

---

23 Selected from *Leadership Journal*, Summer, 1993, Vol.XIV #3, p.60.

24 Edwin Conklin. As quoted in *The New Speakers Source Book* by Eleanor Doan, p. 108.

25 Robert G. Lee. *Sourcebook of 500 Illustrations.* (Grand Rapids, MI: Zondervan Publishing House, 1968), p.157-158.

In Paul's former life, the thing that threw him off course was his misguided sense of self-righteousness. The "hyphen" that put him back on an accurate course for life was *the cross*. Without the cross, we will be, forever, lost in space.

9-163

CROSS

Galatians 6:11-18

All Direction Comes from the Cross

(POSB, note 3, point 4.)

If you need good directions to get somewhere, the last person you want to ask is someone who is just as lost as you. Like you, he needs a point of reference: how to get there from here.

The geographical heart of London is Charing Cross. All distances are measured from it. This spot is referred to simply as "the cross." A lost child was one day picked up by a London "bobby." The child was unable to tell where he lived. Finally, in response to the repeated questions of the bobby, and amid his sobs and tears, the little fellow said, "If you will take me to the cross I think I can find my way from there."

The cross is the point where men become reconciled to God. If we [are to] find our way to God and home we must first come to the cross.[26]

The only road sign that will do you any good is the one which points you to the cross. There, the lost can be found.

9-164

CROSS

Galatians 2:11-21

The Purpose of the Cross

(POSB, note 5, point 4.)

Have you ever thought about what it means to live a crucified life? Imagine the following happening to a church in your community:

In the middle of a church service, Jesus Christ Himself walked right down the center aisle and positioned Himself behind the pulpit. As you can imagine, there was great excitement. A pulsating electricity ran through the congregation.

On the edge of their seats, the people waited for His profound words. *"Go with Me today to the local shopping mall and witness for Me."* The assembly was a little shocked by His request. After all, their church was trying to do all the right things to bring people in. But, because it was Jesus doing the asking, they decided to do as He said and follow Him to the mall. It would be hard to witness, but they would.

The next week, Jesus came back to the church again. By this time, the congregation was feeling honored that He would take the time to visit their church. Again, they sat in their chairs, wondering what He would say. Truthfully, they expected Him to ease up after the last week's difficult challenge. *"Go with Me and comfort those who are in the prison. And*

---

[26] Walter B. Knight. *Knight's Treasury of 2,000 Illustrations*, p.97-98.

then, reach out to their families by including them in your times of fellowship." Everyone was shocked! The mall was a safe place to share with people that they would never see again (hopefully). But now, He was asking them to get close to people they had no desire to be around.

But again, because it was Jesus, they did everything He asked them to do. It was awkward at times, but they all lived through the experience, and those who were visited seemed to really appreciate their efforts.

Jesus came back to the same church for the final time the following week. By this time they had gotten used to His visits. They figured they had passed His test of faithfulness and that He would bless them and go on His way. As was His custom, He walked to the pulpit. One man in the congregation shouted out: *"Jesus, what do you want us to do for you today? We've blocked out the whole afternoon to go with you. What's it going to be today? Nursing homes, soup kitchens, visiting widows? Like I've said; we've scheduled you in for the whole afternoon."* With eyes that pierced through their shallow hearts, He said, *"Today, I want you to take up your cross, deny yourself, and follow Me up that hill and die." "Die?! We don't understand. How can we serve you if we die? We're doing a lot of good things down here and dying on a cross would ruin everything that we've done."*

Like these church people, many of us have missed the purpose of the cross. Crosses were not made for carrying...they were made for dying. There should be no pride in the number and weight of the crosses we carry. Their purpose is for our death to self.

9-165

DISCIPLINE

Philippians 2:1-4

(POSB, note 7.)

Focus on Things Above

Do you know anyone who is always focusing on himself at the expense of others? A person who is the center of his own world? Many a person has defined success as being able to climb the corporate ladder, climbing on the backs of others to get there.

To many, success is also buying a big house on the right side of town, owning new cars, and wearing the latest style of clothes that shout "Success!" But when their families fall apart or their children rebel or they fall victim to the ravages of disease, they quickly realize that material possessions matter little. The problems and tragedies of life should serve as God's wake-up call to those who focus their lives upon this world and its possessions. But will they listen? Will they lose everything that they thought was important, and lose eternity too?

What is the focus of your life? What is important to you?

> **"For what is a man profited, if he shall gain the whole world, and lose his own soul? or what shall a man give in exchange for his soul" (Mt. 16:26).**

9-166

DISCIPLINE

Philippians 3:4-16

(POSB, note 3, point 5.)

Focusing on the Prize

J. Vernon McGee paints an excellent description of focusing on the prize:

Now Paul, after receiving eternal life, is out running for a prize. Christ became everything to him, and he is running a race that he might win Christ. In what way? Well, someday he is going to appear in His presence. His whole thought is: "When I come into His presence, I don't want to be ashamed." John said that it is possible to be ashamed at His appearing.

"And now, little children, abide in him; that, when he shall appear, we may have confidence, and not be ashamed before him at his coming" (1 Jn. 2:28).

There are a great many Christians today talking about wishing Christ would come, [but] if they really knew what it will mean to them, [they] would probably like to postpone it for awhile. If you think that you can live a careless Christian life and not have to answer for it, you are entirely wrong. One of these days you will have to stand before the judgment seat of Christ to give an account of the way you lived your life. I suggest that you get down on the racecourse and start living for Him.[27]

9-167

DISOBEDIENCE

Ephesians 2:1-3

(POSB, note 3.)

Disobedience: The Path to Self-Destruction

Those who are on the path of disobedience are blinded to its destructive consequences. This point is illustrated graphically:

In 1982, "ABC Evening News" reported on an unusual work of modern art—a chair affixed to a shotgun. It was to be viewed by sitting in the chair and looking directly into the gunbarrel. The gun was loaded and set on a timer to fire at an undetermined moment within the next hundred years.

The amazing thing was that people waited in lines to sit and stare into the shell's path! They all knew that the gun could go off at point-blank range at any moment, but they were gambling that the fatal blast wouldn't happen during their minute in the chair.

Yes, it was foolhardy, yet many people who wouldn't dream of sitting in that chair live a lifetime gambling that they can get away with sin. Foolishly they ignore the risk until the inevitable self-destruction.[28]

---

27 J. Vernon McGee. *Thru The Bible*, Vol.5. (Nashville, TN: Thomas Nelson Publishers, 1983), p.316.
28 Craig B. Larson, Editor. *Illustrations for Preaching and Teaching*, p.226.

9-168

DRUNKENNESS

Ephesians 5:15-21

(POSB, note 4.)

God's Amazing Power to Deliver

Does the gospel of Jesus Christ offer any hope at all for those who have fallen into the grips of alcoholism? Listen to this exciting testimony:

As a Christian businessman concluded his business with a lawyer in St. Louis some years ago, he said to the lawyer: "I have often wanted to ask you a question, but I have been a coward." "Why?" replied the lawyer, "I did not think you were afraid of anything. What is the question?" The man said, "Why are you not a Christian?" The lawyer hung his head. He said, "Is there not something in the Bible that says no drunkard shall have any part in the Kingdom of God? You know my weakness." "That is not my question," answered the Christian man. "I am asking you why you are not a Christian?" "Well," answered the lawyer, "I cannot recall that anyone ever asked me if I were a Christian, and I am sure nobody ever told me how to become one."

Then the Christian drew his chair close to the lawyer, read him some passages from the Bible, and said simply, "Let us get down and pray."

The lawyer prayed first: "O Jesus, Thou knowest what a slave I am to drink. Here this morning Thy servant has shown me the way to God. Oh, break the power of this habit in my life."

Giving his testimony later, this drinking lawyer said, "[Write] it down big, [write] it down plain, that God broke that power instantly." Who was this drunken lawyer? Dr. C. I. Scofield, famous editor of the Scofield Reference Bible![29]

9-169

DRUNKENNESS

Ephesians 5:15-21

(POSB, note 4.)

Drunkenness: Disease or Desire?

Is liquor a disease? If it is—

1. It is the only disease that is contracted by an act of the will.
2. It is the only disease that requires a license to propagate it.
3. It is the only disease that is bottled and sold.
4. It is the only disease that requires outlets to spread it.
5. It is the only disease that produces a revenue for the government.
6. It is the only disease that provokes crime.
7. It is the only disease that is habit-forming.
8. It is the only disease that is spread by advertising.
9. It is the only disease without a germ or virus cause, and for which there is no human corrective medicine; and
10. It is the only disease that bars the patient from heaven.[30]

29 Dr. P. W. Philpott in *Evangelical Christian*. Walter B. Knight. *Knight's Treasury of 2,000 Illustrations*, p.400.

30 The Gospel Banner. Walter B. Knight. *Knight's Treasury of 2,000 Illustrations*, p.401.

9-170

ENCOURAGEMENT

Philippians 1:3-11

(POSB, note 6.)

Compassion: The Arm of Encouragement

Are you regularly in tune with the needs of other people around you?

Jackie Robinson was the first black [man] to play major league baseball. While breaking baseball's color barrier, he faced jeering crowds in every stadium.

While playing one day in his home stadium in Brooklyn, he committed an error. His own fans began to ridicule him. He stood at second base, humiliated, while the fans jeered.

Then shortstop "Pee Wee" Reese came over and stood next to him. He put his arm around Jackie Robinson and faced the crowd. The fans grew quiet. Robinson later said that arm around his shoulder saved his career.[31]

Who needs your arm around their shoulder today?

9-171

ENCOURAGEMENT

Philippians 2:1-4

(POSB, note 1.)

Receiving Signals from the Lord

Is encouragement a part of your daily agenda? "My Favorite Martian" was a popular old television program that featured an unusual fellow who could sense incoming signals around him. You see, he was equipped with a set of antennae.

God has equipped His people with a similar device: spiritual antennae that can pick up signals from the Lord, directing them to other Christians who need encouragement.

What a miracle it is that we often receive a signal, a prompting from the Lord, that burdens us to encourage and minister...

- to the sick and dying
- to the poor and needy
- to the brokenhearted and backslidden
- to the unsaved and lost
- to the lonely and empty
- to the orphan and widow

9-172

EVANGELISM

Colossians 4:2-6

(POSB, note 2.)

Staying Sensitive to the Needs of the Lost

As believers, our days are numbered. Even more important, the days of an unbeliever are also numbered. Every day God gives us opportunities to plant the seed of the gospel into the hearts of the lost.

---

31 Craig B. Larson, Editor, *Illustrations For Preaching and Teaching*, p.144.

The Christian believer must be aware of the needs of the lost. The great temptation is to get caught up in our own spiritual accolades and success. Listen to this sobering story.

The Times-Reporter of New Philadelphia, Ohio, reported in September 1985 a celebration at a New Orleans municipal pool. The party around the pool was held to celebrate the first summer in memory without a drowning at any New Orleans city pool. In honor of the occasion, two hundred people gathered, including one hundred certified lifeguards.

As the party was breaking up and the four lifeguards on duty began to clear the pool, they found a fully dressed body in the deep end. They tried to revive Jerome Moody, thirty-one, but it was too late. He had drowned surrounded by lifeguards celebrating their successful season.

I wonder how many visitors and strangers are among us drowning in loneliness, hurt, and doubt, while we, who could help them, don't realize it. We Christians have reason to celebrate, but our mission, as the old hymn says, is to "rescue the perishing." And often they are right next to us.[32]

9-173

EVANGELISM

Galatians 2:1-10

(POSB, note 4.)

Keeping Alert for "Hidden People"

As we share the gospel, we need to make sure that every aspect of our community is exposed to the love of God. No one should be left out.

There are many "hidden people" throughout the world—and some even close to home.

A great life insurance company in New York invited all its agents throughout the country to a conference in New York, and while in attendance one of the agents from the West insured the barber, the elevator man, and a waiter in the restaurant, all of whom had been employed for years by the insurance company in its great building. No one had thought to offer policies to these men in the home office building!

Exactly so. That is the reason the professional evangelist sweeps in so many; he simply improves the chance that has been there all the time. But why must we wait for him?[33]

Closer to home, who needs to hear the gospel from you *today*?

---

32 Craig B. Larson, Editor. *Illustrations for Preaching and Teaching*, p.152.

33 *Sunday School Time*. Paul Lee Tan. *Encyclopedia of 7,700 Illustrations: Signs of the Times.* (Rockville, MD: Assurance Publishers, 1985), p.1327.

9-174

FAITH

Philippians 3:4-16

(POSB, note 1, point 2.b.)

Need for a Relationship with Christ

Goodness and righteousness are not found in religion, not even in being a follower of the true religion. Yet, how many feel the very opposite? Dr. J. Vernon McGee says:

I remember hearing Dr. Carroll say, "When I was converted, I lost my religion." A great many people need to lose their religion and find Jesus Christ as Paul did. He was so revolutionized that what had been his prized possession is now relegated to the garbage can![34]

9-175

FAITH

Philippians 1:12-19

(POSB, note 1.)

The Comfort of Faith

How can we live such a victorious life in Christ, a life so victorious that it conquers even the most terrible circumstances?

The superintendent of a mission school read the text, "My yoke is easy." Turning to the children she asked, "Who can tell me what a yoke is?" A little girl said, "Something they put on the necks of animals." Then she inquired, "What is the meaning of God's yoke?" All were silent for a moment, when the hand of a four-year-old child went up and she said, "God putting his arms around our necks." What could be more comforting than that?[35]

9-176

FAITH

Galatians 3:1-5

(POSB, note 4.)

The Great Benefit of Struggling

Where is it written in the Bible that a Christian believer is exempt from suffering? Unfortunately, many have bought into a false doctrine that says "bad things don't happen to good people." We need to rest in God's ability to provide everything that we need in order to become more like Jesus.

A man found a cocoon of the emperor moth and took it home to watch it emerge. One day a small opening appeared, and for several hours the moth struggled but couldn't seem to force its body past a certain point.

Deciding something was wrong, the man took scissors and snipped the remaining bit of cocoon. The moth emerged easily, its body large and swollen, the wings small and shriveled.

---

34 J. Vernon McGee. *Thru The Bible*, Vol.5. p.314.

35 Rev. Mark Guy Pearse. Quoted in *Three Thousand Illustrations for Christian Service* by Walter B. Knight, p.69.

He expected that in a few hours the wings would spread out in their natural beauty, but they did not. Instead of developing into a creature free to fly, the moth spent its life dragging around a swollen body and shriveled wings.

The constricting cocoon and the struggle necessary to pass through the tiny opening are God's way of forcing fluid from the body into the wings. The "merciful" snip was, in reality, cruel. Sometimes the struggle is exactly what we need.[36]

9-177

FAITH

Galatians 3:23-29

(POSB, note 2, point 2.a.)

The Meaning of Being "In Christ"

Picture this illustration. Let your left hand represent Christ, and your right index finger represent you. Now, wrap your left hand around your index finger. What do you see? You see Christ, not yourself, for Christ is covering you. So it is with faith. When you believe in Jesus Christ, your faith covers you with Jesus Christ and His righteousness.

> **"For he hath made him to be sin for us, who knew no sin; that we might be made the righteousness of God in him" (2 Cor. 5:21).**

9-178

FAITH

Galatians 3:23-29

(POSB, Introduction)

Trust the Lord to Show the Way

How many times have you begun a journey, only to realize that you made a wrong turn along the way? You wanted to go south, but you were actually heading west. Sincere as you were about wanting to go south, your destination was westward bound.

Many of us have turned down the wrong road in life, trusting in our works and the law to save us. We have been sincere, but we have been sincerely wrong. How can we make a mid-course correction? By faith, we must begin to trust the Lord to show us the way.

9-179

FAITH

Galatians 3:23-29

(POSB, Summary)

What Faith Must Be

As you picture your life on a road map, are you on course, trusting and living for God? Or have you focused your eyes on the things of this world?

---

36 Craig B. Larson, Editor. *Illustrations for Preaching and Teaching*, p.266.

God is the supreme, all-knowing Guide who will never lead you astray. Listen to these lyrics from the pen of Christian song writer Michael Card:

To hear with my heart,
To see with my soul,
To be guided by a hand that I cannot hold,
To trust in a way that I cannot see,
That's what faith must be.[37]

9-180

FAITHFULNESS

Colossians 4:7-18

(POSB, note 11.)

Faithful Even unto Death

How can your faithfulness to Christ be measured? Paul remained faithful—even in the most adverse circumstances.

A Baptist pastor from Latvia spoke in Chicago. When his country was taken over by the Communists, many were put to death, and many others were sent to death, and many others were sent to a living death in slave-labor camps. The pastor spoke of the horrible persecution which Christians there have suffered. He related the story of a brave boy to whom the Communists had said, "If you will deny Christianity and Christ, we will let you live!" The brave boy had answered, "I will not deny my Lord Jesus Christ!" Thinking that they might change his steadfastness, the Communists then said, "We will give you two hours to think over your fate and change your mind." Bravely the boy replied, "I don't need two hours. I know what I will do. I will not deny my Lord Jesus Christ."

He was put to death.[38]

9-181

FAITHFULNESS

Ephesians 6:21-24

(POSB, note 1, point 3.)

Being Faithful Where Christ Puts You

An essential quality needed to be a Christian soldier is faithfulness. But no one ever said that faithfulness was an easy assignment.

In the eleventh century, King Henry III of Bavaria grew tired of court life and the pressures of being a monarch. He made application to Prior Richard at a local monastery, asking to be accepted as a contemplative [one devoted to prayer and penance] and spend the rest of his life in the monastery.

"Your Majesty," said Prior Richard, "do you understand that the pledge here is one of obedience? That will be hard because you have been a king."

"I understand," said Henry. "The rest of my life I will be obedient to you, as Christ leads you."

---

37 Written by Michael Card. *That's What Faith Must Be* (Birdwing Music [a division of The Sparrow Corporation] and BMG Songs, Inc./ Mole End Music [ASCAP], 1988).

38 Walter B. Knight. *Knight's Treasury of 2,000 Illustrations*, p.122.

"Then I will tell you what to do," said Prior Richard. "Go back to your throne and serve faithfully in the place where God has put you."

When King Henry died, a statement was written: "The king learned to rule by being obedient."

When we tire of our roles and responsibilities, it helps to remember God has planted us in a certain place and told us to be a good accountant or teacher or mother or father. Christ expects us to be faithful where he puts us, and when he returns, we'll rule together with him.[39]

9-182

FAITHFULNESS

Ephesians 6:21-24

(POSB, Introduction)

Christian Soldiers Serve Eternally

The great American General Douglas MacArthur said at the end of his illustrious career: "Old soldiers never die. They just fade away." He was speaking of mortal soldiers who would eventually die. But Christian soldiers are not like mortal soldiers who die; Christian soldiers have the promise of eternal life which will never fade away.

9-183

FALSE TEACHERS

Philippians 3:1-3

(POSB, note 3, point 3.)

Warning: Beware of False Teachers

J. Vernon McGee gives an excellent illustration on watching out for false teachers.

This is not a word of warning to the mailmen. I once had a dog that hated mailmen, and I don't know why. We changed mailmen several times during the period we had him, and he had the same attitude toward each of them. But Paul is not referring to animals in this verse. We will get some insight into his thinking by turning back to the prophecy of Isaiah who warned against the false prophets of his day: "His watchmen are blind: they are all ignorant, they are all dumb dogs, they cannot bark; sleeping, lying down, loving to slumber" [Isaiah 56:10]. Isaiah was warning the people against the false prophets who were attempting to comfort the people and were telling them that everything was find instead of warning them of coming disaster....

In Isaiah's day there were a great many false prophets who were comforting the people when they should have been warning them. Isaiah likens the false prophets to dumb dogs. You see, a good sheep dog is constantly alert to danger. If a lion or a bear makes a foray into the flock, that dog will bark like mad and run it away if he can. He gives warning of the approach of any kind of danger. But the false prophets gave no warning at all. Therefore the southern kingdom had been lulled to sleep and resented Isaiah's effort to arouse them.

---

39 Craig B. Larson, Editor. *Illustrations for Preaching and Teaching*, p.166.

America today is in the same position. We are going to sleep, my friend, under the comfortable blanket of affluence. We like the idea of comfort, of getting something for nothing, of taking it easy, of having a good day. My feeling is that somebody ought to do a little barking.

So Paul warned, "Beware of dogs"—beware of men who are constantly comforting you and are not giving you the Word of God.[40]

9-184

False Teaching

Galatians 3:1-5

(POSB, note 1, point 4.)

A Commitment to Quality

When you were in school, how many papers did you begin to write only to ball them up later and throw them away? Did you ever give up and quit? Probably not, because you needed to turn in your assignment in order to pass the class.

If you were to spend some time in the shop of a potter, you would be fascinated to watch the potter at work. Working with a lump of unimpressive clay, the potter beings to form a civilized shape on his wheel. When it appears that he is almost finished, he suddenly smashes his work back into a lump of clay again. "What a waste of time," you think to yourself. It looked pretty good from your perspective.

But, to the trained eye of the potter, an error was easily detected. Because he took pride in what he did, he was not willing to overlook the flaw. His product was going to be a cut above the rest—because of his commitment to quality.

In the same sense, the Christian believer must have the same commitment to correcting errors in the church. Is it any wonder that a lot of non-Christians are searching for answers elsewhere because the "Christian potters" are not committed to quality? We must be willing to look for and recognize false teachings and then to get rid of the erroneous teachings. Only then will our witness be pure and appealing to non-believers.

9-185

False Teaching

Galatians 1:6-9

(POSB, Introduction)

Beware the Advances of Wolves

How would your church respond if your young people were approached by an organized cult? One night at a church skating party, a group of teenagers were "befriended" by several men who asked about their spiritual lives. The teenagers were given an invitation to join them for a series of special studies. These strangers also invited themselves to the church of these teens. Like a sinister snake, this cult was moving in for the kill.

40 J. Vernon McGee. *Thru The Bible*, Vol.5, p.311.

Fortunately, the parents of these teenagers knew enough of God's Word to make them cautious and wise. After the next church service, the leaders of this cult were spoken to and in blunt terms told to leave their kids alone and to never return to their church again.

Were these adults being ugly and unloving? No. On the contrary, they were carrying out the Biblical charge: to protect the innocent sheep from the advances of wolves.

9-186

FALSE TEACHING

Galatians 1:6-9

(POSB, note 1.)

Protecting the Gospel

Why is it so important to protect the gospel from falsehood? Dave Bass shares this shocking story:

Every day, striking incidents are accumulating in the experience of overseas missionaries and North American Christians alike:

The candidate for elder in an independent suburban church in the Midwest sat with the board for his interview. From all the church's appearances—doctrinal statement, sermons, worship, teaching—he had no reason to doubt that this was a solid, biblical church. In discussing his qualifications, however, he discovered that he was chosen partly because his astrological sign was in harmony with those of the board members. They urged him to pray for a "spirit guide" who would give him wisdom in his new office. They said he could expect to benefit from "deep" teachings from the elders themselves. Now the man understood why a friend had earlier declined the position and had been reluctant to discuss it.[41]

9-187

FALSE TEACHING

Galatians 2:1-10

(POSB, note 2.)

Keeping Your Heart in Tune with Christ

Throughout the ages, men have attempted to improve the gospel. Some call it old-fashioned. Others want to repackage it in order to make it *more relevant for today*. And there are some who want to change it by replacing it with something else altogether.

In composing a "new gospel," these people convince themselves that they are right on key. But to a trained ear, the obvious is apparent: this vain rendition is as flat as a pancake!

When Lloyd C. Douglas, author of The Robe and other novels, was a university student, he lived in a boarding house, says Maxie Dunnam in Jesus' Claims—Our Promises. Downstairs on the first floor was an elderly, retired music teacher, now infirm and unable to leave the apartment.

41 Selected from *Christianity Today*. (Carol Stream, IL: Christianity Today, Inc. April 29, 1991), p.14.

Douglas said that every morning they had a ritual they would go through together. He would come down the steps, open the old man's door, and ask, "Well, what's the good news?"

"The old man would pick up his tuning fork, tap it on the side of his wheelchair, and say, "That's middle C! It was middle C yesterday; it will be middle C tomorrow; it will be middle C a thousand years from now. The tenor upstairs sings flat, the piano across the hall is out of tune, but my friend, that is middle C!

The old man had discovered one thing upon which he could depend, one constant reality in his life, one "still point in a turning world."[42]

We live in a world filled with a variety of noises. But, there is still only one middle C, only one gospel of Jesus Christ. Make certain that your song is in tune with Him!

9-188

FALSE TEACHING

Colossians 2:1-7

(POSB, note 3.)

Why Is False Teaching So Appealing?

What makes false teaching attractive to so many people? If it is so destructive, how can it be so appealing to people? Rick Green writes:

A former policeman...told me about being on duty during an ice storm. The ice was a half-inch thick on every tree in the area. He was called to a site where the ice and falling branches had caused a power line to come down; his duty was to keep people away from the area.

"There was a small tree near the fallen power line," he said, "the kind with a short trunk and lots of long thin branches. While that fallen power line was crackling and popping with electricity, it was throwing out sparks through the branches of that small tree. The sparks would reflect off the ice-covered branches sending out a rainbow of glimmering colors. I stood there and watched, and wondered how anything so beautiful could be so deadly."[43]

Like any other sin, false teaching can look good and sound good. But a mature, believer (one whose faith is grounded in God's Word) is able to see beyond the outer appearance and discern the truth.

42 Craig B. Larson, Editor. *Illustrations for Preaching and Teaching*, p.27.

43 *Ibid.*, p.257.

9-189

FELLOWSHIP

Philippians 1:3-11

(POSB, note 4, point 2.)

The Benefits of Christian Fellowship

Becoming a part of a church fellowship will expand your life. In the following quote, David Bryant challenges the church to unite for the cause of world missions.

World missions cannot happen without a vital, growing, global community of disciples who burn with the fire of a world vision. Christians aren't meant to be a collection of spectators....We're not to sit by passively waiting for the Kingdom to suddenly materialize before our eyes. The Church is the agent of God's worldwide purpose. We're to be more like a caravan of ambassadors, going forth to bless the families of the earth, than a royal entourage basking in the sunlight of God's love for us.[44]

9-190

FORGIVENESS

Colossians 2:11-12

(POSB, note 2, point 1.)

Christ Has Cleansed the Believer's Heart

A good story is told of old Thomas K. Beecher, who could not bear deceit in any form. Finding that a clock in his church was habitually too fast or too slow, he hung a placard on the wall above it, reading in large letters: "Don't blame my hands—the trouble lies deeper."

That is where the trouble lies with us when our hands do wrong, or our feet, or our lips, or even our thoughts. The trouble lies so deep that only God's miracle power can deal with it. Sin indeed goes deep; but Christ goes deeper.[45]

Thank God! Jesus has the power to remove the grossness of sin by cutting it out of our hearts.

9-191

FORGIVENESS

Colossians 3:12-14

(POSB, note 8.)

Forgiveness: The Power to Set People Free

Many of us remember the "Watergate" episode that nearly tore America apart in the early 1970's. President Richard Nixon had just resigned in disgrace and the new President, Gerald Ford, granted Nixon a free, full, and absolute pardon.

Many Americans struggled with that decision. President Ford did the very thing that God wants each of us to do when someone hurts us: we need to forgive the person and go on with our lives.

---

[44] David Bryant. *In the Gap.* (Madison, WI: Inter-Varsity Missions, 1981), p.109-110.

[45] *Christian Witness.* Walter B. Knight. *Three Thousand Illustrations for Christian Service,* p.368.

In a portion of Ford's statement he said, "My conscience tells me clearly and certainly that I cannot prolong the bad dreams that continue to reopen a chapter that is closed. My conscience tells me that only I, as President, have the constitutional power to firmly shut and seal this book." [46]

And so it is with the Christian believer. When we put on the garment of forgiveness, we have the power to set people free.

9-192

FORGIVENESS
Philippians 3:4-16
(POSB, note 3, point 2)

Forgiveness Sets Us Free from the Past

The believer should be future-oriented, "forgetting those things which are behind." Please keep in mind that in Bible terminology, "to forget" does not mean "to fail to remember." Apart from senility, hypnosis, or a brain malfunction, no mature person can forget what has happened in the past. We may wish that we could erase certain bad memories, but we cannot. "To forget" in the Bible means "no longer to be influenced by or affected by." When God promises, "And their sins and iniquities will I remember no more" [Hebrews 10:17], He is not suggesting that He will conveniently have a bad memory! This is impossible with God. What God is saying is, "I will no longer hold their sins against them. Their sins can no longer affect their standing with Me or influence My attitude toward them."[47]

9-193

FORGIVENESS
Colossians 1:12-14
(POSB, Summary)

Sins Are Remembered No More

As far as the east is removed from the west,
My sins are remembered no more;
Forever my soul is at perfect rest,
My sins are remembered no more.

Forgiven, forgotten, all cleansed in the Blood,
My sins are remembered no more;
Atoned for by Jesus in Calv'ry's flood,
My sins are remembered no more.[48]

[46] Paul Lee Tan. *Encyclopedia of 7,700 Illustrations: Signs of the Times*, p.459.
[47] Warren W. Wiersbe. *The Bible Exposition Commentary*, Vol.2, p.89.
[48] Walter B. Knight. *Three Thousand Illustrations for Christian Service*, p.290.

9-194

FULLNESS OF GOD

Ephesians 3:14-21

(POSB, note 7.)

Prayer is the Method for Being Filled

Picture a glass filled half way with water. Is the glass of water half full or half empty? Some people would say half full; others half empty. Full is a matter of perspective in this case. Some Christians are content with either condition of being half full or half empty.

But the praying believer is not content with a partial filling of God. His heart's cry is "fill me up!" Prayer gives the Christian the passion needed to seek the fullness of God. **"O taste and see that the Lord is good" (Ps. 34:8).**

9-195

GENTLENESS

Philippians 4:1-5

(POSB, note 4, point 2.)

Strength under Control

Have you wanted to flatten, put down, or squash someone lately? You feel the person has had it coming for a long time and your patience has run out? Listen to this story:

The classroom became steamy as the heated debate grew increasingly intense. The professor was a meek-looking sort of fellow, short in stature but long on patience.

The arguing student had the audacity to try and prove the mild-mannered professor wrong. Brains were not a gift of this particular student for two reasons:

- One, he had all the facts about the subject mixed up—he was just flat-out wrong.
- Two, he was challenging a man who was a leading authority in the field.

Finally, having heard enough, the professor spoke sharply: "I know enough about this subject to blow you out of the water."

The class sat in absolute silence, waiting for a pen to drop.

Then in a soft voice, the professsor humbly apologized to the class for his outburst. "I had no right to say what I did."

What the professor said that day spoke volumes, picturing exactly what God expects from His followers. God wants followers who are gentle: followers who have mastered the art of "strength under control."

9-196

GIVING

Philippians 4:10-19

(POSB, Introduction)

Examine the Strength of Your Giving

Would you consider yourself to be a generous person—a giver? See if this shoe fits. C.S. Lewis remarked:

If our expenditure on comforts, luxuries, amusements, etc., [is equal to] those with the same income as our own, we are probably giving away too little. If our charities do not at all pinch or hamper us...they are too small. There ought to be things we should like to do and cannot do because our charitable expenditure excludes them.[49]

What does the Bible say about giving? A lot! One such area is the giving of money to meet the needs of ministers and missions or the spread of the gospel to the world. Have you examined the strength of *your* giving lately?

9-197

GIVING

Philippians 4:10-19

(POSB, note 1.)

A Spiritual Checkup

Do you give until it hurts or do you hurt when you give? Have you had a spiritual checkup lately? Listen carefully to this illustration:

When you go to a doctor for your annual checkup, he or she will often begin to poke, prod, and press various places, all the while asking, "Does it hurt? How about this?"

If you cry out in pain, one of two things has happened. Either the doctor has pushed too hard, without the right sensitivity, or, more likely, there's something wrong, and the doctor will say, "We'd better do some more tests. It's not supposed to hurt there!"

So it is when ministers preach on financial responsibility, and certain members cry out in discomfort, criticizing the message and the messenger. Either the pastor has pushed too hard, or perhaps there's something wrong. In that case, I say, "My friend, we're in need of the Great Physician because it's not supposed to hurt there."[50]

---

49 R. Kent Hughes. *Discipines of a Godly Man.* (Wheaton, IL: Crossway Books, 1991), p.179.

50 Craig B. Larson, Editor. *Illustrations for Preaching and Teaching*, p.157.

9-198

Giving

Philippians 4:10-19

(POSB, note 2, point 1.)

Achieving Contentment through Giving

Lehman Strauss says:

In those early days of my Christian experience I could not see how some Christians I knew could be content with so little of this world's goods. I sincerely trust that I am learning the secret. From what I see about me I do not hesitate to say that it is a secret many Christians have yet to learn. Paul needed to learn it. He said, "I have learned...." The lesson of contentment was one he learned by degrees in varying circumstances. As a young unbelieving Jew, he had no want insofar as this world's possessions are concerned. He did not always know the divine provision of satisfaction, but after he was saved he came to learn it, not in the academic classroom, but as the result of a lengthy experience of trials and discipline. "I have learned" is the language of a good student. Have you learned to be satisfied with your place and position and possessions in this life?[51]

9-199

Godly Examples

Philippians 3:17-21

(POSB, Introduction)

Your Example Speaks Volumes

How many times have we heard parents tell their children, "Don't do as I do; just do as I say"? Unfortunately, we hear the same conversation take place in the church. It has been said that the clearest sermon spoken is spoken by our actions. Where are the teachers of the faith: those men and women who instruct by a godly example?

Your life is a sermon. What kind of example are you setting for those who follow you?

9-200

Gospel

Ephesians 6:10-20

(POSB, note 5, point 3.)

The Soldier's Shoes

Lehman Strauss makes a statement about this point that startles the mind of modern man:

The soldier's shoes are not the dancing slippers of this world or the lounging slippers of the slothful, but the shoes of the Christian warrior who knows Christ and makes Him known.[52]

51 Lehman Strauss. *Devotional Studies in Philippians.* (Neptune, NJ: Loizeaux Brothers, 1959), p.321.

52 Lehman Strauss. *Galatians and Ephesians.* (Neptune, NJ: Loizeaux Brothers, 1957), p.232f.

9-201

GRACE

Galatians 6:11-18

(POSB, note 4.)

Bind Your Fate to the Grace of God

The choice is clear: either we choose a life that is bound to the law and its legalism, or we choose to bind our fate to the grace of God.

Lillie Baltrip is a good bus driver. In fact, according to the Fort Worth Star-Telegram of June 17, 1988, the Houston school district nominated her for a safe-driving award. Her colleagues even trusted her to drive a busload of them to an awards ceremony for safe drivers. Unfortunately, on the way to the ceremony, Lillie turned a corner too sharply and flipped the bus over, sending herself and sixteen others to the hospital for minor emergency treatment.

Did Lillie, accident free for the whole year, get her award anyway? No. Award committees rarely operate on the principle of grace. How fortunate we are that even when we don't maintain a spotless life-record, our final reward depends on God's grace, not on our performance![53]

9-202

GRACE

Philippians 1:1-2

(POSB, note 5, point 1.)

The Need for Grace

D.L. Moody, a famous evangelist of a former day, made this statement while preaching:

It is well that man cannot save himself; for if a man could...work his own way to Heaven, you would never hear the last of it. Why, if a man happens to get a little ahead of his fellows and scrapes a few thousand...dollars together, you'll hear him boast of being a self-made man. I've heard so much of this sort of talk that I am sick and tired of the whole business; and I am glad that...in Heaven we will never hear anyone bragging of how he worked his way to get there.[54]

9-203

GRACE

Ephesians 2:8-10

(POSB, Introduction)

The Need for the Master Craftsman

As you browse through the employment section of a newspaper's classified ads, you will usually find a variety of entries to meet almost any need. Here is one you *will not* see, but any one of us might have placed at sometime in our lives:

---

53 Craig B. Larson, Editor. *Illustrations for Preaching and Teaching*, p.101.

54 From *Mid-Continent*. Quoted in *Three Thousand Illustrations for Christian Service* by Walter B. Knight, p.326.

WANTED: MASTER CRAFTSMAN NEEDED TO REMODEL DAMAGED LIFE. Current life has been damaged beyond normal repairs due to original sin. Owner has tried a variety of ways to correct the problem but has failed every time. The qualified applicant must have the following:

1. Must have own tools.
2. Must be willing to work .
3. Must have impeccable references.
4. Must have a previous successful track record with similar restorations.
5. Must be willing to work for nothing. Owner cannot pay anything.

The owner will be willing to work for the Master Craftsman upon successful completion of his remodeled life.

There is an immediate need to fill this position.

Call 1-800-REMODEL for an appointment.

This classified ad closely resembles the cry of every Christian prior to salvation. Our damaged lives are beyond human repair, and all of our own efforts to correct the problem have failed.

Thankfully, the Master Craftsman, our Lord Jesus, was qualified to answer our ad. He had all of the tools needed to save us. He was willing to provide the work needed to save us. He was referred to us by His Father. His track record is all of the other saints that have gone before us. Finally, He would not accept any payment for our salvation. As the great hymn reminds us, **"Jesus paid it all. All to Him I owe. Sin had left a crimson stain. He washed it white as snow"** (*Jesus Paid it All.* Text by Elvina M. Hall).

9-204

HEART

Colossians 3:15-17

(POSB, Introduction)

The Heart Must be Empowered by the Holy Spirit

When Dr. Christian Bernard performed the first human heart transplant, the medical world basked in the glow of human achievement. Sick and dying people were given hope that in receiving a brand new heart, their lives would be extended.

As great as this is, it pales in comparison to what God has done for His followers. He has been in the heart transplant business for a much longer time and, unique to His surgery, His patients live forever.

When a new life enters the world, a new heart enters the world too. There is no life apart from a physical heart. So it is with the believer: the believer receives a new heart when he receives a new life in Christ. The heart of the new life *is Christ.*

9-205

HEAVEN

Ephesians 1:19-23

(POSB, note 3.)

Heaven: A Customized Place

Do you ever imagine what heaven will be like? If you are a Christian believer, there will be a special place waiting just for you.

Joe Thompson was a master at his trade. Time and time again people would marvel at his talents. Joe's job was to customize passenger vans. He would take a van with only four wheels and an engine to craft a beautiful vehicle for its proud owner.

Joe had a real gift of being able to see the potential while staring at the present. Where others saw only a shell, Joe saw a customized van. But even greater than that: he could build what he saw—a van especially customized for its owner.

That is exactly what Jesus has done for us:

> **"In my Father's house are many mansions: if it were not so, I would have told you. I go to prepare a place for you. And if I go and prepare a place for you, I will come again, and receive you unto myself; that where I am, there ye may be also" (Jn. 14:2-3).**

The word "prepare" literally means to customize. Jesus has taken a shell and is building a place according to your heart's desire. It will be perfect. Just for you.

Need a customized job? Joe can help you with your van, but only Jesus can help you with your eternal home.

9-206

HEAVEN

Philippians 1:27-30

(POSB, note 1.)

The Glorious Benefits of Heaven

Have you ever traveled to another country? For those who have, they understand the need for a passport. If you travel abroad, one of your most valuable possessions is your passport. Your passport validates your citizenship, permits you to travel across international borders, grants you all the rights as a citizen of your *home country*—if you should ever need help from your embassy or consulate. Your passport has another important feature: it allows you to come home.

So it is with our *heavenly passport.* Being sealed by the Holy Spirit is for us a precious possession. His work in our hearts validates the fact that our citizenship is in heaven. We are just passing through this world: in it, but not of it.

Because we belong to Him, He has given us His Kingdom and all of its rights. When we need help in this world, He invites us to call upon Him for help. Finally, having a heavenly passport grants us immediate access to the Father—whenever we need Him (which is all day long). And when He calls us home for good, forever, our heavenly passport (the redemptive work of His Son) will allow us to walk through heaven's gates with a song of rejoicing!

9-207

Heaven

Ephesians 6:21-24

(POSB, note 2, point 2.)

This World Is Not Home to the Believer

When God's grace rests upon us, it helps put everything we experience here on earth in a better perspective. Listen to this vivid illustration from the pen of Ray Stedman and his book, *Talking to My Father*:

An old missionary couple had been working in Africa for years, and they were returning to New York City to retire. They had no pension; their health was broken; they were defeated, discouraged, and afraid. They discovered they were booked on the same ship as President Teddy Roosevelt, who was returning from one of his big-game hunting expeditions.

No one paid attention to them. They watched the fanfare that accompanied the President's entourage, with passengers trying to catch a glimpse of the great man.

As the ship moved across the ocean, the old missionary said to his wife, "Something is wrong. Why should we have given our lives in faithful service for God in Africa all these many years and have no one care a thing about us? Here this man comes back from a hunting trip and everybody makes much over him, but nobody gives two hoots about us."

"Dear, you shouldn't feel that way," his wife said.

"I can't help it; it doesn't seem right."

When the ship docked in New York, a band was waiting to greet the President. The mayor and other dignitaries were there. The papers were full of the President's arrival, but no one noticed this missionary couple. They slipped off the ship and found a cheap flat on the East side, hoping the next day to see what they could do to make a living in the city.

That night the man's spirit broke. He said to his wife, "I can't take this; God is not treating us fairly."

His wife replied, "Why don't you go in the bedroom and tell that to the Lord?"

A short time later he came out from the bedroom, but now his face was completely different. His wife asked, "Dear, what happened?"

"The Lord settled it with me," he said. "I told Him how bitter I was that the President should receive this tremendous homecoming, when no one met us as we returned home. And when I finished, it seemed as though the Lord put His hand on my shoulder and simply said, 'But you're not home yet!'"[55]

[55] Craig B. Larson, Editor. *Illustrations for Preaching and Teaching*, p.197-198.

9-208

HEAVEN

Philippians 1:20-26

(POSB, note 3.)

Where Will You Spend Eternity?

How strong is your perception of eternity?

We live in a day and time where medical technology has made great strides by keeping people alive who years ago would have died. There are both positive and negative points for the Christian believer to consider.

For example, look at the life of a young lady whom we will call Karen. At the prime of her life, Karen was stricken by a devastating disease which put her in a coma. Years went by as she lay asleep. The only thing keeping her alive was a series of tubes.

Karen's parents finally made the difficult decision to turn off the life-support machines and remove the tubes from their daughter's wasted body. Their decision was not easy. It was so hard to let her go. But it was bearable because of Karen's commitment to Christ. When she finally left this world, she fell into the arms of her loving heavenly Father.

When you let go of this old world, will you fall into His arms also?

9-209

HOLY SPIRIT

Ephesians 1:8-14

(POSB, note 4.)

Holy Spirit Given as a Pledge

Have you ever heard of a lay-a-way plan? For example: *a dollar down will secure your lay-a-way for Christmas.* This phrase is spoken in hundreds of stores as merchandise is set aside until it has been paid for in full. If payments are made on a timely basis, the customer picks up the merchandise and is finally able to enjoy what has been previously laid away.

Of course, for a variety of reasons, some people fail to make the scheduled payments and consequently lose what they wanted.

In the same sense, God has a lay-a-way program. However, His program is a guaranteed payment for the believer. In fact, we are not allowed to pay on anything that He has done. The cross took care of it all, and the most wonderful thing has happened: the Holy Spirit has been given to us, given as a pledge or down payment of God's great promise to us, that we shall live forever with Him.

9-210

Holy Spirit

Ephesians 1:8-14

(POSB, Introduction)

The Great Blessings of God

We live in an age where knowledge is king. Through the inventions of video, fax, computer, and other technologies to come, instant knowledge is at our fingertips. But for the Christian believer, knowledge is not the end; it is only a means to the end (knowing God and learning more and more about God). Without wisdom, we will be poor stewards of the knowledge that we collect.

God gives us wisdom and understanding in order that we might be able to comprehend His will, His inheritance, and His sealing us with the Holy Spirit.

9-211

Honesty

Galatians 2:11-21

(POSB, note 2, point 2.)

Passing the Honesty Exam

If you were given an honesty test, would you pass or fail? The Lord gave Peter an honesty test in the area of relationships...and he failed, proving to be hypocritical. The Christian believer is charged to be honest in his relationships with others.

In Moody Monthly...George Sweeting writes about the desperate need for honesty in our culture. He refers to Dr. Madison Sarratt, who taught mathematics at Vanderbilt University for many years. Before giving a test, the professor would admonish his class something like this:

"Today I am giving two examinations, one in trigonometry and the other in honesty. I hope you will pass them both. If you must fail one, fail trigonometry. There are many good people in the world who can't pass trig. But there are no good people in the world who cannot pass the examination of honesty"[56]

9-212

Hope

Colossians 1:3-8

(POSB, note 4, point 8.)

Hope Is Focused on Eternal Life

There are a lot of different ideas in the world about filling the "God-void" in the hearts of people. Man is prone to put his hope in the things of this world. But Scripture tells us that our hope must have a certain focus in order to attain eternal life. Warren W. Wiersbe shares this story:

When I was a young pastor, one of my favorite preachers was Dr. Walter Wilson of Kansas City. He had a unique way of making old truths seem new and exciting. I once heard him quote John 3:16 and ask, "If you were to give a gift that would be suitable for the whole world, what would you give?"

56 Paul Lee Tan. *Encyclopedia of 7,700 Illustrations: Signs of the Times*, p.560.

He then listed several possibilities and showed how those gifts could not suit everybody: books (many people cannot read); foods (people eat different things in different parts of the world); clothing (climates are different); money (not every culture makes use of money). He came to the logical conclusion that only the Gospel, with its gift of eternal life, was suitable for the whole world; and he was right.[57]

9-213

Hope

Colossians 1:3-8

(POSB, note 3.)

The Believer's Hope Is in Christ Alone, Not in Religion

God loves you! Think of what God has provided for you in Jesus Christ and how Christianity differs from other religions in what it offers. A major distinction is pointed out by Donald Barnhouse in this story:

In the lobby of the Imperial Hotel in Tokyo, Japan, the girl at one of the airline desks spoke Chinese, Japanese and English; she was obviously from a cultured background. I asked her if she was a Christian. She replied that she was a Buddhist. Further questions elicited the information that she had heard of Christ and knew that there was a sacred book, the Bible; but she had never read it and knew nothing of Christian truth. I then asked her, "Do you love Buddha?" She was startled and said, "Love? I never thought about love in connection with religion." I said to her, "Do you know that in the whole world no God is truly loved except the Lord Jesus Christ? Other gods are hated and feared. You have statues of fierce monsters to guard the gates of your temples, and the people stand at a distance and try to awaken their gods by clapping their hands. They burn incense and offer sacrifices to them as though they were gods who had to be appeased. But Jesus Christ loves us; He came to die for us, and those of us who truly know Him have learned to love Him in return...Mohammedans do not love Allah; Hindus do not love their gods, and neither do you love Buddha. But we love the Lord Jesus because He died for us."[58]

What a hope! What a powerful reason to follow the Lord Jesus Christ!

---

57 Warren W. Wiersbe. *The Bible Exposition Commentary,* Vol.2, p.107.

58 Donald Grey Barnhouse. *Let Me Illustrate.* (Grand Rapids, MI: Fleming H. Revell, 1967), p.163-164.

9-214

HUMILITY

Colossians 3:12-14

(POSB, note 4.)

Humility: Helps Keep the Focus on the Gospel

The garment of humility is often overlooked in today's culture. We have been told that "the biggest is the best." "You are the show, so show off." And so, we find ourselves wearing pride instead of humility.

Howard was a most talented church choir director. His life was filled with humble service to the Lord and to His church. He was truly a "glory-deflector"—one who was always careful to give God the glory.

One afternoon before the Christmas cantata, a choir member approached Howard and said, "Tonight, all of the men are going to wear colorful bow-ties to celebrate the season. Do you want to wear one also?"

In a very loving but direct response, Howard said, "I do not want to do anything that would distract others from clearly hearing our message of the gospel."

Is your humility helping others to clearly hear the gospel?

9-215

HUMILITY

Galatians 6:1-5

(POSB, note 5.)

Qualifications for Spiritual Service

All ground at the foot of the cross is level. There is no spiritual hierarchy for men to climb in this life. A dynamic example of this truth was Saint Francis of Assisi, who was the founder of the Order of Friars (Franciscans). He lived out his life in an attempt to imitate Christ, to live just as Christ had lived upon earth. He set a dynamic example for all of us in one primary thing: he had a firm grasp on the concept of humility.

When someone asked [him] why and how he could accomplish so much, he replied: "This may be why. The Lord looked down from Heaven upon the earth and said, 'Where can I find the weakest, the littlest, the meanest man on the face of the earth?' Then He saw me and said, 'Now I've found him, and I will work through him. He won't be proud of it. He'll see that I am only using him because of his littleness and insignificance.'"[59]

Could God say the same things about you?

[59] From *The Christian Herald.* Walter B. Knight. *Three Thousand Illustrations for Christian Service*, p.367.

9-216

Humility

Philippians 2:5-11

(POSB, note 1.)

The Example of Christ

Every believer should cultivate the mind of Christ, that of humbling himself and going forth to meet the needs of a lost world. D.B. Rote worded it well:

Every [believer] should cultivate a lowly spirit....No one is so much in need of a lowly spirit as servants of the Lord. It is one of the first and last qualifications for service.

It is related of [the missionary] Francis Xavier, that as he was preaching in one of the cities of Japan, a man went up to him as if he had something to say to him privately. Xavier leaned his head near to hear what he had to say, and the scorner spit upon the face of the devoted missionary. Xavier, without a word or the least sign of annoyance, took out his pocket handkerchief, wiped his face and went on with his important message as if nothing had happened. The scorn of the audience was turned to admiration. The most learned doctor of the city, who happened to be present, said to himself that a law which taught men such virtue, inspired them with such courage, and gave them such complete mastery over themselves, could not but be from God. Afterwards he desired baptism, and his example was followed by others....

"Learn of Me;" Jesus said, "for I am meek and lowly in heart."

"Though the Lord be high, yet hath He respect unto the lowly," and "He giveth grace unto the lowly."

Dear coworkers, let Christ be your Example.[60]

9-217

Humility

Philippians 2:5-11

(POSB, Introduction)

Walking in the Humility of Christ

Have you ever bought something that was an imitation—it looked like the real thing but lacked the quality of the original? Chances are your imitation wore out or broke or became tarnished before too long. There is nothing like the real thing, whether it be a cherished painting, a treasured piece of jewelry, or a precious relationship. Nothing quite meets our expectations except the real thing. But there are times in life when we are supposed to try to imitate something or someone—times when we want to model ourselves after an ideal or a role model. We don't expect to be as good or perfect as the original, but it is in our best interests to try. Why? Because our sinful nature is so depraved, and because we have a perfect model for all we do in Jesus Christ!

No one has ever come close to humbling himself like Jesus Christ did, and no one ever will. Unity among Christians depends upon our walking in the humility of Jesus Christ.

---

[60] D.B. Rote. Quoted in *Three Thousand Illustrations for Christian Service* by Walter B. Knight, p.366.

9-218

IDOLATRY

Galatians 1:6-9

(POSB, note 2, point 3.)

A Warning to Those Who Want to Save Their God

Have you ever thought about the things that pierce God's heart? One of the major things is idolatry, especially when a person whom He has called turns to a false religion or a false god.

Years ago, a photographer captured on film four men who were struggling to carry a ent typhoon. As water was rushing up to their knees, their faces grimaced as they attempted to save their god.

Isaiah the prophet framed this tragic irony—a god who cannot save and has to have the help of people.

> **"They lift it upon the shoulder and carry it; they set it in its place and it stands there. It does not move from its place. Though one may cry to it, it cannot answer; it cannot deliver him from his distress" (Is. 46:7, NASB).**

Are you ever tempted to serve this kind of god? Christian believer, let go and let it drown. And then reach out to the one who says...

> **"When you pass through the waters, I will be with you; and through the rivers, they will not overflow you. When you walk through the fire, you will not be scorched, nor will the flame burn you" (Is. 43:2, NASB).**

9-219

IDOLATRY

Galatians 4:8-11

(POSB, note 1, point 2.)

Living in the Midst of Idolatry

Have you ever wondered what it would be like to stumble upon a community of idolaters? What kinds of things would offend you? Take a glimpse into one such community:

As we peek into one of their homes, several things strike us as *unChristian-like.* It seems that their worship is centered in the main living area. The entire room has been arranged to give honor to this inanimate object (which makes all kinds of noises and appeals to the senses of those who worship it). All of the available seating in this room is angled in order to provide the best seating and viewing arrangement possible.

Upon further investigation, closets are found full of beautiful sewn fabrics displayed on metal hangers. One can only guess about this culture, but there seems to have been a lot of value placed in this area of the living quarters.

Seeing their bookkeeping records might give additional insight into what they valued; the only entry you find on the ledger is entitled "self."

Let's leave this uncivilized culture behind. What kind of people are they? Sad to say, but it looks a lot like our culture. The inanimate object displayed in the main living area is a television. For many, it has become an object of worship as its pull has overcome many a Christian.

The closet represents the value our culture places on apparel—especially the trendy and expensive type. Many are judged for what they wear on the outside and not for what dresses the heart.

Finally, how we invest our financial resources tells a lot about what we consider important. Our culture is one that promotes "me first" and then others if anything is left over (by accident).

Some would respond and say, "But we don't have idols. We are civilized." However, the evidence is clear: anything that is placed before Jesus Christ is an idol. Let this rule of thumb keep you from the sin of idolatry.

9-220

INHERITANCE

Ephesians 1:8-14

(POSB, note 3, point 4.b.)

Joint-Heirs with Jesus Christ

Through God's infinite wisdom, He has given His Son an inheritance. Because of God's mercy and grace, we have been made joint-heirs with the Son. Listen to this striking story of how one man received his inheritance.

A man who was blessed with wisdom, virtue, and wealth had only one son. He offered him the best education, sending him to Jerusalem to learn. He made certain the young man's every need was met.

Shortly after his son left, [the father] became sick and died. His death caused immense grief throughout the community, for he was a benefactor for both rich and poor....

When the period of mourning was over, the dead man's executor opened the man's will and read it aloud. To the astonishment of everyone, the man left all of his property and wealth to his slave. There was a final clause that his beloved son should have the privilege of choosing only one thing out of the entire estate.

Immersed in grief over the loss of his father, the young man asked his teacher to assist him in selecting one thing from his father's estate. In the meantime, the slave began to live the life of a wealthy man.

When the teacher read the will, he at once discovered the intention of the father. "We must leave at once for your home," the teacher told the pupil, "where you will take possession of all your property."

"But I am a pauper," the boy cried. "All I have are the clothes on my back and one item from my father's house."

"I suggest," the teacher said, "that you choose your late father's slave out of his estate, and with him will go over to you all he possesses, since a slave can own nothing, and all he has belongs to his master."

"That indeed was your father's clever device. He knew that if the will were to state that all was left to you, the slave, in your absence, would take for himself all the valuables on which he could lay his hands. Whereas, if he thought all belonged to him, he would take care of everything that was left. Your father knew that the one thing he gave you the power to choose would be no other than his slave, and with him you will become the just and rightful owner of everything."[61]

This young man's father was very clever. But our Heavenly Father is even wiser. Have *you* claimed your inheritance?

9-221

INTEGRITY

Galatians 4:12-20

(POSB, note 2, point 3.)

Placing the Greatest Value on the Truth

If the minister of God tells the truth, will he be exempt from persecution? John wished it were so. Let's hear his painful story:

John was a man of God who had forsaken all to follow Christ. He was willing to go wherever God wanted. It looked like a golden opportunity for a young minister. This congregation wanted him, and he felt led to the church. Right up front he told the congregation that he would never compromise the truth. And they replied, "Pastor, that's great! We're sure glad to have you with us."

As the years went by, the truth from God's Word forced the congregation to face their sins. The old saying that the truth hurts was proven accurate. But instead of responding in repentance to the Lord, many in the church began to shift the blame for their guilt to the pastor's sermons.

The result was tragic. John was spiritually tarred and feathered. The people were looking for something that would tickle their ears. To his credit, John refused to give in to the pressure, counting the truth more important than acceptance by man.

9-222

JOY

Philippians 2:1-4

(POSB, note 5.)

Concern for One Another's Joy

Do your words fill others with joy? Listen to what Gary Smalley and John Trent have to say to us:

Spoken words of blessing are so vital. They fortify relationships. They nurture and bolster self-esteem. They stimulate growth. And sometimes they can keep a worn-out traveler from stumbling on the road of life...A few carefully chosen words of comfort, encouragement, empathy, or insight—perhaps accompanied by a hug—can make all the difference between stumbling and moving on.[62]

---

61 William R. White. *Stories for the Journey.* (Minneapolis, MN: Augsburg Publishing House, 1988), p.86-87.

62 Gary Smalley & Dr. John Trent. *Giving The Blessing: Daily Thoughts On The Joy Of Giving.* (Nashville, TN: Thomas Nelson, 1993), March 30th entry.

9-223

JUDGMENT

Galatians 5:16-21

(POSB, note 3.)

Judgment for Those Who Live by the Flesh

The love of God should always be balanced with the judgment of God. Listen to this story from Warren Wiersbe's *Meet Yourself in the Psalms:*

[He] tells about a frontier town where a horse bolted and ran away with a wagon carrying a little boy. Seeing the child in danger, a young man risked his life to catch the horse and stop the wagon.

The child who was saved grew up to be a lawless man, and one day he stood before a judge to be sentenced for a serious crime. The prisoner recognized the judge as the man who, many years before, had saved his life; so he pled for mercy on the basis of that experience.

But the words from the bench silenced his plea, "Young man, then I was your savior; today I am your judge, and I must sentence you to be hanged."

One day Jesus will say to rebellious sinners, "During that long day of grace, I was the Savior, and I would have forgiven you. But today I am your Judge. Depart from me, ye cursed, into everlasting fire!"[63]

If you play with fire, you will get burned. Allow Christ to be your Savior, so you will not stand before Him ashamed in the terrible day of judgment that is coming upon all the world.

9-224

JUDGMENT

Philippians 2:5-11

(POSB, note 5, point 3.)

You Cannot Hide from God

No one is smart enough to fool God. Everyone will have to stand before Him one day and there will be no way to hide who we are:

The Queen Mary was the largest ship to cross the oceans when it was launched in 1936. Through four decades and a world war she served until she was retired, anchored as a floating hotel and museum in Long Beach, California.

During the conversion, her three massive smokestacks were taken off to be scraped down and repainted. But on the dock they crumbled.

Nothing was left of the ¾-inch steel plate from which the stacks had been formed. All that remained were more than thirty coats of paint that had been applied over the years. The steel had rusted away.

When Jesus called the Pharisees "whitewashed tombs," He meant they had no substance, only an exterior appearance.[64]

63 Craig B. Larson, Editor. *Illustrations for Preaching and Teaching*, p.100.

64 *Ibid.*, p.118.

9-225

Justification

Galatians 3:15-18

(POSB, Introduction)

A Life That Affects the Total Person

Do you really believe that God will keep His promises to you? Have you ever felt that God has forgotten you?

When God made a covenant with Abraham, it was more than just a few legal terms pasted on a piece of paper. God chose to take full responsibility for Abraham's destiny. God guaranteed His commitment to him, unconditionally.

As Christian believers, we also benefit from the Abrahamic Covenant. How? It guarantees our justification. What justification? That we are made righteous and acceptable to God through Jesus Christ. With that guarantee set in place, we need to do something: *live* our lives like we belong to God. Living a justified life affects the total person. Myron Augsburger speaks toward this gripping truth:

The words holiness and sanctification are not prominent in much of Protestant theology. We have tended to speak of justification without [an] emphasis on sanctification...Holiness means that one belongs wholly to God. This is also the meaning of sanctification, being set apart as God's own possession. When this begins internally, with the heart, the transformation becomes something that affects the total person.[65]

9-226

Justification

Galatians 2:11-21

(POSB, note 3, point 3.)

Justification by Faith in Christ Alone

Many a man has tried to make it over to the other side (from earth to heaven) without trusting Christ. Every one of them, without exception, has failed.

The Bible says that we are justified by faith in Christ alone. Remember, justification means that God counts our faith in Christ as righteousness, counts us acceptable to Him.

Years ago a strong wire was stretched across Niagara River, just above the roaring falls. It was announced that a tightrope walker would walk on that suspended wire from the American to the Canadian side. The thrilling moment for the death-defying feat arrived. Great crowds watched with wide-eyed wonderment as the man performed, with calm deliberateness, the awesome stunt. The people cheered wildly!

Then the performer did an even more daring thing. He began to push a wheelbarrow with a grooved wheel across the suspended wire. At the conclusion of this breath-taking performance, thunderous applause went up. The performer observed a boy whose wonderment was clearly discernible on his bright face. Asked the man, "My boy, do you believe that I could put you in this wheelbarrow and push you over the falls?" "Oh, yes," said the boy quickly. "Then, get in the wheelbarrow," said the man. Instantly the boy dashed

65 From *The Christ-shaped Conscience*. Selected from *Christianity Today*. (March 8, 1993), p.45.

66 Walter B. Knight. *Knight's Treasury of 2,000 Illustrations*, p.117.

away! In reality he did not believe that the tightrope walker could take him safely across the falls.[66]

Have you come to the place in your life where you trust Christ enough to place yourself into His hands?

9-227

Knowledge of God

Ephesians 3:14-21

(POSB, note 6.)

Having a Passion for Christ

Are you satisfied with the depth of your love for Jesus Christ? Hopefully not! Believers should never become satisfied with the status quo. God has something much better for you to pursue: a passion for Christ!

As Gustave Dore' was putting the finishing touches on the face of Christ in one of his paintings, an admiring friend stepped quietly into the studio. She looked with bated breath upon the painting. Dore' sensed her presence and said graciously, "Pardon, madam, I did not know you were here." She answered, "Monsieur Dore', you must love Him very much to be able to paint Him thus!" "Love Him, madam?" exclaimed Dore', "I do love Him, but if I loved Him better I could paint Him better!"

If we loved Him better, we could serve Him better.[67]

9-228

Knowledge of God

Ephesians 1:15-18

(POSB, note 3, point 3.)

The Need for the Knowledge of God

There is a story that will help us better understand the need to have a *heart* knowledge of the Lord and not just a *head* knowledge.

The master musician was finally ready to listen to the results of his students' efforts. He had done all that he could do to teach them to play the music. Now, the moment had come for his prize student to play his instrument.

Bill was a very talented fellow. He had mastered every note of the difficult composition and did so with great pride. On cue, he proceeded to show off his talent as the notes flew out of his instrument. When he had finished his piece, he took a deep breath and asked his teacher, "Well, what do you think professor? Did I pass?"

To Bill's amazement, his professor was not pleased with his performance. Using phrases filled with passion, the master musician said, "You played all of the notes...but, you did not play the music."

It is not good enough merely to *know* the truth; we must *live* it!

---

[67] Walter B. Knight. *Knight's Treasury of 2,000 Illustrations*, p.212.

9-229

Knowledge of God

Ephesians 1:15-18

(POSB, Introduction)

Overcoming All Distractions

Do you ever get distracted as you follow the Lord? All of us can relate to this story:

It was a fog-shrouded morning, July 4, 1952, when a young woman named Florence Chadwick waded into the water off Catalina Island. She intended to swim the channel from the island to the California coast. Long-distance swimming was not new to her; she had been the first woman to swim the English Channel in both directions.

The water was numbing cold that day. The fog was so thick she could hardly see the boats in her party. Several times sharks had to be driven away with rifle fire. She swam more than fifteen hours before she asked to be taken out of the water. Her trainer tried to encourage her to swim on since they were so close to land, but when Florence looked, all she saw was fog. So she quit...only one-half mile from her goal.

Later she said, "I'm not excusing myself, but if I could have seen the land, I might have made it." It wasn't the cold or fear or exhaustion that caused Florence Chadwick to fail. It was the fog.

Many times we too fail, not because we're afraid or because of the peer pressure or because of anything other than the fact we lose sight of the goal. Maybe that's why Paul said, "I press toward the mark for the prize of the high calling of God in Christ Jesus" (Phil. 3:14).

Two months after her failure, Florence Chadwick walked off the same beach into the same channel and swam the distance, setting a new speed record, because she could see the land.[68]

And so it is with the knowledge of God. There are many distractions that leave us in a fog. It is vitally important that the believer not lose sight of his one great goal: that of knowing God, of knowing Him personally, of growing in the knowledge of Him more and more.

9-230

Law

Galatians 3:19-22

(POSB, note 1.)

How the Law Reveals Sin

What does God use to get your attention, to show that you are a long way from perfection? Does He use other people or circumstances?

Long ago a story was told about a proud fishing pond and a fish. Across the land, fishermen would come and exclaim how clear the water was in this pond. Upon hearing yet another positive accolade, the pond's level of pride began to reach flood stage. "I must be the best and clearest pond in the world!" It didn't take long for the old fishat the bottom to grow weary of this overdone pride. He had heard it for years. And he, better than anyone, knew what was really in this pond.

68 Craig B. Larson, Editor. *Illustrations for Preaching and Teaching*, p.96.

Resting on the bottom of the pond, the old fish began to rapidly flutter his fins. As he did, the motion of the water began to stir up the silt on the bottom. It did not take long for the pond to fill up with a murky cloud.

"Stop! What are you doing to me? How dare you dirty me up?!" screamed the offended pond. The fish responded in measured and striking words: "I haven't done a thing to you except to show what has been in you all the time."

And that is what the law does to us. It simply shows us the sin that has settled in the bottom of our hearts. Just in case we forget who we really are, the law reminds us how desperately we need the cleansing power of our precious Savior, the Lord Jesus Christ.

9-231

LAW

Galatians 3:19-22

(POSB, Introduction)

The Law: Intimidating but Powerless

One of the corny gags from the days of Vaudeville theater was someone pointing a gun at someone else, pulling the trigger and...BANG! said the flag as it hung from the barrel. The gun looked real and sounded real, but it proved to be harmless.

The law has the same affect on the Christian believer. It looks intimidating and it sounds intimidating, but it is powerless. The law cannot justify us. Those who claim that the law does justify are just shouting BANG!

9-232

LAW

Galatians 3:19-22

(POSB, note 4, point 2.)

The Law: Lacks the Power to Grant Eternal Life

Doing all the right things and having all the right titles are of no benefit to the Christian believer. There is only one thing that will grant us justification. David Seamands ends his book *Healing Grace* with this story:

For more than six hundred years the Hapsburgs exercised political power in Europe. When Emperor Franz-Joseph I of Austria died in 1916, his was the last of extravagant imperial funerals.

A procession of dignitaries and elegantly dressed court personages escorted the coffin, draped in the black and gold imperial colors. To the accompaniment of a military band's somber dirges and by the light of torches, the cortege descended the stairs of the Capauchin Monastery in Vienna. At the bottom was a great iron door leading to the Hapsburg family crypt. Behind the door was the Cardinal—Archbishop of Vienna.

The officer in charge followed the prescribed ceremony, established centuries before. "Open!" he cried.

"Who goes there?" responded the Cardinal.

"We bear the remains of his Imperial and Apostolic Majesty, Franz-Joseph I, by the grace of God Emperor of Austria, King of Hungary, Defender of the Faith, Prince of Bohemia-Moravia, Grand Duke of Lombardy, Venezia, Styriga..." The officer continued to list the Emperor's thirty-seven titles.

"We know him not," replied the Cardinal. "Who goes there?"

The officer spoke again, this time using a much abbreviated and less ostentatious title reserved for times of expediency.

"We know him not," the Cardinal said again. "Who goes there?"

The officer tried a third time, stripping the emperor of all but the humblest of titles: "We bear the body of Franz-Joseph, our brother, a sinner like us all!"

At that, the doors swung open, and Franz-Joseph was admitted.

In death all are reduced to the same level. Neither wealth nor fame can open the way of salvation, but only God's grace, given to those who will humbly acknowledge their need.[69]

The law is powerless. It cannot open heaven's door for you. It cannot give you life. Where have you placed your trust? In the law or in Christ?

9-233

Law

Galatians 5:1-6

(POSB, Introduction)

The Law Serves As a Tyrant

It was the American patriot Patrick Henry who said, "Give me liberty or give me death." Henry knew what it was like to live under the thumb of a tyrant. Along the way, he had the good fortune to get a small taste of liberty. And once he tasted liberty, his taste buds exploded with flavor. The bland taste of bondage would never satisfy him again.

In the same sense, the law serves as a tyrant. It shows no mercy and hates anything related to freedom. Anyone who weds himself to the law will be entangled in the chains of bondage. What is the alternative for the Christian believer? Liberty in Christ.

9-234

Law

Galatians 3:19-22

(POSB, note 5, point 3.)

No Man Can Break the Law of Gravitation

No matter who we are, the law pulls us down. No one can defy the law's lethal gravitational pull. J. Vernon McGee illustrates this point for us:

Picture a building about twenty-four stories high. There are three men on top of the building, and the superintendent goes up to see them and warns, "Now be very careful, don't step off of this building or you will be killed. It will mean death for you." One of the fellows says, "This crazy superintendent is always trying to frighten people. I don't believe

69 Alan J. White. Selected from *Leadership Journal.* (Fall, 1994), p.42.

that if I step off this building I will die." So he deliberately steps off into the air. Suppose that when he passes the tenth floor, somebody looks out the window and asked him, 'Well how's it going?' and he says, "So far, so good." But, my friend, he hasn't arrived yet. There is death at the bottom...

Now suppose another fellow becomes frightened at what the superintendent said. He runs for the elevator, or the steps, and accidentally slips. He skids right off the edge of the building and falls to the street below....The third fellow...is thrown off the building by some gangsters...Now the man who was thrown off the building is just as dead as the man who deliberately stepped off and the man who accidentally slipped off the building. All of these men broke the law of gravitation, and death was inevitable for all of them. It is in the fact, you see, and not the degree. It is the fact that they went over the edge—they all broke the law of gravitation.[70]

If you are going to take a leap, leap into the waiting arms of the Lord Jesus Christ. Allow Him to pull you close to His side.

9-235

LAW

Colossians 2:13-15

(POSB, note 2, point 2b.)

No Man Can Keep the Law

Do you live the perfect Christian life? Nobody does, but a lot of us try by living according to "the rules"—then fail and fall into defeat and condemnation. This is not God's best for the Christian believer. J. Vernon McGee shares this nugget of truth with us:

You can't...keep the law today in your own strength...the law was given to discipline the old nature. But now the believer is given a new nature, and the law has been removed as a way of life.

...A man once came to me and said, "I'll give you $100 if you will show me where the Sabbath day has been changed." I answered, "I don't think it has been changed. Saturday is Saturday, it is the seventh day of the week, and it is the Sabbath day. I realize our calendar has been adjusted and can be off a few days, but we won't even consider that point. The seventh day is still Saturday and is still the Sabbath day."

He got a gleam in his eye and said, "Then why don't you keep the Sabbath day if it hasn't been changed?" I answered, "The day hasn't changed, but I have been changed. I've been given a new creation. We celebrate the first day because that is the day He rose from the grave."

That is what it means when he says that the ordinances which were against us have been nailed to His cross.[71]

70 J. Vernon McGee. *Thru The Bible,* Vol.5, p.171.

71 *Ibid.,* p.351-352.

9-236

LEGALISM

Galatians 4:21-31

(POSB, note 4, point 2.)

Legalism Stunts Your Growth

There are few things sadder in life than that of a Christian believer who has been bound up by legalism. Charles Simpson, in *Pastoral Renewal*, writes:

I met a young man not long ago who dives for exotic fish for aquariums. He said one of the most popular aquarium fish is the shark. He explained that if you catch a small shark and confine it, it will stay a size proportionate to the aquarium. Sharks can be six inches long yet fully matured. But if you turn them loose in the ocean, they grow to their normal length of eight feet.

That also happens to some Christians. I've seen the cutest little six-inch Christians who swim around in a little puddle. But if you put them into a larger arena—into the whole of creation—only then can they become great.[72]

9-237

LIGHT

Ephesians 5:8-14

(POSB, note 6.)

Light Awakens the Sleeping

For many of us, there is a struggle to get up and go in our Christian walk and service. This is not the time to just lay around and appear dead. Listen to this:

Winston Churchill had planned his funeral, which took place in Saint Paul's Cathedral. He included many of the great hymns of the church and used the eloquent Anglican liturgy. At his direction, a bugler...intoned...the sound of "Taps", the universal signal that says the day is over.

But then came a dramatic turn: as Churchill instructed, after "Taps" was finished, another bugler...played the notes of "Reveille"—"It's time to get up. It's time to get up. It's time to get up in the morning."[73]

Isn't it time for you to get up to serve the Lord with all of your might?

9-238

LIGHT

Ephesians 5:8-14

(POSB, note 4, point 3.)

Light Overcomes Darkness

Does the darkness of sin ever overwhelm you? The gospel of Christ illuminates the way for the Christian believer.

70 J. Vernon McGee. *Thru The Bible,* Vol.5, p.171.

71 *Ibid.,* p.351-352.

A father took his son into an art shop to buy a picture of Christ for him. The boy was shown different pictures of Christ but he didn't like any of them. "No, Daddy, these are not what I want." The father, thinking that his son didn't want a picture of Christ after all, asked, "What kind of picture of Christ do you want?" Promptly the boy replied, "I want a Christ who shines in darkness!" The boy had seen a luminous picture of Christ which shone in darkness.

We greatly need Christ to shine in the night of sorrow, suffering, testing and temptation. Only He can illumine life's dark pathway. As we follow Him, our way grows increasingly bright[74]

9-239

LOVE

Ephesians 3:14-21

(POSB, note 6.)

Sacrificial Love

It is utterly impossible to grasp and experience the love of Christ anywhere close to its full measure. We must pray for God to help us learn more and more of His love—and we must make the request *often every day*. There has never been penned a greater description of the unsurpassing love of Christ than that of F.M. Lehman in the song, *The Love of God*:

Could we with ink the ocean fill,
And were the skies of parchment made;
Were every stalk on earth a quill,
And every man a scribe by trade,

To write the love of God above
Would drain the ocean dry.
Nor could the scroll contain the whole,
Though stretched from sky to sky.

O love of God, how rich and pure!
How measureless and strong!
It shall forever more endure.
The saints and angels song. 75

74 Walter B. Knight. *Knight's Treasury of 2,000 Illustrations,* p.203.

75 *The Love of God.* Words by F. M. Lehman. (Nazarene Publishing House, 1945).

9-240

MAN

Colossians 1:20-23

(POSB, note 2, point 2.)

Unsaved Man's Hatred for God

Just how intense is an unsaved man's hatred for God? J. Vernon McGee illustrates this point with a personal example:

A great many people think that men are lost because they have committed some terrible sin. The reason people are lost is that their minds are alienated from God. I think this explains the fierce antagonism toward God on the part of the so-called intellectuals of our day. There is an open hatred and hostility toward God.

Some time ago I had the funeral of a certain movie star out here in California. The Hollywood crowd came to the funeral. One of the television newscasters commented on the funeral, and I appreciated what he had to say about it. He said, "Today Hollywood heard something that it had never heard before." But I also saw something there at that funeral that I had never seen before. I had never seen so much hatred in the eyes of men and women as I saw when I attempted to present Jesus Christ and to explain how wonderful He is and how He wants to save people. There is an alienation in the mind and heart of man.[76]

9-241

MARRIAGE

Ephesians 5:22-33

(POSB, note 2, point 1.)

Sacrificial Love

Chrysostom, a great minister in the early church, said:

If it be needful that thou shouldst give thy life for her, or be cut to pieces a thousand times, or endure anything whatever, refuse it not....He brought the Church to His feet by His great care, not by threats nor fear nor any such thing; so do thou conduct thyself towards thy wife.[77]

9-242

MARRIAGE

Colossians 3:18-21

(POSB, note 1, point 2.)

Biblical Submission in Marriage

Does Biblical submission mean that the woman is to become a "doormat" and accept physical, emotional, or verbal abuse as God's will for her life? Of course not. Biblical submission is a partnership between the wife and husband. Stephen P. Beck writes:

[76] J. Vernon McGee. *Thru The Bible*, Vol.5, p.342.

[77] William Barclay. *The Letters to the Galatians and Ephesians.* "The Daily Study Bible." (Philadelpia, PA: Westminster Press, 1953), p.206.

Driving down a country road, I came to a very narrow bridge. In front of the bridge, a sign was posted: "Yield." Seeing no oncoming cars, I continued across the bridge and [on] to my destination.

On my way back, I came to the same one-lane bridge, now from the other direction. To my surprise, I saw another "Yield" sign posted.

"Curious," I thought. "I'm sure there was one positioned on the other side."

When I reached the other side of the bridge, I looked back. Sure enough, yield signs had been placed at both ends of the bridge. Drivers from both directions were requested to give the other the right of way. It was a reasonable and gracious way of preventing a head-on collision.[78]

God never intended marriage to be a head-on collision. Biblical submission keeps the traffic of life safe and steady. Without it, the marriage will become a wreck.

9-243

MARRIAGE
Ephesians 5:22-33
(POSB, Introduction)

Keeping Marriage Vows

Every day, all over the world, important words are being spoken to some men and women: *"I now pronounce you man and wife."* And with that charge, married couples make daily discoveries that cloud their ideas on what makes a marriage good. For many, the wedding day was the pinnacle. As they experience trials and tribulations, the promises they made to each other become faint memories. They ignore their vows by going from "until death do us part" to "How soon can I get out of this?"

What has gone wrong with the marriage that God has ordained as His will? Why are so many missing so much in their marriage? Is a good Christian marriage out of reach? Is Christian marriage just too much of a burden to be endured?

When dealing with wives and husbands, we must always remember that God's instructions are not grievous. In fact, they are easy and light. God instructs and guides us down the easiest and lightest path possible. As Christ said:

> **"Come unto me, all ye that labour and are heavy laden, and I will give you rest. Take my yoke upon you, and learn of me; for I am meek and lowly in heart: and ye shall find rest unto your souls. For my yoke is easy, and my burden is light" (Mt. 11:28-30).**

If we walk down the path God has laid for us—if we do just what He says—we can experience the most loving, peaceful, rich, and full life imaginable. This is doubly true for husband and wife, for they have the companionship of each other as well as of the Lord.

[78] Craig B. Larson, Editor. *Illustrations for Preaching and Teaching,* p.249.

9-244

Marriage

Ephesians 5: 22-33

(POSB, note 2, point 1.c.)

Protecting a Marriage with Hedges

The devil takes great pleasure when a Christian marriage hits the rocks and destroys what God had joined together. Are we at the mercy of the desires of the devil? Only if men fail to put up "hedges" around their marriages. As you listen to this illustration, take care that it will not be your story:

Stanley was a Sunday school teacher who wanted to relate to his adult students. He prided himself on being able to talk up a storm about anything. Through the years, he noticed that his gift of gab appealed to the ladies. Stanley was married and had a couple of kids who wanted to be just like Dad. From all observations, he had the perfect marriage and family. Any one who knew Stanley would agree that he was very relational—a real "touchy-feely" man. It was this attribute which led to his demise.

Mary was in Stanley's class and made it a point never to miss a Sunday or any other time the class met for fellowship. She liked Stanley a lot because he always made it a point to greet her with a warm embrace that tended to linger. Everything appeared to be innocent at first, but the fuse was lit shortly after that first embrace. Without saying a word, they both knew the fire that was burning was rapidly becoming a wildfire which would consume their lives. They tried to fight those feelings...for awhile...sort of...not really. To tell you the truth, they just gave up and gave in to a temptation which would destroy his marriage and devastate the church.

In his book, Hedges—Loving Your Marriage Enough To Protect It, Jerry B. Jenkins sheds a warning light on men:

> Call it what you will, but a man with as perfect a wife as he could ever want is still capable of lust, of a senseless seeking of that which would destroy him and his family. If he does not fear his own potential and build a hedge around himself and his marriage, he heads for disaster.
>
> Shall we all run scared? Yes! Fear is the essential. "There are several good protections against temptation," Mark Twain said, "but the surest is cowardice."[79]

9-245

Marriage

Colossians 3:18-21

(POSB, note 2.)

Protecting Your Marriage

William Bennett, the former U.S. Secretary of Education, has said that a divorce is like the death of a small civilization. Statistics tell us that about one out of every two marriages fail in America. How close has divorce come to wiping out your "small civilization," your marriage? If you have yet to do so, now would be a great time to plant some protective hedges around your marriage. Protecting your marriage is a wonderful way to love your wife.

---

[79] Jerry B. Jenkins. *Hedges—Loving Your Marriage Enough To Protect It.* (Chicago, IL: Moody Press, 1989), p.26-27.

In the excellent book, *Hedges: Loving Your Marriage Enough to Protect It,* author Jerry Jenkins shares this hedge with us:

Evangelist Robert M. Abbott writes that, just as the fact that "a certain percentage of people die annually through traffic accidents does not mean we stop searching for ways to remedy the situation," neither should we be ready to shrug off moral impurity among our leaders.

Abbott continues, "None of us plan[s] to have moral accidents, but we must also plan not to! Danger rides with us all the time." He compares the moral danger to that of a driver pulling several tons of equipment behind his car. "[This] requires more braking power and a longer stopping time...Brakes! Thank God for brakes!"

Abbott writes that "[we] must learn to keep plenty of space between us and sinful acts, so we can start braking soon enough to stop before it is too late." He offers a list...when we might "need to put on the brakes early and well." Among them:

⇒ When you are so busy there is no time to be alone with God.
⇒ When you are too busy to spend at least one relaxed evening a week with your wife and family.
⇒ When you feel you deserve more attention than you are getting at home.
⇒ When you wouldn't want your wife [or a colleague] to see what you are reading or looking at.
⇒ When the romance in your marriage is fading.
⇒ When your charisma, appearance, and personality are attractive to women, and you are tempted to make the most of it.
⇒ When you enjoy fantasizing about an illicit relationship.
⇒ When a woman makes herself available by her behavior.
⇒ When some woman [not your wife] tells you how wonderful you are and how much she loves you.
⇒ When Scriptures concerning adultery are for others, not you
⇒ When you start feeling sorry for yourself.
⇒ When you hope God isn't looking or listening.[80]

God will provide the brakes...if you choose to use them. What do you need to start pumping the brakes for today?

[80] Jerry B. Jenkins. *Hedges: Loving Your Marriage Enough to Protect It,* p.81-83.

9-246

MARRIAGE

Ephesians 5:22-33

(POSB, note 2, point 5.)

The Need to Cleave to Christ

To whom are we to cleave? Only to each other? A great Christian marriage exists when both the man and the woman cleave to the Lord Jesus. Listen closely as this point is illustrated by Dr. Larry Crabb:

Consider what may really be happening when a couple gets married: Two people, each with personal needs pressing for fulfillment, pledge themselves to become one. As they recite their vows to love and respect each other, strong but hidden motivations stir inside them. If a tape recorder could somehow tune into the couple's unconscious intentions, I wonder if perhaps we would hear words like these:

Bridegroom: I need to feel important and I expect you to meet that need by submitting to my every decision, whether good or bad; by respecting me no matter how I behave; and by supporting me in whatever I choose to do...My goal in marrying you is to find my significance through you. An arrangement in which you are commanded by God to submit to me sounds very attractive.

Bride: I have never felt as deeply loved as my nature requires. I am expecting you to meet that need through gentle affection even when I'm growling, thoughtful consideration whether I am always sensitive to you or not, and an accepting, romantic sensitivity to my emotional ups and downs. Don't let me down.

A marriage bound together by commitments to exploit the other for filling one's own needs...can be legitimately described as a "tic on a dog" relationship...The rather frustrating dilemma, of course, is that in such a marriage there are two tics and no dog![81]

9-247

MARRIAGE

Colossians 1:15

(POSB, Introduction)

The Truth Was Never Known

A married couple can live together for years but fail to really know each other. An example: for many years a wife made her husband beets for supper because she thought he liked them. One day, the husband let the cat out of the bag and told her:

"I do not like beets; I never have liked beets; I never will like beets! Why are you fixing me beets?" Her reply, "You never told me!" Obviously, they had failed to communicate. An assumption here, a guess there—and the truth was never known! There are many Christians whose experience with Jesus Christ is also based on the "best guess" method. Assumptions of who He is and what he likes have been programmed into their minds.

81 Dr. Lawrence J. Crabb, Jr. *The Marriage Builder.* (Grand Rapids, MI: Zondervan Publishing House, 1982), p.31-32.

9-248

MATURITY

Ephesians 3:14-21

(POSB, note 3.)

The Key to Maturity

Spiritual maturity takes time to grow deep roots. The temptation for many of us is just to put on the appearance of being mature. Of course, the danger in this is when the first good wind of tribulation blows our way, we fall over because our roots in the Lord are not deep and developed. Listen closely to this testimony:

I'll never forget a lesson the Lord taught me some time ago. I was walking beside a pond of water that was lined with towering pine trees on the opposite bank. Looking at the pond, I saw a reflection of the trees. I saw the tops of the trees, the branches, and the trunk. But the roots remained unseen for obvious reasons—they were hidden in the ground. In that still, small voice, the Lord impressed this great truth upon my heart: "the key to maturity is not the height of the trunk but the depth of the roots. If your roots fail to hold, the whole tree will fall."

9-249

MATURITY

Philippians 1:3-11

(POSB, Introduction)

The True Measure of Maturity

A tape measure is a must when you need an accurate measurement. How long is that bolt that you need? About 4 inches? Maybe 5? If you need one that is exactly 4 inches, you'll need an exact measurement. A random measurement is not effective when you need to be precise.

Do you live your life randomly? Have you measured your maturity in Christ accurately? A random measurement is not good enough. The Bible teaches us that we are to measure our spiritual maturity.

What are the marks of a mature Christian believer? A thankful heart, prayer, joy, fellowship, confidence in God's salvation, partnership, growing and discerning love, and righteousness.

9-250

MENTORING

Galatians 6:6-10

(POSB, Introduction)

Ministering Together

One day, a frustrated teacher decided to pull out all the stops. He decided to take a risk and take a personal interest in each one of his students. The teacher concluded that "the cold facts" were not enough to attract the interest of his students. The only thing which would break down the walls of apathy was the power of relationships.

Months later, his class was the most exciting class in the entire Sunday school. When one of his students was asked what made the difference, the reply was: "Before, our teacher just read us the Bible stories. Now, we have so much more—he challenges us to act out the stories in the Bible and to join him in doing so. For the first time, we feel like we are *ministering together*."

9-251

MENTORING

Galatians 6:6-10

(POSB, note 1.)

The Joy of Shared Ministry

One of the most rewarding experiences for a teacher is when his or her students capture the truth and apply it to other people.

Years ago, a Christian football coach invested a good portion of his life in his players and coaches. A stickler for details, his philosophy on offense and defense was branded into the minds of his assistant coaches. He spent just as much energy sharing his philosophy on what made up good character as he did on the actual game of football. An active member of the Fellowship of Christian Athletes, his faith in Christ became contagious. Through his witness, many of his coaches and players became believers.

As the years went by, some of his players and assistant coaches went on to coach at other schools. Showing striking evidence that they had been mentored by this great coach, the philosophy for each of their teams mirrored what they had learned. The offense was the same. The defense was played the same. And in more important matters, godly character was stressed and expected. Like their former coach—their mentor, their teacher—Christ was seen in each of their lives. Through one man's influence, many young men came to know Jesus Christ personally. His students were sharing in his ministry—literally—both on and off the field of play.

A good teacher reproduces what is in him. A good student shares what he has learned with others. Just as we are all teachers in some areas of life, we are all students in others areas. Are you sharing in the ministry of your teachers by passing on what you have learned to others?

9-252

MERCY

Ephesians 2:4-7

(POSB, Introduction)

Getting What You Do Not Deserve

Does the name Uwe Holmer mean anything to you? Perhaps not. How about the name of Erich Honecker? The lives of these two men crossed in 1990 and became a vivid example of God's mercy to the entire world.

Uwe Holmer is a pastor who served the Lord in what was formerly known as East Germany, a former communist nation. Like many other believers, he suffered from the 40 years of Erich Honecker's iron-fisted rule. But history has changed things. Honecker had been disposed of as leader and was facing trial on the charges of treason. While awaiting his trial, he was operated on for cancer and needed a place to recover. This beaten and sick man had no where to go: he was too sick to stay in prison and no one dared to open up his home to him because he was so hated.

Pastor Holmer's church ran a convalescent center in the secluded village of Lobetal. Unfortunately, there was no room for Honecker. Pastor Holmer could have easily rationalized this situation and closed his heart, but instead, he opened up his own home to Honecker and his wife. The gospel compelled Uwe Holmer to reach out and minister to this man's needs. After all, that was the Christian thing to do...wasn't it?

Torrents of rage were directed at Pastor Holmer: hate mail, bomb threats and threats to cut off funding to his ministry—all because Holmer had offered mercy to an enemy.

Uwe Holmer explained to the nation (and to the world) why he had mercy on Erich Honecker in a letter to an East German newspaper, Neue Zeitung:

"In Lobetal" he wrote, "there is a sculpture of Jesus inviting people to Himself and crying out: 'Come unto Me all ye that labor and are heavy laden, and I will give you rest.' We have been commanded by our Lord Jesus to follow Him and to receive all those who are weary and heavy laden, in spirit and in body, but especially the homeless...What Jesus asked His disciples to do is equally binding on us."[82]

Pastor Holmer did not do the politically correct thing at all, which would have been to join the others in throwing stones at Honecker. Instead, Uwe Holmer did things the Jesus way: **"Love your enemies, do good to those who hate you, bless those who curse you, pray for those who mistreat you" (Lk. 6:27-28)**. Erich Honecker deserved to die a horrible death, alone. Pastor Holmer did not give him what he deserved. Instead, he gave him mercy.

9-253

MERCY

Colossians 3:12-14

(POSB, note 2.)

Putting Feet on Your Prayers by Granting Mercy

Sometimes we can get so close to the forest that we fail to see the trees around us. Many times we pray for those around us, asking *God* to meet their needs. Perhaps *we* are that answer!

A lady answered the knock on her door to find a man with a sad expression.

"I'm sorry to disturb you," he said, "but I'm collecting money for an unfortunate family in the neighborhood. The husband is out of work, the kids are hungry, the utilities will soon be cut off, and worse, they're going to be kicked out of their apartment if they don't pay the rent by this afternoon."

"I'll be happy to help," said the woman with great concern. "But who are you? "I'm the landlord," he replied.[83]

In today's hectic, fast-paced society, we often get so wrapped up in our own lives that we fail to see the small ways in which we can help each other.

82 Reported by Bud Bultman. *Christianity Today*, 11/11/91, p.25.

83 Craig B. Larson, Editor. *Illustrations for Preaching and Teaching*, p.161.

9-254

Ministry

Ephesians 1:1-2

(POSB, note 2, point 2.b.3)

Ministry to Other Believers

Do you struggle with God's call upon your life? You can find great comfort in the presence of other Christians. For example, this is a story that could happen in any Christian church when God's people fulfill their call.

"Unemployed!" In the eyes of many, Bobby became just another impersonal statistic to join the ranks of the unemployed. At one moment, he had a secure position in his company; but the next moment saw him with his pink slip in hand—the victim of an unforgiving economy. For many people like Bobby, they would have to go it alone. But this was not Bobby's testimony.

Bobby found himself surrounded by people in his church who understood God's call upon their lives. Because God had called them, they were to live like saints and be faithful to His call as they became a vessel of God's grace and peace.

They were sensitive to Bobby's struggles and reached out to him in practical ways. Several of them committed to pray for him on a regular basis. Others in the church began to network with the business world in seeking the right career job for Bobby. Still, there were others who used their spiritual gift of encouragement to minister to Bobby when he needed another boost.

Like a light bulb that brightens a dark room, Bobby began to see for himself that God had a special call upon his life. God had not called him to trust in a career. Instead, God had called him to trust in the One who provides everything—including careers.

9-255

Ministry

Galatians 4:12-20

(POSB, note 4, point 3.)

Receiving the Ministry of Other Ministers

How open is your church's pulpit to visiting ministers? Does your pastor have every gift in the Bible and a resume that lists every possible spiritual experience? Of course not. A healthy church wants and needs input from other parts of the body of Christ. Without an extended vision, a church will never grow; eventually it will dry up and die.

About 350 years ago a shipload of travelers landed on the northeast coast of America. The first year they established a town sight [sic]. The next year they elected a town government. The third year the town government planned to build a road five miles westward into the wilderness.

In the fourth year the people tried to impeach their town government because they thought it was a waste of public funds to build a road five miles westward into a wilderness. Who needed to go there anyway?

Here were people who had the vision to see three thousand miles across an ocean and overcome great hardships to get there. But in just a few years they were not able to see even five miles out of town. They had lost their pioneering vision.

With a clear vision of what we can become in Christ, no ocean of difficulty is too great. Without it, we rarely move beyond our current boundaries.[84]

Without a vision from outside our walls of comfort, we'll never know what God is doing in His world. Don't you want to know?

9-256

MINISTRY

Colossians 1:24-29

(POSB, note 4, point 4.)

The Goal: To Present Every Man Perfect in Christ

The challenge to present every man perfect in Christ is the bottom line for a minister. Either he does or he doesn't.

A sailor had just returned from a whaling voyage. He heard an eloquent preacher. Asked how he liked the sermon, the sailor replied: "It was shipshape. The masts just high enough, the sails and the rigging all right, but I did not see any harpoons. When a vessel goes on a whaling voyage, the main thing is to get whales. They do not come because you have a fine ship. You must go after them and harpoon them. The preacher must be a whaler!"[85]

The preacher *must go* after men in order to present them to Christ. The preacher must be a worker!

9-257

MINISTRY

Philippians 2:19-24

(POSB, note 2.)

The Requirements of Ministry

A true minister of God must consider his ministry as more than a job: it must be his life. He must have a genuine concern for people. Listen to this conversation between two lay teachers, one of whom had grown weary of teaching:

"Well, how is it going for you in your Bible class?"

"Going well, thank you. And how are things in your Bible class?"

"Well, I love teaching and studying. I love the class socials and fellowship meetings we have. And I love the teaching conferences our church sends us to every year. I love it all except one thing."

"Which is?"

---

84 Craig B. Larson, Editor. *Illustrations for Preaching and Teaching*, p.276.

85 Dr. W. H. Griffith Thomas. Quoted in *Knight's Treasury of 2,000 Illustrations* by Walter B. Knight, p.280.

"The visiting. The church wants me to visit every class member, and I just do not have the time to become involved in their lives and problems. Some of them have already called me to share their problems and illnesses at all hours of the day and evening. And, frankly, I just do not have the time to visit and give them the attention needed."

"I know where you are coming from. But I need to remind you of one important detail: Without the people, there would be no Bible class and no church and no witness for Christ upon the earth. Can you imagine what the earth would be like without the witness of Christ? Your witness and gift of teaching is needed. I hope you will continue and somehow make time to visit and care for your class."

9-258

Miracle (s)

Galatians 3:1-5

(POSB, note 5.)

When God Does the Impossible

In the U.S. Navy, the Seabees have a saying: "The difficult, we do immediately. The impossible takes a little time."

Author Jamie Buckingham shares this story from the missionary adventures of JAARS (Jungle Aviation and Radio Service—the flying arm for Wycliffe Bible Translators). We pick up his story about a pilot who was fighting to keep his plane from a fatal crash:

Never for an instant did Ralph believe they could live through the pending crash...He could feel his wife's warm hand on the back of his clammy knuckles where he gripped the stick. "We do our best, God does the rest." It was the motto of JAARS. During all the time of the emergency, he had not called upon God. Why had he waited? Why had he not cried out at ten thousand feet? Now, with death only seconds away, he gulped the words. "Father, if You still have work for me and for my passengers, please bring on the engine..."

It was a sensible prayer. He could have prayed for a giant hand to rise up out of the jungle and cushion his fall. He could have asked for ten thousand angels to bear him up on wings of down. But like Moses at the Red Sea, he was content for God to work in natural ways—not by sending a strong east wind to blow back the sea—but by bringing the engine back to life...The carburetor heat!...[It] was used primarily to prevent ice from forming in the carburetor...But there were no known instances of icing at this altitude.

The carburetor heat! Again he tried to dismiss the thought, to spit it out of his mind. But it pounded against the inside of his temples. It rang in his head. And his hand was obedient. He reached down and jerked the carburetor heat handle and at the same time pulled back on the stick. The jungle had arrived. The only thing to do was flatten his glide just at the treetops, lose as much speed as possible, and settle into the foliage. Certainly forever.

Suddenly there was a mighty roar up front. The big prop, which had been slowly windmilling in the streaming air, roared to life. As if they had never quit, the thousand horses were up and running again, straining at the traces, trying with all of their might to pull the sinking old Duck out of the jaws of death.

Ralph's Canadian dignity, shaken all the way to the soles of his soggy socks, finally broke. It came forth like the sound of a shipwrecked sailor thrown at last upon a sandy beach. From the very inner part of his soul, there came forth an utterance of thanksgiving.

"Praise the Lord!" he said with deep reverence. And then repeated it. "Praise the Lord!"[86]

9-259

MISSIONS

Ephesians 1:8-14

(POSB, note 2, point 5.b.)

The Subtle Trap of Materialism

Is your church making a difference for the cause of Christ? Beware of the subtle trap that substitutes material wealth for God's true work.

There is a story of an artist who was asked to paint a picture of a decaying church. To the astonishment of many, instead of putting on the canvas an old, tottering ruin, the artist painted a stately edifice of modern grandeur. Through the open portals could be seen the richly carved pulpit, the magnificent organ, and the beautiful stained glass windows. Within the grand entrance was an offering plate of elaborate design for the offerings to missions. A cobweb was over the receptacle for foreign missions![87]

What a tragedy! To have a beautiful, grand facility for believers to enjoy and give nothing toward the spread of the gospel to the lost of the world!

9-260

MONEY

Philippians 4:10-19

(POSB, note 2, point 3.)

Control of Money

Do you control your money or does your money control you? Bill Hybles shares this personal story:

When I left the family business to enter the ministry, I turned down a golden opportunity for affluence, I say that with no credit to myself. I felt God's call so definitely that I simply could not refuse. For two years I ministered with no salary. Lynne (his wife) taught music lessons and we took in boarders to cover the rent. Then I began receiving thirty-five dollars a week, and later eighty-five. We were thrilled!

---

86 Jamie Buckingham. *Into the Glory.* (Plainfield, NJ: Logos International, 1974), p.13-14.

87 *Gospel Herald.* Walter B. Knight. *Three Thousand Illustrations for Christian Service*, p.133.

Eventually our salary was set at twelve thousand dollars a year. I remember thinking, "Who would ever want more than twelve thousand dollars a year?" Soon I found the answer. Me.

As the church grew and my job description enlarged, the board of directors periodically increased my salary. Each time I thought, "Wow, this is far more than I need. Who would ever want more than this?" Twelve months later, I would find out. Me.

Finally, in a late night truth-telling session, I came to grips with an ugly reality. The more I had, the more I wanted. I'd been believing the Money Monster's lie that just a little bit more would be enough. But when would the drive to accumulate stop? Lynne and I decided then and there to cap my salary. The board agreed to our request, and helped us strike a deadly blow to the Money Monster.[88]

9-261

Morality

Ephesians 5:1-7

(POSB, note 3.)

Example of Christian Leaders in Morality

If we are going to follow the Lord, we must do it on His terms and not on ours. Read this sobering thought from *Disciplines of a Godly Man* by R. Kent Hughes:

Recently Leadership Magazine commissioned a poll of a thousand pastors. The pastors indicated that 12 percent of them had committed adultery while in the ministry—one out of eight pastors!—and 23 percent had done something they considered sexually inappropriate. Christianity Today surveyed a thousand of its subscribers who were not pastors and found the figure to be nearly double, with 23 percent saying they had had extramarital intercourse and 45 percent indicating they had done something they themselves deemed sexually inappropriate. One in four Christian men are unfaithful, and nearly one half have behaved unbecomingly! Shocking statistics! Especially when we remember that Christianity Today readers tend to be college-educated church leaders, elders, deacons, Sunday school superintendents, and teachers. If this is so for the Church's leadership, how much more for the average member of the congregation? Only God knows![89]

Continuing on with Hughes' analysis of the above statistics, he makes the following conclusions:

This leads to an inescapable conclusion: The contemporary evangelical Church, broadly considered, is "Corinthian" to the core. It is being stewed in the molten juices of its own sensuality so that it is:

⇒ No wonder the Church has lost its grip on holiness.

⇒ No wonder it is so slow to discipline its members.

⇒ No wonder it is dismissed by the world as irrelevant.

---

88 Bill Hybles. *Honest to God?* (Grand Rapids, MI: Zondervan Publishing House, 1990) p.154.

89 R. Kent Hughes. *Disciplines of a Godly Man,* p.23-24.

⇒ No wonder so many of its children reject it.

⇒ No wonder it has lost its power in many places—and that Islam and other false religions are making so many converts.

Sensuality is easily the biggest obstacle to godliness among men today and is wreaking havoc in the Church.[90]

9-262

New Man

Ephesians 4:25-32

Exhortation: Don't Go Back to the Old Man

(POSB, note 7, point 4.)

The excellent expositor John R.W. Stott says this in his writings:

I find it helpful to think in these terms. Our biography is written in two volumes. Volume one is the story of the old man, the old self, of me before my conversion. Volume two is the story of the new man, the new self, of me after I was made a new creation in Christ. Volume one of my biography ended with the judicial death of the old self. I was a sinner. I deserved to die. I did die....Volume two of my biography opened with my resurrection. My old life having finished, a new life to God has begun.

We are simply called to "reckon" this—not to pretend it, but to realize it. It is a fact. And we have to lay hold of it. We have to let our minds play upon these truths. We have to meditate upon them until we grasp them firmly. We have to keep saying to ourselves, "Volume one has closed. You are now living in volume two. It is inconceivable that you should reopen volume one. It is not impossible, but it is inconceivable.[91]

9-263

New Man

Ephesians 4:17-24

Putting on the New Man

(POSB, Deeper Study #3)

Some people are constantly changing their outward appearance by varying their style of clothes, wearing a different hairstyle, or even focusing on different jewelry or makeup. But underneath, they are still the same people. Who have they fooled? What looks good to them now will be dissatisfactory to them in a week or two or maybe a month. Then they will change their appearance again. There is an ongoing lack of contentment with their looks. But our heavenly Father has given us a new life in Him that never tarnishes or looks bad or wears out. It is the inward man that is changed; it is the new man. The new man is a permanent part of our lives; the old way of sin is no longer acceptable. And it is only through Christ that we can receive this new nature. It is up to us to accept or reject what God has offered us.

---

90 R. Kent Hughes. *Disciplines of a Godly Man,* p.24.

91 John R. W. Stott. *Men Made New: An Exposition of Romans 5-8.* (Grand Rapids, MI: Baker Book House, 1978), p.49-50.

9-264

Obedience

Galatians 5:13-15

(POSB, note 1, point 2.)

Is the Grass Really Greener on the Other Side?

There is an old saying that says, "give him enough rope and he'll hang himself." In the same way, some Christians feel that God's love gives them enough rope (license) to explore the sins of the world. Listen to this example of one who took advantage of God's love.

My name is Sidney the Sheep. I had the good fortune of belonging to the Good Shepherd. He treated me with great respect and provided me with the finest care.

I really had it made. He made me to lie down in green pastures. And when I got thirsty, He led me beside quiet waters. When I felt bad inside, He restored my soul. I could always count on Him to lead me in the right path—a path of righteousness.

Sometimes, life got really scary as I faced the shadows of death. But my Good Shepherd stayed with me and brought comfort to my troubled heart. He kept me secure against the enemies who surrounded me. Life with Him has been wonderful.

He has promised to help me—even when I stray from His side. I could kick myself (with each of my four legs) when I allow myself to be drawn to the other side of the fence. The grass just looks greener at times. But as I sample the grass, I quickly realize that I have been deceived! When will I ever learn to trust Him for everything that I need?

Have you tried the world's green pastures? Then you have also come to realize, or will shortly, what Sidney did: looks can be deceiving!

9-265

Obedience

Galatians 5:7-12

(POSB, note 1, point 1.)

Listening to the Umpire of Your Soul

Has anyone tried to hinder you in your spiritual race? Listen to this illustration about a little boy who knew how to keep on course.

Dennis wasn't a big fellow, but as he played Little League Baseball, his knowledge of the game made up for any lack of size. On a particular summer day he swung at the ball with all his might, and to his amazement, the ball rocketed off his bat in the general direction of left field.

Off he ran! As he rounded first base, his head was down. In doing so, he failed to see whether or not the ball had landed in fair or foul territory. Before he arrived at second base, the second baseman on the other team flagged Dennis down and said, "Go back. It was a foul ball."

Without hesitation, Dennis ignored the second baseman and slid safely into second base. The umpire, whose opinion mattered the most, signaled that the ball was fair.

What is the lesson for us here? Keep on running until the Umpire of our souls, the Lord Jesus Christ, tells us to go back. We need to ignore any other voice that would hinder our running ahead to the next base.

Fair or foul? Fair ball—keep on running to the Lord. In Him, you'll always be called safe!

9-266

OBEDIENCE

Philippians 3:1-3

(POSB, note 2.)

Obedience: No Negotiations with God

Have you ever tried to bargain with God...

- by trying to find loopholes?
- by obeying Him in the easy things?
- by passing up His hard instructions?
- by highlighting the wonderful promises of the Bible and overlooking the difficult sayings that require tough decisions?

Doctor Charles Stanley of Atlanta, Georgia, has said in his teaching that *obedience* to God is defined as *Doing...*

- what He says
- when He says
- how He says
- all He says

Anything less than this is not obedience, but disobedience.

The Christian who wants to press on must obey the Scriptures in all points. Anything less than obedience is disobedience.

9-267

OBEDIENCE

Colossians 2:16-19

(POSB, note 1, point 2.)

Obedience to the Voice of God

Do you attempt to approach God on your own terms? Listen closely to this story:

The captain of the ship looked into the dark night and saw faint lights in the distance. Immediately he told his signalman to send a message: "Alter your course 10 degrees south."

Promptly a return message was received: "Alter your course 10 degrees north."

The captain was angered; his command had been ignored. So he sent a second message: "Alter your course 10 degrees south—I am the captain!"

Soon another message was received: "Alter your course 10 degrees north—I am seaman third class Jones."

Immediately the captain sent a third message, knowing the fear it would evoke: "Alter your course 10 degrees south—I am a battleship."

Then the reply came: "Alter your course 10 degrees north—I am a lighthouse."

In the midst of our dark and foggy times, all sorts of voices are shouting orders into the night, telling us what to do, how to adjust our lives. Out of the darkness, one voice signals something quite opposite to the rest—something almost absurd. But the voice happens to be the Light of the World, and we ignore it at our [own] peril.[92]

Whose rules do you follow? Whose voice do you listen to—the god and false teachings of this world or the God of heaven?

9-268

Occult

Colossians 2:8-10

(POSB, note 1.)

Warning: Avoid Attraction to Horoscopes

Do you glance at the horoscopes in your daily paper—just for the fun of it? Have you ever dabbled in the occult? Be warned! Listen to this man's testimony:

A minister paid an expensive fee to have a horoscope cast for himself, with [the] purpose of trying to prove it wrong and that astrology is nothing but ignorance and superstition.

So, he waited confidently. BUT he was astonished to find his prophecies coming true, even to the smallest details. As [the] years [went] by, he [became] uneasy and tried to find a rational explanation for this.

Finally, he concluded that he had sinned in the experiment—becoming a victim of evil spirit powers through the horoscope. He immediately repented and renounced all connections with astrology![93]

9-269

Parenting

Ephesians 6:1-4

(POSB, note 2, point 2.f.)

Building a Relationship with Children

Practically speaking, how are parents to bring their children up in the nurture and admonition of the Lord? "How To" books are helpful but are lacking. Material gifts fail to work. The only way Christian parents can obey this verse is to actively build a *relationship* with their children. Christian child psychologist, Dr. James Dobson, shares a story from his childhood with us:

My dad and I would arise before the sun came up on a wintry morning. We would put on our hunting clothes and heavy boots and drive twenty miles from the little town where we lived. After parking the car and climbing over a fence, we would enter a wooded area,

92 Craig B. Larson, Editor. *Illustrations for Preaching and Teaching*, p.134.

93 Paul Lee Tan. *Encyclopedia of 7,700 Illustrations: Signs of the Times*, p.913.

which I called the "big woods" because the trees seemed so large to me. We would slip down to the creek bed and follow that winding stream several miles back into the forest.

Then my dad would hide me under a fallen tree, which made a little room with its branches. He would find a similar shelter for himself around a bend in the creek. Then we would await the arrival of the sun and the awakening of the animal world. Little squirrels and birds and chipmunks would scurry back and forth, not knowing they were being observed. My dad and I then watched as the breathtaking panorama of the morning unfolded, which spoke so eloquently of the God who made all things.

But most importantly, there was something dramatic that occurred between my dad and me out there in the forest. An intense love and affection was generated on those mornings that set the tone for a lifetime of fellowship. There was a closeness and a oneness that made me want to be like that man...that made me choose his values as my values, his dreams as my dreams, his God as my God.[94]

Are you making memories that are nurturing?

9-270

PARENTING

Ephesians 6:1-4

(POSB, Introduction)

God's Design for the World

A strong, Christian family is God's design for the world. God wants every family to be strong and to be a follower of Him. God wants every family to be under His authority, under His care and protection, secure in His love. Day by day, the home is to be a place of safety where mistakes can be made and where love will cover a multitude of sins. How safe is your home?

Think for a moment: What happens in your home when someone spills his drink at the dining room table? Does everybody get uptight and make the offender of this "malicious" crime feel like crawling under the table in shame? One family decided to challenge this emotional event by agreeing together that accidents were simply a part of life. To prove the point in a graphic way, the mother put a table cloth on the table and slowly poured a glass of water on it. Her little child's eyes widened in disbelief! "Mom, you'll get in trouble. You'll get in trouble." She softly responded, "From now on, it's O.K. to make a mistake in our family. We are going to learn to love a lot more and yell a lot less."

Children are a gift from the Lord (Psalm 127:3). What does the Bible have to say about protecting this gift, God's gift of children? It is a crucial issue for every day and time. Every generation has its *problem children and problem parents*, and one of the major causes of the tension is the failure to heed the instructions of God's Word. Children and parents are to walk together under God's authority.

---

[94] Rolf Zettersten. *Dr. Dobson: Turning Hearts Toward Home.* (Dallas, TX: Word Publishing, 1989), p.25-26.

9-271

PARENTING

Ephesians 6:1-4

(POSB, note 1, point 2.)

Training a Child to Obey Willingly

How do you get a child to obey you? Parents have a choice to *either* threaten a child or to train a child to follow willingly. Unfortunately, a lot of us find it easier to threaten our children to obey. For example, let's take a look at a sports field as the little ones practice for the next big game.

"If you don't pay attention to the game, I'm going to jerk you off the field!" shouted the coach. He was a pretty intense fellow who hated to lose. In fact, he refused to lose. His philosophy in life was pretty simple: drive people into the ground by yelling at them. Name-calling was a valid part of the menu.

During one of these intense practices, seven year old Andy could not take any more. He was doing the best he could, he really was, but it was not enough to please the coach. "Be a leader or get out of the way!" the coach yelled. After another verbal barrage, Andy left the field, straining so the tears would not gush out. "I'm no good...I'm a failure...I'll never amount to anything, ever."

What Andy did not understand was that the negative messages he had heard were lies. Unfortunately, he grew up with a view that equated being yelled at with obedience. How many "Andys" do you know?

9-272

PATIENCE

Colossians 3:12-14

(POSB, note 6, point 2.)

Example of Patience

In the days of instant coffee and fast-food service, we have come to expect short waiting periods for things. We struggle with patience day by day; we get tied up in knots. Why? Because God is not on our schedule. We want to hurry up and wait while He wants us to be patient, to wait on Him.

William Carey, the father of a modern missions movement, had to be patient before the first Hindu convert was baptized in India. Did he wait for a few months? Was he patient for a year or two? The Lord gave him the grace to wait *seven* years until he could see the fruit of his labor.

The next time you have to wait for a slow traffic light to change, put on the garment of patience...and use the time to pray or think or plan. Make use of the time, patiently so; enjoy the wait!

9-273

PEACE

Philippians 4:1-5

(POSB, Introduction)

The Value of Peace

What kind of value do you place on having peace? Billy Graham writes about the value of peace:

I know men who would write a check for a million dollars if they could find peace. Millions are searching for it. Every time they get close to finding the peace that you have found in Christ, Satan steers them away. He blinds them. He throws up a smoke screen. He bluffs them. And they miss it! But you have found it! It is yours now forever. You have found the secret of life.[95]

Once we possess the peace of God, how do we keep and maintain it? How do we keep the peace of God ruling and reigning within our hearts? How do we keep a consciousness of God's very own presence within us—an awareness that the "God of peace" lives within our very being?

9-274

PEACE

Philippians 4:6-9

(POSB, Introduction)

Holding on to the Peace of God

Have you ever tried to squeeze a wet bar of soap? It tends to shoot right out of your hands, doesn't it? It is kind of like the peace of God—one minute you think you have it and the next minute it's gone! But the problem isn't with the soap or with God's peace—the problem is with our grip. Is there a secret that could help us hold on to the peace of God—regardless of the circumstances? The answer is yes!

9-275

PEACE

Colossians 3:15-17

(POSB, note 1, point 3.)

Do You Argue with Peace?

What kind of respect do you give to the "umpire" in your heart? Do you tend to argue the call, going nose-to-nose with the umpire?

Years ago, there was a Major League Baseball manager by the name of Leo "the Lip" Durocher. He picked up his nickname from newspaper writers who took notice of his brash and bullying conversations with the umpires. On more than one occasion, the umpire would grow weary of this onslaught and put Leo the Lip in his place—off the field and in the shower. His involvement in the game that day was finished.

How often does God send you to the showers? Notice the first phrase of Col.3:15: **"And let the peace of God rule in your hearts...."** Do you *let* His peace work in your heart?

---

[95] Billy Graham. *Peace With God.* (Garden City, NY: Doubleday & Co., 1953), p.217.

9-276

Perseverance

Philippians 3:1-3

(POSB, Introduction)

Pressing On: Guarding Oneself

You can take almost any scenario in life—cleaning house, building a house, raising kids, working at a job—and understand that each area needs maintenance. It is not enough just to do something once and expect that it will forever keep working, stay fixed, stay clean, or take care of itself. Everything and everyone needs to be nurtured to keep on track. The same is true with our Christian faith.

It is a terrible misconception to believe that personal growth for a Christian believer is natural and easy. Pressing on in our faith requires hard work and effort.

9-277

Position in Christ

Ephesians 2:4-7

(POSB, note 2.)

The Believer's Place

Have you ever gone somewhere for a special event, and you could not see because your vision was blocked? Do you remember how frustrating it was to be where you wanted to be but not have a good view? This little boy's story is for all of us who have experienced this:

"I can't see anything!" cried the little boy. The circus had come to his town, and the parade was passing him by. He could hear the instruments playing with excitement. He could hear the oohs and aahs from the crowd as the circus passed by. All he could see was a sea of legs.

Fortunately, the little boy's father took notice of his son's plight and immediately picked him up to place him high above the crowd on his shoulders.

"Wow! Look at all of those colorful costumes. The clowns are so funny to watch. Daddy, daddy, look at the elephants!"

The little boy's perspective had changed from only listening to what others were seeing; now he could also enter in, enjoying everything about the parade. His view of life was much richer upon his father's shoulders.

9-278

Positive Thinking

Philippians 4:6-9

(POSB, note 2, point 3.)

The Habit of Right Thinking

Does positive thinking really made a difference? Listen to this statement:

We do not advance upward unless we yearn upward," it has been said. Our thoughts shape our lives. We grow little or big by the ideals we cherish and the thoughts upon which we dwell.

"Avoid worry, anger, fear, hate, and all abnormal and depressing mental states," said an eminent authority on health. This victory over harmful thoughts cannot be achieved by suppressing these feelings, but by supplanting them with right thinking which is becoming to the followers of Jesus Christ, and which is the outgrowth of a close walk with the Lord.[96]

9-279

Resurrection Power Needed to Live the Christian Life

POWER

Colossians 2:11-12

(POSB, note 2, point 3.b.)

How much of the power needed to live the Christian life do you attempt to provide? Even when you get creative and give it your best shot, failure is inevitable.

In a seminary missions class, Herbert Jackson told how, as a new missionary, he was assigned a car that would not start without a push.

After pondering his problem, he devised a plan. He went to the school near his home, got permission to take some children out of class, and had them push his car off. As he made his rounds, he would either park on a hill or leave his car running. He used this ingenious procedure for two years.

Ill health forced the Jackson family to leave, and a new missionary came to that station. When Jackson proudly began to explain his arrangement for getting the car started, the new man began looking under the hood. Before the explanation was complete, the new missionary interrupted, "Why Dr. Jackson, I believe the only trouble is this loose cable." He gave the cable a twist, stepped into the car, pushed the switch, and to Jackson's astonishment, the engine roared to life.

For two years needless trouble had become routine. The power was there all the time. Only a loose connection kept Jackson from putting the power to work.

J.B. Phillips paraphrases Ephes. 1:19-20, "How tremendous is the power available to us who believe in God." When we make firm our connection with God, His life and power flow through us.[97]

9-280

The Power of the Gospel

POWER

Galatians 1:10-16

(POSB, note 2, point 3.)

The gospel of Jesus Christ is not a figment of man's imagination. When preached or taught in the power of God, the gospel will produce results. The lives of people will be changed. No man-made gospel can change the hearts of men.

When George Whitefield was shaking England with the thunders of his revival preaching, a certain baronet said to a friend: "This man Whitefield is a truly great man. Surely he will be the founder of a new religion." "A new religion!" exclaimed the friend. "Yes," said

[96] *Gospel Herald.* Walter B. Knight. *Three Thousand Illustrations for Christian Service*, p.690.

[97] Craig B. Larson, Editor. *Illustrations for Preaching and Teaching*, p.182.

the baronet, "if it is not a new religion, what do you call it?" "I say of it that it is nothing but the old religion revived and heated with divine energy in a man who really means what he says."

The old-fashioned Gospel produces old-fashioned conversions when it is reached under the power of the divine Spirit.[98]

What kind of gospel does your life proclaim? A "new religion" or the only true gospel of Jesus Christ?

9-281

Power

Colossians 1:9-11

(POSB, note 3, point 3.)

Warning: Do Not Run Out of Gas

God has designed us so that we can possess His power. Unfortunately, many of us tend to run out of gas.

On New Year's Day in the Tournament of Roses parade, a beautiful float suddenly sputtered and quit. It was out of gas. The whole parade was held up until someone could get a can of gas.

The amusing thing was this float represented the Standard Oil Company. With its vast oil resources, its truck was out of gas.

Often Christians neglect their spiritual maintenance, and though they are "clothed with power" (Luke 24:49) "[they] find themselves out of gas."[99]

9-282

Power of Darkness

Colossians 1:12-14

(POSB, note 2, point 1.b.)

Delivered from the Power of Darkness

A man asked an old Christian woman, "Does the devil ever trouble you about your past sins?" She said, "Yes." "What do you do then?" "Oh, I just send him [the devil] to the east." "Does he come back after that?" "Aye." "And what do you do then?" "I just send him away to the west." "And when he comes back from the west what do you do?" "Man, I just keep him going between the east and the west."[100]

> **"As far as the east is from the west, so far hath he removed our transgressions from us" (Ps. 103:12).**

Just like the Christian woman, you have to constantly be on guard against the devil. The devil will never quit trying to lure you into the power of darkness!

---

98 *Pentecostal Herald.* Walter B. Knight. *Knight's Master Book of 4,000 Illustrations,* p.252-253.

99 Craig B. Larson, Editor. *Illustrations For Preaching & Teaching,* p.181.

101 Walter B. Knight. *Three Thousand Illustrations for Christian Service,* p.288.

9-283

Power of Darkness
Colossians 1:12-14
(POSB, note 2, point 3.)

The Gospel Turns on the Light

The Bible tells us that before Christ came into our lives, our existence was spent in the darkness. Thankfully, God had a plan:

Bob Woods, in Pulpit Digest, tells the story of a couple who took their son, 11, and daughter, 7, to Carlsbad Caverns. As always, when the tour reached the deepest point in the cavern, the guide turned off all the lights to dramatize how completely dark and silent it is below the earth's surface.

The little girl, suddenly enveloped in utter darkness, was frightened and began to cry.

Immediately [she] heard the voice of her brother: "Don't cry. Somebody here knows how to turn on the lights."

In a real sense, that is the message of the gospel: light is available, even when darkness seems overwhelming.[101]

9-284

Power of Darkness
Ephesians 6:10-20
(POSB, note 3.)

The Believer's Spiritual Struggle

Kenneth Wuest has a descriptive picture of the believer's great spiritual struggle:

In the word "wrestle," Paul uses a Greek athletic term....When we consider that the loser in a Greek wrestling contest had his eyes gouged out with resulting blindness for the rest of his days, we can form some conception of the Ephesian Greek's reaction to Paul's illustration. The Christian's wrestling against the powers of darkness is no less desperate and fateful.[102]

9-285

Power of God
Ephesians 1:19-23
(POSB, Introduction)

A Lack of the Power of God

After a powerful storm of nature strikes an area, many homes experience a power failure.

"Where were you when the lights went out?" then becomes the topic of conversation. The storm's ferocious hands, winds, and water are hurled at earth like a demon loosed from hell. It takes men years to connect the various parts of our land with electrical lines linked to sources of power. In one devastating night, all of their work can be swept up and scattered into a chaotic mess. For days, weeks, months, and even years after, many people have to make a change in lifestyle. Old habits are not easily broken: reading at night, cooking on an electric stove, getting cold drinks from the refrigerator, turning on the heat or air conditioning, just to name a few. Not having any power causes great hardships for many.

---

101 Craig B. Larson, Editor. *Illustrations For Preaching & Teaching*, p.133.

102 Kenneth S. Wuest. *Ephesians and Colossians.* "Word Studies in the Greek New Testament." (Grand Rapids, MI: Eerdmans Publishing Co., 1966), p.141.

There is a great feeling of dependency on others at times like these. Among the people who are able to help are those who work for the power company. They can fix the problem to restore the power. And once the power is restored again, every one feels grateful and has a new appreciation for the power they once took for granted.

This is also true in the spiritual realm of life. There are a variety of storms that come our way that can cut us off from our Source of spiritual power. Sometimes circumstances are at fault, but usually the blame for not having power to live the Christian life lies with us. Without God's power, we find ourselves severely disabled.

"Where were you when the lights went out?" You were probably standing there holding the plug.

9-286

POWER OF GOD

Ephesians 1:19-23

(POSB, note 2, point 3.)

Concerning the Resurrection

Does your Christianity work during a crisis? This true story is about a Christianity that works.

The phone call came to a pay phone at the end of the dormitory hall. In calm words that were cased in sadness, the voice on the other end said, "Linda has gone home to be with the Lord." My friend Linda: a faithful wife, a wonderful mother, and a trusted friend had gone ahead of the rest of us to be with the Lord forever.

When a loved one walks through the gate of death, the resurrection assures us of God's promise to raise the dead. After taking that phone call, the Lord immediately reminded me of this great promise:

> **"O death, where is thy sting? O grave, where is thy victory?...But thanks be to God, which giveth us the victory through our Lord Jesus Christ" (1 Cor.15:54-56).**

9-287

POWER OF GOD

Ephesians 3:14-21

(POSB, Introduction)

Prayer: The Source of God's Power

I have never met a person who took a test without wanting to know what to study. Nor have I met a soldier who was willing to go into battle without his gun. Also, I have never met a pilot who wanted to lose power while still in the air.

But I have met Christians who were perfectly willing to live their lives without God's power. Why is this so? Possibly, there are some who are ignorant of how to tap into God's vast resource of power. Others know about God's power but would rather supply their own source of strength.

If we as Christians fail to plug into God's power, the results spill out in how we live: The fruit within us spoils. We take our relationship with God and turn it into just a religion. Without the power of God, Christianity becomes an empty form (or as Paul told Timothy, **"having a form of godliness, but denying the power"**—2 Tim. 3:5). Without the power of God, the joy of salvation is gone. The power of sin overwhelms us, and life becomes an endurance, not something to be enjoyed.

Do you want the power of God in your life, the power to conquer sin and to become victorious in life? God's power will come only when we learn to pray—to pray consistently and fervently.

9-288

PRAYER

Colossians 4:2-6

(POSB, note 1, point 4.)

Prayer: A Strategic Operation

Prayer is such a vital part of the believer's life. God has sovereignly chosen to change and do certain things through those who pray. Who is counting on your faithful prayers today?

There is a story told about underwater divers who worked during World War II. As fighting raged above the water, they performed their work under the water. While at work, their only connection with the world above was an air line which was hooked up to an air pump. While the underwater divers did their work, a man was stationed next to the pump to make sure it remained operational. If this man left his post, the diver would be at risk if the pump quit pumping air to his lungs.

God has stationed His people in key places. While some go "underwater" and work at bringing down the strongholds of the enemy, others have been assigned to pray for them. Prayer is the life-support system that requires our devotion. All over the world, God's workers are at war with the powers of darkness. Prayer warriors: don't forsake your post. Keep the air coming!

9-289

PRAYER

Galatians 4:12-20

(POSB, note 1, point 4.)

Praying for Your Pastor

Several Christian men who had been touched by the Lord decided to do something practical for their pastor: pray for him. What is so unusual about that, you might ask. Well, for one particular pastor, it was a brand new sensation.

These few laymen had just returned from a Bible study that encouraged them to approach their pastor and tell him that they were committing to pray for him on a regular basis. They liked their pastor but had never thought that such a great man of God needed their awkward prayers. After all, they were just laymen and *he* was the pastor.

During their appointment with their pastor, they shared with him what God had led them to do. In response to their offer, the pastor took a deep breath and told them a sad truth: "In all of my fifteen years of being in the ministry, no group of men have ever come to me to tell me that they were praying for me." He was truly touched by their Christian love; and make no mistake about it, from that day forward he preached, pastored, and prayed with a greater confidence knowing that he was not in the battle alone.

Does your pastor know that you are praying for him?

9-290

Prayer

Colossians 2:1-7

(POSB, note 1.)

Responsibility: To Hear God's Heart

Are your personal prayer times like a sprint or a marathon? In other words, how fast do you pronounce the benediction in order to move on to other busy parts of your day? Here is a story about a man who is known as "Praying Hyde"—and for good reason.

Dr. Wilbur Chapman wrote to a friend: I have learned some great lessons concerning prayer. At one of our missions in England the audiences were exceedingly small; but I received a note saying that an American missionary was going to pray God's blessing down on our work. He was known as Praying Hyde.

Almost instantly the tide turned. The hall became packed, and at my first invitation fifty men accepted Christ as their Saviour. As we were leaving I said, "Mr. Hyde, I want you to pray for me." He came to my room, turned the key in the door, and dropped on his knees, and waited five minutes without a single syllable coming from his lips. I could hear my own heart thumping, and his beating. I felt hot tears running down my face. I knew that I was with God.

Then, with upturned face, down which the tears were streaming, he said, "O God." Then for five minutes at least he was still again; and then, when he knew that he was talking with God there came from the depths of his heart such petitions for me as I had never heard before. I rose from my knees to know what real prayer was. We believe that prayer is mighty and we believe it as we never did before.[103]

Before we can pray God's will, we must be able to hear His heart.

103 *Gospel Herald.* Walter B. Knight. *Knight's Master Book of 4,000 Illustrations,* p.493.

9-291

Prayer

Ephesians 6:10-20

(POSB, note 6, point 5.)

The Christian Soldier's Responsibility

As a Christian soldier, are you serious about prayer? "How To Pray" books fill the shelves in bookstores, libraries and offices. But the haunting question that we must answer before God is: Are you seriously committed to pray? Listen closely to this story from John R. Rice:

I once visited a home in Chicago where for purpose of exercise they had an "electric horse." As a horseman of long experience in my youth, I was asked to ride the electric horse. I got on, pressed the button, and presto, I galloped a fine imitation of the gallop of a horse. But it was only an imitation after all, for when I pressed the button, the galloping stopped, and I got off exactly where I got on! I had not been anywhere at all! That is exactly like the prayer of [so many]—purely for exercise, not to get things from a prayer-hearing, prayer-answering God![104]

9-292

Prayer

Colossians 1:9-11

(POSB, Introduction)

The Partnership of Faith and Prayer

Our faith must be real, and faith becomes real when we commit ourselves to prayer. Pastor Jim Cymbala shares his experience with us:

After I had been pastor of Brooklyn Tabernacle for about a year, the church had grown to fifty people, but we were facing problems: little money, few people coming to faith in Christ. One Tuesday afternoon I sat in my cubbyhole office on Atlantic Avenue, depressed. I knew that later that day, fifteen people, at most, would come to church to pray. *How could God call me and my wife to this city not to make a difference? I wondered.*

I walked into our empty, little sanctuary and recited to God a list of my problems: "Look at this building, this neighborhood...Our offerings are laughable...I can't trust So-and-so...There's so little to work with."

Then the Holy Spirit impressed upon me, "I will show you the biggest problem in the church. It's you."

In that moment I saw with excruciating clarity that I didn't really love the people as God wanted me to. I prepared sermons just to get through another Sunday. I was basically prayerless. I was proud.

I fell on my face before God and began to weep. "God, whatever it takes, please change me. I would rather die than live out some useless ministry of catch phrases."

---

104 John R. Rice. *Prayer: Asking and Receiving.* (Murfreesboro, TN: Sword of the Lord Publishers, 1970), p.48.

The Brooklyn Tabernacle began to turn around, and twenty years later, we are still learning about the tremendous power of prayer. Every Tuesday evening many hundreds of people come together simply to pray.[105]

How often we go through life expecting God to meet our needs! And we never grasp the critical importance of our own involvement—that of prayer, constant prayer.

9-293

PRAYER

Philippians 4:6-9

(POSB, note 1, point 3.)

Getting What Only God Can Do

Dr. A.C. Dixon of Spurgeon's Tabernacle once said...."When we rely upon organization, we get what organization can do, when we rely upon education, we get what education can do; when we rely upon eloquence, we get what eloquence can do.... But...when we rely upon prayer, we get what God can do."[106]

When God answers our prayers, peace floods our hearts and lives. Anxiety is conquered and overcome.

9-294

PRIDE

Galatians 5:22-26

(POSB, note 4, point 2.)

Pride Comes When the Cross Is Forgotten

There is a fine line to walk between living in the Spirit and in the flesh. One of the things that will trip us up is pride. Pride comes when we forget the cross. Listen to this practical illustration and see how you relate to its point:

The growth chart had slipped from the playroom wall because the tape on its corners had become dry and brittle. Five-year-old Jordan hung it up again, meticulously working to get it straight. Then he stood his sister against the wall to measure her height.

"Mommy! Mommy! Anneke is forty inches tall!" he shouted as he burst into the kitchen. "I measured her."

His mom replied, "That's impossible, Sweetheart. She's only 3 years old. Let's go see." They walked back into the playroom, where the mother's suspicions were confirmed. Despite his efforts to hang the chart straight, Jordan had failed to set it at the proper height. It was several inches low.

We easily make Jordan's mistake in gauging our spiritual growth or importance. Compared to a shortened scale, we may appear better than we are. Only when we stand against the Cross, that "Great leveler of men" as A. T. Robertson called it, can we not think of ourselves "...higher than we ought to think." Christ, Himself, must be our standard.[107]

105 Jim Cymbala. Selected from the article *"How To Light The Fire," Leadership Journal.* (Fall 1994), p.57.
106 *The European Harvest Field.* Walter B. Knight. *Three Thousand Illustrations for Christian Service,* p.500.
108 Craig B. Larson, Editor. *Illustrations for Preaching and Teaching,* p.246.

9-295

Pride

Colossians 2:20-23

(POSB, note 3.)

Wrongly Taking Credit

For a person with natural gifts and abilities, the temptation is to think more highly of himself than he should. Listen closely to this fable:

A woodpecker was pecking away at the trunk of a dead tree. Suddenly lightning struck the tree and splintered it. The woodpecker flew away, unharmed. Looking back to where the dead tree had stood, the proud bird exclaimed, "Look what I did!"[108]

If you are like the woodpecker, who are you trying to fool? Certainly not God!

9-296

Priorities

Ephesians 1:15-18

(POSB, note 1.)

Doing the Best Things

Sometimes our days are filled with a lot of good things, yet we often neglect to do the best things. Think about this fact as the following illustration is shared:

Film maker Walt Disney was ruthless in cutting anything that got in the way of a story's pacing. Ward Kimball, one of the animators for Snow White, recalls working 240 days on a 4 1/2-minute sequence in which the dwarfs made soup for Snow White and almost destroyed the kitchen in the process. Disney thought it was funny, but he decided the scene stopped the flow of the picture, so out it went.[109]

9-297

Pure

Philippians 2:12-18

(POSB, note 4, point 3.)

How to Be Pure

The theory that is used for mixing paint at a hardware store is really quite simple: the more colored tint that you add to the can of white paint, the darker the paint will become.

It only takes a drop of black tint to change the color of pure white to off-white. Once that first drop of tint goes into the can of white paint, it can never be taken out. That can of paint will never be pure white again; it can only get darker.

A Christian can work at being pure. True, sin is sin and that cannot be denied. But unlike the tainted can of white paint, the Christian has hope in this great truth: **"Create in me a clean heart and renew a right spirit within me" (Ps.51:10).**

Literally, God makes something out of nothing and gives to people who are truly repentant of their sins a brand new start. In other words, He forgets about the impure can of paint and gives us a brand new can of white paint. **"Though our sins be as scarlet, He makes us as white as snow" (Is.1:18).**

108 Walter B. Knight. *Knight's Treasury of 2,000 Illustrations,* p.299.

109 Craig B. Larson, Editor. *Illustrations for Preaching and Teaching,* p.186.

9-298

Purpose of God

Ephesians 2:4-7

(POSB, note 4.)

God Wants to Show Believers His Grace

Take a look at two trophy cases and what it takes to be a proud owner of one of the trophies.

A loser again. Satan thought for sure this time that he would add Martin to his trophy collection. He had his game plan outlined in sinister detail: blind him from seeing the gospel during his formative youthful years, offer him the lie that he could take care of his own problems, hook him with addictions, and destroy his marriage. "By the time I'm through with him, he will be all mine," Satan thought to himself. So confident was he, that he began his celebration early by giving a thumbs-up to his demon henchmen. "Boys, take some time off. Martin is going in our trophy case."

Martin lived most of his adult life in the gutter. Over the years, his heart had become as hard as a rock. He would scoff with disdain whenever anyone would share the gospel with him.

"I don't need any religion. I'm a man's man," was his rehearsed speech. Over the course of life, he became an alcoholic which ruined his career and marriage. By the time he was 50 years old, he was as good as dead, an accident waiting to happen.

Unknown to Martin, God was at work in his life. Martin did not know that God also has a trophy case that is filled with trophies that resembled Martin. God takes personal pleasure in redeeming prople just like Martin and in showing them off as trophies of His mercy.

Thus God had a plan for Martin's life: replace his heart of stone with a heart of flesh, open his eyes to see his need for a Savior, and allow other believers to have a burden for him. God wanted to heal Martin from his addictions and provide a new Christian wife who would be a helpmate to him.

The result: Martin became a trophy of God's mercy. He was saved. He was added to God's great trophy case of believers, of people who have experienced God's great mercy.

Now, whose trophy are you?

9-299

Reconcilitation

Colossians 1:20-23

(POSB, note 4, point 1.)

Conditional Reconciliation

It has been said that if you are not growing then you are dying. This is particularly true with the believer. Here is a practical illustration which shows us that growth is not always easy. Here's why.

Every member of a family was puzzled over the mystery of a fern that would not grow. Sulking, seemingly, the plant refused to put out new stems. That there might be no injury from transplanting, it had been taken up carefully, and sheltered until it should have been well rooted. Everything in the way of plant food had been provided, but there it stood, no larger than when brought to the house, an awkward, ugly thing, in a mockingly large flower pot.

Then arrived a guest who was a horticulturist. He forced a wire down into the earth about the fern's roots, and diagnosed the trouble at once. The plant had been set in stiff clay, and this had become packed hard. Reset in loose soil, the fern grew luxuriously. Even the flower of God's planting cannot find root in a heart choked by the cares and riches and pleasures of this life.[110]

Where are your roots? In a hard heart of clay? Or in a heart filled with fertile soil?

9-300

Reconciliation
Galatians 1:17-24
(POSB, note 2.)

Getting a Second Chance at Life

One of the hardest things for people to do is to make things right with those whom they have hurt. But to get a fresh start, it is a necessary action. In the book *Is it Real When it Doesn't Work?*, Doug Murren and Barb Shurin recount:

Toward the end of the nineteenth century, Swedish chemist Alfred Nobel awoke one morning to read his own obituary in the local newspaper: "Alfred Nobel, the inventor of dynamite, who died yesterday, devised a way for more people to be killed in a war than ever before, and he died a very rich man."

Actually, it was Alfred's older brother who had died; a newspaper reporter had bungled the epitaph.

But the account had a profound effect on Nobel. He decided he wanted to be known for something other than developing the means to kill people efficiently and for amassing a fortune in the process. So he initiated the Nobel Prize, the award for scientists and writers who foster peace.

Nobel said, "Every man ought to have the chance to correct his epitaph in midstream and write a new one."

Few things will change us as much as looking at our life as though it is finished.[111]

Nobel was fortunate—he had a warning that jolted him out of his comfort zone. If you are reading this or listening to this, it is not too late for you to go back and make things right with someone you have hurt—or even to seek peace with someone who has hurt you!

9-301

Redemption
Ephesians 1:3-7
(POSB, note 4, point 3.)

Redemption Is Expensive, but Christ Paid It All

Do you think you are worth the price that God paid to ransom you? The Bible says that you did not come cheap. For example:

---

110 *Methodist Times*. Walter B. Knight. *Three Thousand Illustrations for Christian Service*, p.328.
111 Craig B. Larson, Editor. *Illustrations for Preaching and Teaching*, p.123.

Suppose you are standing outside of a great auction room...and you hear a clerk say, "He paid $25.00 for a picture, another man paid $600,000.00 for one." You know quite a lot about the two pictures: The twenty-five dollar picture may be any one of 10,000 little dogs done by amateur artists who paint...hoping to get paid for them. The six hundred thousand dollar picture—was it a Gainsborough, Rembrandt, Reubens?... You can judge the painting by the price that is paid for it.

We can judge ourselves by the price Christ paid for us...when I form conclusions that are justified from other portions of the Scripture—how great was my sinfulness, the depths of my nature and the height of His love.[112]

9-302

REJOICING

Philippians 3:1-3

(POSB, note 1.)

Rejoicing Keeps the Right Perspective

Rejoicing in the Lord gives the Christian believer a different perspective of life than what the world offers, for example:

A Coloradan moved to Texas and built a house with a large picture window from which he could view hundreds of miles of rangeland. "The only problem is," he said, "there's nothing to see."

About the same time, a Texan moved to Colorado and built a house with a large picture window overlooking the Rockies. "The only problem is I can't see anything," he said. "The mountains are in the way."[113]

Rejoicing in the Lord will bring contentment—no matter where you are or what is happening to you.

9-303

REJOICING

Philippians 4:1-5

(POSB, note 3.)

Radiating Joy

Are you waiting for your circumstances to improve before you begin to rejoice? Is your ability to rejoice related to your happiness? Dr. J. Vernon McGee shares this humorous story about what it means to radiate joy. Is your joy radiating?

The Fuller brush man calls at our house on Saturdays. He is not a sorrowful fellow by any means. I don't know whether he is having trouble at home or not, but he sure radiates joy. One Saturday morning my wife had gone to the market, and from my study window I saw him coming. I thought, I'll ignore him because I'm busy, and I'm not going to fool with brushes today. So he came and pushed the doorbell. I let him push it. He pushed it two or three times. I thought, He'll leave now. But he didn't leave. He knew somebody was in the house, so he just put his thumb down on the doorbell and held it.

---

112 Donald Grey Barnhouse. *Let Me Illustrate,* p.262.

113 Craig B. Larson, Editor. *Illustrations for Preaching and Teaching,* p.241.

Finally in self-defense I had to go to the door. When I opened the door, I expected him to be a little irritated because I had made him wait. But no, he was happy about it. Everything pleased him. He greeted me joyfully,

"Dr. McGee, I didn't expect to see you today!" With a scowl I said, "My wife has gone to the market. She'll see you the next time you are around." But that wasn't enough for him. I do not know how he did it, but in the next ten seconds he was in the living room and I was holding a little brush in my hand. Then I couldn't order him out—he'd given me a little brush. And so I stood there listening to his sales pitch.

When he had finished, I said, "Now look, I don't buy brushes and I don't need one. My wife generally buys from you, and she'll probably buy next time, but I haven't time to look at them. I'm busy this morning." So he thanked me and started down the walkway whistling! You would have thought I had bought every brush he had! I met a man who trains Fuller brush salesmen, and I told him about this experience. He said that they were so instructed; they are trained to radiate joy.

Now I do not know if that Fuller brush man was happy or not, but a child of God ought to have real joy, the joy of the Lord, in his life.[114]

9-304

RESTORATION

Galatians 6:1-5

(POSB, note 1, point 4.)

The Healing Results of Spiritual Surgery

Sometimes Christians can act just like sharks that sense blood in the water: they circle in for the kill. But this is not God's way! Here is an example of how restoration is to be done:

One of the great preachers of the South was marvelously converted when he was a drunkard. His ministry was quite demanding and after a great deal of pressure and temptation he got drunk one night. He was so ashamed that the very next day he called in his board of deacons and turned in his resignation. He told them, "I want to resign." They were amazed. They asked why. He frankly told them, "I got drunk last night. A preacher should not get drunk, and I want to resign."

It was obvious that he was ashamed, and do you know what those wonderful deacons did? They put their arms around him and said, "Let's all pray." They would not accept his resignation. A man who was present in the congregation that next Sunday said, "I never heard a greater sermon in my life than that man preached."

Those deacons were real surgeons—they set a broken bone; they restored him. There are some people who would have put him out of the ministry, but these deacons put that preacher back on his feet, and God marvelously used him after that.[115]

114 J. Vernon McGee. *Thru The Bible*, Vol.5, p.321.
115 *Ibid.*, p.193.

9-305

Restoration

Galatians 6:1-5

(POSB, Introduction)

They Shoot Their Wounded

The Christian army is the only one that shoots its wounded. This is often said, but is it really true? Are Christians really guilty of shooting their wounded? Sadly, Christians do often put other believers down when they fail or fall. For too often, believers become judgmental and critical when others slip and are wounded by the effects of sin.

But note: the issue is not to be why was a believer wounded by sin but how can a believer be restored? We have been given an opportunity that has been birthed in the heart of God. God is a God of restoration. He does not hold a grudge. Just ask the Prodigal Son...just look into the mirror and you will see who He restores. The Christian has been charged with the responsibility to restore fallen saints. Will we be found faithful in this critical ministry?

9-306

Return Of Christ

Philippians 3:17-21

(POSB, note 3, point 2.)

Focus upon the Return of Christ

Lehman Strauss makes a strong point in the following:

The greatest event in any country on earth is a visit from its chief emperor. History records the most elaborate preparations and memorials for such an event. Special coins have been minted, commemorative stamps issued, and highways built. Looking forward to the Coming of our Lord Jesus Christ is the highlight of Christian expectation. We should be dwelling daily in this thought of His return....Imagine how the residents in your neighborhood would feel if the President of the United States had announced that he was making a personal appearance in your community. I feel certain there would be some special preparations for his coming.[116]

9-307

Revelation

Ephesians 3:1-13

(POSB, note 2, point 2.)

Understanding the Mind of God with the Human Mind Is Futile

Natural man does not have a clue about solving the mystery of Christ. His attempt to figure out God's mind by using his own reason is futile. Use your imagination for a moment if you will:

116 Lehman Strauss. *Devotional Studies in Philippians,* p.207.

Imagine a family of mice who lived all their lives in a large piano. To them in their piano-world came the music of the instrument, filling all the dark spaces with sound and harmony. At first the mice were impressed by it. They drew comfort and wonder from the thought that there was Someone who made the music—though invisible to them—above, yet close to them. They loved to think of the Great Player whom they could not see.

Then one day a daring mouse climbed up part of the piano and returned very thoughtful. He had found out how music was made. Wires were the secret; tightly stretched wires of graduated lengths which trembled and vibrated. They must revise all their old beliefs: none but the most conservative could any longer believe in the Unseen Player.

Later, another explorer carried the explanation further. Hammers were now the secret, numbers of hammers dancing and leaping on the wires. This was a more complicated theory, but it all went to show that they lived in a purely mechanical and mathematical world. The Unseen Player came to be thought of as a myth.

But the pianist continued to play.[117]

9-308

RIGHTEOUSNESS

Philippians 3:4-16

(POSB, note 2, point 5.b.)

How hungry are you for the things of the Lord?

Having a Hunger for Righteousness

In the Antarctic summer of 1908-09, Sir Ernest Shackleton and three companions attempted to travel to the South Pole from their winter quarters. They set off with four ponies, to help carry the load. Weeks later, their ponies dead, rations all but exhausted, they turned back toward their base, goal not accomplished. Altogether, they trekked 127 days.

On the return journey, as Shackleton records in The Heart of the Antarctic, the time was spent talking about food—elaborate feasts, gourmet delights, sumptuous menus. As they staggered along, suffering from dysentery, not knowing whether they would survive, every waking hour was occupied with thoughts of eating.

Jesus, who also knew the ravages of food deprivation, said, "Blessed are those who hunger and thirst for righteousness." We can understand Shackleton's obsession with food, which offers a glimpse of the passion Jesus intends for our quest for righteousness.[118]

117 Reprinted from *The London Observer.* Craig B. Larson, Editor. *Illustrations for Preaching and Teaching,* p.81.

118 Craig B. Larson, Editor. *Illustrations for Preaching and Teaching,* p.199.

9-309

RIGHTEOUSNESS
Philippians 3:4-16
(POSB, note 2, point 3.)

The Blessings of Having Christ's Righteousness

"Christ, the righteousness which is of God (Ph.3:9).

This is the verse that came to John Bunyan as he walked through the cornfields one night, wondering how he could stand before God. He said that suddenly he saw himself—not just as a sinner, but as sin from the crown of his head to the soles of his feet. He realized that he had nothing, and that Christ had everything.[119]

9-310

SACRIFICE
Ephesians 5:1-7
(POSB, note 2, point 2.)

Giving All

The hardest thing for any person to do is to deny his selfish desires and offer his life as a sacrifice. All of us can relate to the following story:

Once upon a time a pig and a chicken went for a walk together down the main street of town. As they were walking, the chicken noticed a sign in the restaurant that looked like a pretty good deal to him.

"Hey, pig. Look at that sign in the window: 'Ham and eggs—all that you can eat.' That's a great deal."

The pig paused for a moment while he carefully chose his words. "A good deal you say. Well, for you its only an offering; but for me its a sacrifice."

9-311

SALVATION
Philippians 1:12-19
(POSB, note 3.)

A Confident Assurance of Salvation

A popular story is told about a man who was hiking on the edge of a very high cliff. In his haste to get to his destination, he slipped and found himself in a free-fall. Desperately, luckily, he was able to grab a branch of a tree that was growing out of the side of the cliff. Thankful that there was a tree there to save him from his sudden collision on the sharp rocks below, he quickly began to plot how to save himself.

His options were few: hang on to the branch with all his might; let go and finish his surely fatal free-fall; or hope that someone on top of the cliff could hear him. *"Hey! Is there anyone up there?!"* In response to his desperate cry, an unseen voice from above called out to him, *"Let go of the branch. I can help you then!"* The hiker in peril spent little time meditating on the unseen voice's offer... *"Is anybody else up there?!"*

Unlike this hiker, when the Christian finds himself out on a limb for God, he can have the assurance of a happy ending: God will save him.

---

119 J. Vernon McGee. *Thru The Bible*, Vol.5, p.314.

9-312

SALVATION

Galatians 3:1-5

(POSB, Introduction)

An Experience with Jesus Christ

Christian songwriter Andrae Crouch captured the essence of salvation by faith when he wrote, "I didn't think it could be until it happened to me. And you'll never know that it's true until it happens to you." (From *Andrae Crouch and the Disciples: Live at Carnegie Hall.* Light Records, a division of Word).

Until someone has had a spiritual experience with Jesus Christ, their concept of salvation will be built on a foundation of works. The natural mind has no concept of grace and faith. The Christian believer's experience validates the truth of this line from a great hymn: "Just as I am without one plea." You will note that the rendition does not say "Just as I *will* be," but "just as I am." Hallelujah! We can not add one thing to our salvation. Christ comes to each one of us...just as we are.

9-313

SALVATION

Colossians 4:7-18

(POSB, note 5.)

Salvation: From a Religion to a Relationship

One of the most difficult things for a lost person to do—a lost person who has been raised in a religious family—is to break free and become born again (converted). Why? Because too many people have substituted *religion* in the place of a *relationship* with Jesus Christ. Charles Spurgeon, the great preacher of an earlier generation, had this insight:

Have you ever read "The Ancient Mariner"? I dare say you thought it one of the strangest imaginations ever put together, especially that part where the old mariner represents the corpses of all the dead men rising up to man the ship,—dead men pulling the rope, dead men steering, dead men spreading sails. I thought what a strange idea that was.

But do you know, I have lived to see that time. I have gone into churches, and I have seen a dead man in the pulpit, a dead man as deacon, a dead man handling the plate, and dead men sitting to hear.[120]

Have you made the journey from a life of religion to a relationship which has given you life?

120 Paul Lee Tan. *Encyclopedia of 7,700 Illustrations: Signs of the Times*, p.1128.

9-314

Salvation

Ephesians 2:11-18

(POSB, Introduction)

Lost in Space

Have you ever felt like you were cut off from everyone, like you were free-falling through space with no chance for a soft landing?

James Lovell, John Swigert, and Fred Haise had this feeling also. These men served as the crew for Apollo 13 of the US space program. On Monday, April 13, 1970, their space craft became disabled on their way to the moon. A supply tank of oxygen exploded and left the crew with little provisions and plenty of worry.

There they were: three mortal men floating in space, piloting a disabled ship and sinking fast. They were helpless men who needed help. Their present reality was very sobering; chances were they would either float through the black space forever or burn in the earth's atmosphere in a blazing inferno. There was one glimmer of hope. The men at Mission Control were trying to find a way to keep them alive while salvaging what was left of the ship. For the next several days, every effort was made to rescue these astronauts from their captivity in space.

Miraculously, their lives were spared, and they returned to earth safe and sound.

This illustration reminds us of what Jesus Christ has done for us. For we, too, were "lost in space." We were separated by a gulf of space from God's presence, and our landing was bound for an eternity in hell away from His presence.

The Apollo 13 astronauts had a Mission Control to count on for help. The Christian can improve on that because it is Jesus Christ who controls the mission, and He has rescued us with reconciliation and peace. Let's look to Him and His Word, rejoicing for what He has done for us.

9-315

Salvation

Galatians 5:1-6

(POSB, note 2, point 3.)

Man Cannot Add One Thing to Salvation

Accepting the grace of God at face value is difficult for many Christians: "How can God be that *good* to us? What is the catch? Surely, we have to add something to what God has done to be saved." J. Vernon McGee illustrates this point for us:

Years ago a tonic called Hadacol was advertised. I don't think it is sold any more. I am not sure of the details, but they found it was about seventy-five percent alcohol. A lot of people were using it. The company that made it was giving out glowing testimonials about its product.

Now suppose a testimonial read something like this: "I took 513 bottles of your medicine. Before I began using Hadacol, I could not walk. Now I am able to run....I really have improved. But I think you ought to know that during that time I also concocted a bottle of my own medicine and used it also."

Now, my friend, that final sentence certainly muddied the water. There is no way to tell if it was the 513 bottles of Hadacol that cured him or his own concoction. The minute you put something else into the formula, you are not sure.

Now notice carefully what Paul is saying. If you trust Christ plus something else you are not saved...How can He profit you anything when you have made up a bottle of your own concoction rather than trusting Him alone for your salvation?[121]

9-316

Salvation

Ephesians 6:10-20

(POSB, note 5, point 5.)

The Helmet of Salvation—Staying Focused

Having the right mind-set is important for the Christian. God knew that the battle for the mind would be ferocious at times. What does this helmet of salvation do for Christians? It keeps us focused on our salvation. For example:

Take a look around where you're sitting and find five things that have blue in them. Go ahead and do it.

With a "blue" mindset, you'll find that blue jumps out at you: a blue book on the table, a blue pillow on the couch, blue in the painting on the wall, and so on...In like fashion, you've probably noticed that after you buy a new car, you promptly see that make of car everywhere. That's because people find what they are looking for.[122]

What's been getting your attention lately?

9-317

Satan

Colossians 2:13-15

(POSB, note 3, point 4.)

A Dangerous Foe Not to Be Ignored

Are your steps restrained by the adversary (the devil)? If he has bound you, be warned: he plays for keeps!

Spurgeon told of a wicked king who wished to impoverish and destroy one of his subjects, a blacksmith. He ordered him to make a chain of a certain length. When he was finished, he ordered him to make it longer, and after that still longer. Finally, the blacksmith had no more money to buy metal. Then the wicked king commanded that he be bound with the chain.[123]

121 J. Vernon McGee. *Thru The Bible,* Vol.5, p.183-184.
122 Craig B. Larson, Editor. *Illustrations for Preaching and Teaching,* p.243.
123 Walter B. Knight. *Knight's Treasury of 2,000 Illustrations,* p.107.

The devil is like this evil king: he draws us in a little at a time and then snatches us into his firm grip to enslave us. But praise God—Jesus came to destroy the works of the devil. The enemy has *already* been disarmed and has been made a public display. The victory is yours through Christ, through His finished work on the cross. Calvary *does* cover our sin and death. But you must *choose* to accept Christ and His victory. You must choose Christ to be saved from sin and death. You can conquer and be victorious only through Christ.

9-318

Satan

Ephesians 6:10-20

(POSB, note 2, point 2.)

How to Fight Satan

How often do you attempt to fight off the devil in your own strength? How many times have you won?

A little Christian [girl] was once asked if Satan [ever tempted] her to do wrong things and how she kept from doing them.

The answer was: "Yes, I know he wants to get me, but when Satan knocks at the door of my heart I just say, 'Jesus, won't You go to the door?' and when Satan sees Jesus, he runs away every time."

The strongest man that ever lived is not strong enough to meet Satan alone![124]

9-319

Satan

Colossians 2:16-19

(POSB, note 2, point 1.)

Warning: Do Not Dabble with Satan

For good reason, God warns us against dabbling in the world of spiritism, in the world of the devil and his horde of evil spirits.

Marlowe's drama, Dr. Faustus, tells the story of the man who sold his soul to the devil, signing the contract with his own blood, in return for which he was to have everything he wants in this life. During the twenty-four years, Faustus had a big time, gratifying every wish for wealth, power, wisdom, and pleasure....At last the time was up. Still not satisfied, Faustus hoped he may have an eleventh hour repentance, but it was not to be. As the clock struck twelve a horde of devils came to carry off the screaming victim.

Alas, many are selling out for much less than Dr. Faustus did.[125]

124 *S. S. Quarterly*. Walter B. Knight. *Three Thousand Illustrations for Christinan Service,* p.234.

125 Paul Lee Tan. *Encyclopedia of 7,700 Illustrations: Signs of the Times,* p.920.

9-320

Security

Colossians 2:8-10

(POSB, note 2, point 3.)

Christ Is the Solid Rock

Our God is a rock to the Christian believer, a rock that resists the crashing waves of false teaching.

A vessel was wrecked one stormy night off the coast of England. All were drowned except an Irish boy. The waves swept him onto a great rock. In the morning he was rescued. "Lad, didn't you tremble out there on the rock during the night?" "Sure I trembled, but the rock didn't tremble once all night long!"[126]

As you live day by day, are you clinging to the solid rock? Or are you floundering around on your own, losing ground and losing strength?

9-321

Security

Galatians 4:21-31

(POSB, note 6.)

God Has a Firm Grip on Your Life

God gives each one of His children an eternal assurance of His care for them. Legalism cannot have us anymore—we are now children of grace. This reality gives the Christian believer peace of mind. This story illustrates the truth:

Two brethren who differed on the question of the believer's safety in Christ were discussing the question, and one said to the other:

"I tell you a child of God is safe only so long as he stays in the lifeboat. He may jump out, and if he jumps out he is lost."

To this the other person replied, saying: "You remind me of an incident in my own life. I took my little son out with me in a boat. I realized, as he did not, the danger of his falling or even jumping, into the water. So I sat with him all the time, and all the time I held him fast, so he could neither fall out, nor jump out, of the boat."

"But," said the first speaker, "he could have wriggled out of his coat and got away in spite of you."

"Oh," said the other, "you misunderstood me if you supposed I was holding his coat; I was holding him."[127]

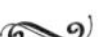

Do you understand that your heavenly Father is holding you tightly? That He has a grip on your life, not just your hand? You can rest assured that once you have genuinely placed your faith in Christ, you have eternal life. But you must take that step of faith!

126 Walter B. Knight. *Knight's Treasury of 2,000 Illustrations*, p.183.

127 J. Vernon McGee. *Thru The Bible*, Vol.5, p.311.

9-322

Service

Colossians 4:7-18

Qualifications of a Servant

(POSB, note 1.)

What qualifies a person to be used by God to serve others?

Paul has told us, by inspiration, just what they are. D.L. Moody is quoted in the Keswick Calendar as follows:

Paul sums up five things that God uses: "the weak things," "the foolish things," "the base things," "the despised things," and "the things which are not." When we are ready to lay down our strength and our weakness before the Lord, He can use us.[128]

9-323

Service

Philippians 1:20-26

The Challenge of Service

(POSB, note 4.)

What kinds of thoughts enter the heart of a Christian believer who willingly serves Christ? Here is one example:

Dwight L. Moody was the Billy Graham of the nineteenth century. On his first trip to England a young Moody heard these challenging words which would radically alter his life:

The world has yet to see what God will do with, and for, and through, and in, and by, the man who is fully and wholly consecrated to Him.

He said "a man," thought Moody; "he did not say a great man, nor a learned man, nor a rich man, nor a wise man, nor an eloquent man, nor a smart man, but simply a man. I am a man, and it lies with the man himself whether he will, or will not, make that entire and full consecration. I will try my utmost to be that man."[129]

9-324

Service

Galatians 1:1-5

The Foundation of Christian Service

(POSB, Introduction)

Have you ever felt intimidated by people who had more credentials to serve than you did? They had all the right papers, went to all of the right schools, and had been approved by all the right agencies? Have you ever felt that you just did not measure up? If you have had these kinds of feelings, you are not alone.

But rest assured, the foundation of Christian service does not rest upon such man-made things as human credentials, schools, and papers of commendation. As helpful as

128 Walter B. Knight. *Three Thousand Illustrations for Christian Service*, p.615.

129 Pat Morley. *The Rest Of Your Life.* (Nashville, TN: Thomas Nelson, 1992), p.237-238.

these things may be, they are not the foundation of our service to Christ. The foundation for service is Christ and the great work He has called us to do: that of bearing witness to His death, to the glorious truth that we can be delivered from this present evil world. Men only confirmed the great work and will of God that already works in us.

9-325

SERVICE

Galatians 5:13-15

(POSB, note 2.)

The Richest Reward Is in Helping Others

What motivates your service to others? Keep your thoughts close to the heart as you read this story:

A young woman in New York held what was considered a splendid position in a school attended by children from wealthy homes. Suddenly she gave it up and went to teach in one of the most squalid districts on East Side.

"These East Side kiddies have so little," she explained. "School is the one bright spot in their lives. I feel almost like a fairy godmother when in their midst. The children in my other school had everything. They even were [brought] to the schoolroom door by nurses and chauffeurs. There was no 'kick' in it for me."

Such confessions as this prove that Jesus was right when He stressed the fact that the joy that comes from helping others is the richest reward one can experience in life.[130]

9-326

SERVICE

Philippians 2:1-4

(POSB, Introduction)

What Would Jesus Do?

In the classic novel by Charles Sheldon, *In His Steps*, the community is challenged to live their lives just as if Jesus were physically living among them.

The attitudes of the people were dramatically changed as each one began to filter his thoughts and actions through this challenge. Needless to say, people began to change. Love and unity became the norm: just because they were walking in His steps.

What a challenge for us as well! Jesus has promised to be with us and to offer us the privilege of walking in His steps. As each of us know, saying we will do it is a whole lot easier than actually doing His will.

130 Walter B. Knight. *Three Thousand Illustrations for Christian Service,* p.614.

9-327

SERVICE

Colossians 2:20-23

(POSB, note 2.)

The Wrong Motivation for Service

What motivates you in your faith? A genuine love for Christ? Or a list of rules and regulations?

Mike grew up in a home where he was taught that the only way to please God was to be in church every time the doors were open. From his parents, he learned by example the art of saying "yes" to every opportunity to get involved in religious work.

As Mike became an adult, he quickly rose up through the ranks of church leadership. One day, his pastor asked him for permission to place his name in nomination for chairman of the board. Mike thought about it for awhile and measured the pros and cons. "Becoming chairman of the board would be great for my insurance business. My client base should increase as they see me at work in the church. It would be a real honor. Just think: God, the preacher, and *me*! It will mean more time away from my wife and children, but I'm sure they'll understand."

His wife and children did not understand. They never did see much of him after he became the chairman. His excuse was, "I'm doing it for God. Quit being so selfish." Who was being selfish? Mike or his family? In the book *Toxic Faith*, the authors make this appropriate statement:

Churchaholics have embraced a counterfeit religion. God is not honored, and the relationship with Him in not furthered. Work is the focus of everything. It—and not God—allows the person to feel safe. Rather than retreat to the loving arms of God, they literally bury themselves in their compulsive acts. The harder they work, the better they feel because they convince one another that God is applauding their efforts. They are so entangled in the world of the church that they no longer have time for the family. They are trying to work their way to heaven or pay the price for their guilt. Without intervention, they lose all sense of reality and rarely come to understand God as He really is.[131]

9-328

SERVICE

Philippians 2:19-24

(POSB, Introduction)

Learning to Serve as Number Two

The competitive culture in which we live scorns being number two. It is seen as a failure to measure up to acceptable standards of excellence.

A national car rental firm has attempted to place a positive spin on being number two. For in their eyes, "number two tries harder." In other words, number two will always be seeking to excel. They will stay responsive to the customers. They will not get lazy. You can count on number two to get the job done for you.

In the same sense, when God calls a "Timothy" to serve as *number two*, He expects him to serve willingly. It takes a special person to serve in a support capacity. None of us can do it until God calls us and equips us to serve.

---

131 Stephen Arterburn & Jack Felton. *Toxic Faith: Understanding & Overcoming Religious Addiction.* (Nashville, TN: Oliver-Nelson Books, 1991), p.120.

9-329

SIN

Ephesians 2:1-3

(POSB, note 2, point 3.)

A Lifetime of Sin

Do you know anyone who has lived a life of trespasses and sins? A story is told of a 94-year-old man who had over the course of his life been charged with 46 crimes, convicted of five felonies, placed on probation three times and served eight prison sentences.

Facing the judge for his latest crime, he stated that he would rather go to jail than to be sentenced to a nursing home. He said, "If I go to a jail, I may be out in a couple of years, If I go to a nursing home, I may be there the rest of my life."

This is a vivid example of a man who chose to walk after the course of this world. His choice was open and defiant rebellion against the laws of the land. This is exactly the same for those who choose to openly rebel against God. This person is described as a child of disobedience: he is committed to a life of crime against God's law.

9-330

SIN

Colossians 3:5-11

(POSB, note 1, point 2.b.)

Worse for Believers to Sin

Colossians 3:5-11 gives a shocking list of sins: sexual immorality, impurity, lust, evil desires, greed, anger, rage, malice, slander, filthy language, and lying. Surely, Paul must have been addressing non-believers! What kind of believer would practice these kinds of sins? The answer: not a very good believer! Warren Wiersbe adds his insight:

Do believers in local churches commit such sins? Unfortunately, they sometimes do. Each of the New Testament epistles sent to local churches makes mention of these sins and warns against them.

I am reminded of a pastor who preached a series of sermons against the sins of the saints. A member of his congregation challenged him one day and said that it would be better if the pastor preached those messages to the lost. "After all," said the church member, "sin in the life of a Christian is different from sin in the lives of other people."

"Yes" replied the pastor, "it's worse!"[132]

That really hits where it hurts! But, tragically, how true. Sins in the life of a believer are worse than sins in the life of a non-believer. Why? Because as believers we know the truth, and we know the power of God to help us overcome sin. A non-believer has neither the knowledge of God nor access to the power of God!

---

132 Warren W. Wiersbe. *The Bible Exposition Commentary*, Vol.2, p.135.

9-331

Spiriual Blessings

Ephesians 1:3-7

(POSB, Introduction)

The Spiritual Blessings of God

Have you ever heard about a person who did not trust banks, so he hid his money some place in his house? Story after story is told about large sums of money being found in mattresses or hidden under floors. More than once, we have heard of people who went lacking in meeting their basic needs during their life. After their death, fortunes were found that had never been touched.

Do you own treasures that you do not use? Many Christian believers do. Many believers live in spiritual poverty when God intended them to live like royalty.

9-332

Spiritual Blessings

Ephesians 1:3-7

(POSB, note 1, point 5.d.)

Partaking of Christ's Spiritual Blessings

Will your blessings be there when you need them? Warren Wiersbe shares this humorous illustration with us:

One of the funniest cartoons I ever saw showed a pompous lawyer reading a client's last will and testament to a group of greedy relatives. The caption read: "I, John Jones, being of sound mind and body, spent it all!"

When Jesus Christ wrote His last will and testament for His church, He made it possible for us to share His spiritual riches. Instead of spending it all, Jesus Christ paid it all...He wrote us into His will, then He died so the will would be in force. Then He arose again that He might become the heavenly Advocate (lawyer) to make sure the terms of the will were correctly followed![133]

9-333

Spiritual Gifts

Ephesians 4:7-16

(POSB, note 1.)

The Need to Share

The story is told of a simple man who prayed every day for a gift that he could share with his church family. Routinely, he would pray this simple prayer: "Lord, please give me at least one gift that I can share with my church family." After he prayed this prayer, he would go outside to sit by his mail box, waiting for the gift to come. Always being the friendly fellow he was, he made a point to share an encouraging word with the mailman.

Andy had been a mailman for years; and, like most folks, he had his share of problems both at home and at work. Trouble seemed to follow him like a cloud, and it showed on his face. On this particular day, as he had so many other times, he saw this man sitting down by his mail box. Andy really liked this fellow because every time he visited with him,

133 Warren W. Wiersbe. *The Bible Exposition Commentary*, Vol.2, p.10.

he always went away feeling better about himself. The simple man greeted him again with a smile and said, "Have you got a package for me today? I really prayed double-hard that God would send me a gift that I could share with my church family." Andy looked long and hard inside his mail bag but could find no such thing for this man. "I'm sorry friend. I have nothing for you today." Dejected, the simple man walked back to his house with slow, plodding steps. "I'll never get my gift to share with my Christian family," he sobbed out loud.

Suddenly, a light flashed in Andy's mind, and he rushed to embrace the simple man. "Friend! God has sent you a gift. I've seen it with my very own eyes," said Andy as he looked the man in the face. Feeling confused, the simple man asked, "You have... you mean He has...where?"

"For all of these months you have asked God for a gift that you already had with you. There have been days when I was as down and discouraged as I could be. But you were always there to cheer me up. You exhorted me to press on and not to give up. God has given you a great gift, the gift of encouragement to share with your Christian family. Your gift has enriched my life."

The simple man thanked Andy for his time and then went back to his house. "Lord, I've had it all wrong. Now I'm going to use all I have to help others:

⇒ *my voice to encourage them*
⇒ *my hand to help them*
⇒ *my feet to walk and fellowship with them*

And, Lord, I'm trusting you to gift me more and more so that I can help Your people more and more."

9-334

Spiritual Gifts

Ephesians 4:7-16

(POSB, note 4, point 1.)

The Results of Spiritual Gifts

Is every member of your church a minister? Look at this challenging story about a group of Christians who discovered their spiritual gifts and began to minister:

A church of my observation had experienced consecutive years of progressive growth. As attendance increased, buildings were added and the ministerial staff was enlarged. It appeared that there would never be an end to financial increase, but then the bottom dropped out of oil prices and the area slipped rapidly into its own recession.

Every possible cost-cutting measure was implemented, including drastic staff reductions. The pastor expected severe negative responses from the congregation when services that they had taken for granted were no longer available. Instead, the people testified, "We are spoiled brats who have been waited on hand and foot by our paid staff. Now it's time for us to go to work."

...The church not only went on, but it strengthened its family relationships and drew new members into its ranks even though most of the professionals were gone. Getting the people involved in the work of the ministry proved to be a needed tonic for that congregation, for they had been overfed and underexercised for a long season.[134]

9-335

Spiritual Gifts

Ephesians 4:7-16

(POSB, Introduction)

The Search for Significance

Think about it for a moment: Do you know your purpose in life? There are many people who struggle through the day-to-day rigors of life never fulfilling their God-given purpose. These people invest a lot of time and energy expending natural gifts and abilities, but what they do fails to have any lasting significance.

There is a much better way to make a difference in the world in which we live. God has given each one of us a wonderful opportunity to join with Him in His work using His gifts. One of the greatest things we can do is to make a passionate search for significance as we put into practice the spiritual gifts God has entrusted to us. The reward of finding your spiritual gift or gifts is a personal blessing. But as important as it is, your spiritual gift has no value unless you are willing to use it, to give it away. Do you know what your spiritual gift is? Are you willing to share it?

9-336

Thankfulness

Philippians 4:20-23

(POSB, Introduction)

Appreciation for God and for Fellow Christians

"Johnny, what do you say?" Or "Johnny, say thank you!" How many times have you said this as a parent or heard this as a child when receiving a gift or compliment or some act of care and love from someone? Thanking people for being kind and good is ingrained in us, and it should be.

It is just as important for believers in this generation to express their love and appreciation for each other as it was for Paul and the Philippian believers. Too often we just take things for granted and go about our business without saying a word of thanks to others. Too often we allow our own concerns to get in the way of our being gracious, thankful, and appreciative. This passage gives us a dynamic challenge. We should be far more active in expressing appreciation to God and to fellow believers.

---

134 Judson Cornwall. *Leaders Eat What You Serve.* (Shippensburg, PA: Destiny Image Publishers, 1988), p.5.

9-337

THANKFULNESS

Philippians 1:3-11

(POSB, note 1.)

How can you have a thankful heart?

How to Be Thankful

Picture a balance scale with a bowl attached to each side. Now picture this same scale inside your heart. On the left side of the scale the bowl quickly fills up with the various trials of the day: worries, misunderstandings, hurt feelings, financial stress—just to name a few.

It just seems that life is not fair. Your scale has become too weighted with bad things.

A mature believer knows how to bring a balance to life's problems. How? By deciding to fill the bowl on the right with a THANKFUL HEART. No one ever said that it would be easy or that all of your circumstances had to be pleasant.

A THANKFUL HEART comes from two things: asking and trusting God for the strength to bear the trials of life, and deliberately choosing to give thanks. As the believer acts in faith, God comes and fills his heart with an overflowing strength and gratitude.

9-338

TONGUE, THE

Colossians 3:5-11

(POSB, note 2, point 2.c.)

Danger of Poisoned Words

Have you heard the saying, "Sticks and stones may break my bones, but words will never hurt me"? That, of course, is a lie! The tongue has poisoned plenty of people that we know. Look carefully at this story:

One day a dog stole a Quaker's roast. Said the Quaker to the dog, "I will not whip thee, or stone thee, but I will give thee a bad name!" As the dog ran away, the Quaker shouted, "Bad dog! Bad dog! Bad dog!" Soon a group of people were chasing the dog and shouting, "Mad dog! Mad dog! Mad dog!" A blast from a shotgun ended the dog's life.

How easily our words are twisted, sometimes to our embarrassment, but more often to the injury or even death of others!

If you would keep your lips from slips,
Five things observe with care:
To whom you speak, of whom you speak,
And how and when and where.[135]

---

135 Walter B. Knight. *Knight's Treasury of 2,000 Illustrations*, p.413.

9-339

TONGUE, THE

Colossians 4:2-6

(POSB, note 3.)

Have a Ready Witness on Your Tongue

Does your tongue ever become paralyzed when you are given an opportunity to witness, or when you are confronted with the claims of a false religion? God wants each of us prepared to respond with a strong witness when opportunity arises.

Some years ago, Dr. Henrietta Mears visited the Taj Mahal in India. The famed structure is noted for its unusual acoustical qualities. Standing in the center of the white marble mausoleum, the guide said loudly, "There is no God but Allah and Mohammed is the prophet!"

His voice reverberated through all the chambers and corridors of the tomb.

Dr. Mears asked, "May I say something, too?"

The guide courteously replied, "Certainly." In a clear, distinct voice, Dr. Mears said, "Jesus Christ. Son of God, is Lord over all!"

Her voice, too, reverberated from wall to wall and through the corridors of the... shrine, saying, "Lord over all...over all...over all...over all!"[136]

How often we are silent when someone gives us an opening to tell what the difference is in our lives. We need to have an answer for every one who does not know and recognize the only living and true God.

9-340

TONGUE, THE

Philippians 2:12-18

(POSB, note 3, point 4.)

The Need to Control the Tongue

Have you ever been a victim of murmuring? Do you remember what it felt like? You probably had feelings of hurt and anger and a determination to protect yourself—as in this example:

"Betrayed!" The once transparent member of the neighborhood church was crushed. Sue had been so open to trust other Christians with her personal struggles. She had always been taught to share her burdens, but how could anyone take her personal pain and make it the talk of the church grapevine? "Never again will I trust my heart with another person," she vowed. And at that very moment, another member of the body of Christ withdrew into a hard shell of isolation: another victim of murmuring and gossip.

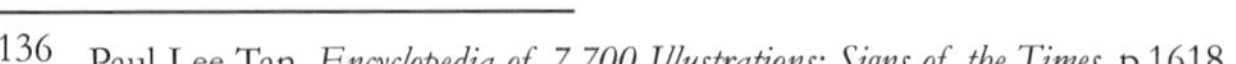

136 Paul Lee Tan. *Encyclopedia of 7,700 Illustrations: Signs of the Times,* p.1618.

9-341

TRUST

Ephesians 5:1-7

(POSB, Introduction)

Need to Follow God's Orders

All of us would probably agree with this statement: you are likely to follow someone whom you trust. Relate this story to your life as you read along:

The night was pitch black, as if every star in the heavens had been snuffed out. And there I was: holding on to the side of a dirt bank waiting for the general's orders to attack an enemy I could not see. The waiting was eating me alive. For days my division had been unable to go forward because of the enemy's intense fire. All I wanted to do was turn around and go back home.

While I was waiting, I began to reflect on all of my training. Follow the leader was a theme that was hammered into each recruit. From the first day, my leader promised to teach me everything that I would need before I fought my first battle.

As I was lost in my thoughts, the command finally came to leave the dirt bank and charge the enemy's position. Are they serious? Do they know something that I do not know? Do they know what they are doing? I could not move. Victory might be just ahead, but I'm afraid if I follow my leader's orders...What if he is wrong?

Like this soldier, we have been trained as Christians to follow orders. There are many times that we do not fully understand why God would have us do certain things. In the final analysis, we must conclude that God is always right, and so we must trust Him even when the way ahead appears hard. Battles are never won by running backwards. For the Christian, the victory comes when we choose to follow God.

9-342

TRUST

Galatians 6:1-5

(POSB, note 3.)

Place Your Trust in Christ, Not in Man

Some of the most inaccurate words that glide across the lips of Christians are these: "I'll never fall. It could never happen to me."

One of the first jokes of the age of automation describes a planeload of people soon after takeoff. A voice comes on the plane's intercom, "Good afternoon, ladies and gentlemen. Welcome aboard. We are climbing to our planned cruising altitude of 39,000 feet. All of the plane's systems are working perfectly, and we expect to land at our destination on time. This is a fully automated plane. There is no pilot or copilot. Everything is guided and monitored by a computer. We want you to sit back, relax, and enjoy the flight. Nothing can go wrong...can go wrong...can go wrong...."[137]

Do not put your trust in man and his abilities, not even in your own. As you well know, we all fail...we all fail...we all fail—far, far too often. Place your trust in Jesus Christ, for He never fails.

---

137 Gordon MacDonald. *Rebuilding Your Broken World.* (Nashville, TN: Oliver-Nelson Books, 1988), p.26.

9-343

TRUST

Philippians 1:27-30

Trust in God

(POSB, note 4, point 4.)

The story is told of a Chinese Christian who lived during the early years when the communists came to power. After being offered his life in exchange for renouncing his faith in Christ, he was finally placed before a firing squad. After the blindfold was in place, the piercing chant from the regiment's officer rang in everyone's ears: "Ready...Aim... Fire," and suddenly this Chinese Christian found himself in the eternal arms of his Savior.

Trusting in Christ will carry the believer from this world to the next.

9-344

TRUTH

Ephesians 4:25-32

Speak the Truth

(POSB, note 1, point 2.)

We can only live in safety because the senses and the nerves pass true messages to the brain. If in fact the senses and the nerves took to passing false messages to the brain, if, for instance, they told the brain that something was cool and touchable when in fact it was hot and burning, life would very soon come to an end. A body can only function accurately and healthily when each part of it passes true messages to thebrain and to the other parts. If then we are all bound into one body, that body can only function when we speak the truth. All deception impairs the working of the body of Christ.[138]

9-345

UNITY

Philippians 2:1-4

A Strong Church Is a United Church

(POSB, Introduction)

When a church is strong, it is always full of vision and planning, and it is always working out a strategy to carry forth the gospel.

A strong church launches ministry after ministry and program after program. It is never still and never complacent—neither the minds of the people nor the hands of the people. Because of this, there is always the danger of differences of opinion: differences in vision, desires, concern, emphasis, and interest. There are always different ideas as to which ministry or project should be undertaken and supported and a host of other differences.

The point is this: the more strength and activity a church has, the more attention it must give to unity. Why? Because a strong church has more minds and bodies working, and where more people are working more differences are bound to arise. Consequently, the members must give more attention to unity.

---

138 William Barclay. *The Letters to the Galatians and Ephesians*, p.184.

9-346

UNITY

Philippians 4:20-23

(POSB, note 2, point 2.)

Example of Unity

There is never to be discrimination and prejudice between believers. We are to greet every believer as a saint, as a true believer in our Lord Jesus Christ. The true brotherhood of believers was graphically demonstrated in the following event:

A Hindu and a New Zealander met upon the deck of a missionary ship. They had been converted from their heathenism, and were brothers in Christ, but they could not speak to each other. They pointed to their Bibles, shook hands, and smiled in each other's face; but that was all. At last a happy thought occurred to the Hindu. With sudden joy, he exclaimed, "Hallelujah!" The New Zealander, in delight, cried out, "Amen!" Those two words, not found in their own heathen tongues, were to them the beginning of "one language and one speech."[139]

As stated, all believers are brothers and sisters in Christ. No matter our nationality or social status, we are to greet and open our hearts, homes, and churches to one another.

9-347

UNITY

Galatians 3:23-29

(POSB, note 3, point 2.)

Ignoring the Petty Things That Divide Believers

If we walk with Christ, we will notice that petty things that divide us will fade away. How is this possible? By the cross. At the foot of the cross, all the ground is level. Look at this humorous, yet sad discussion between two brothers. Comedian Emo Philips tells this story:

In conversation with a person I had recently met, I asked, "Are you Protestant or Catholic?" My new acquaintance replied, "Protestant." I said, "Me too! What franchise?"

He answered, "Baptist."

"Me too," I said. "Northern Baptist or Southern Baptist?"

"Northern Baptist," he replied.

"Me too!" I shouted.

We continued to go back and forth. Finally I asked, "Northern conservative fundamentalist Baptist, Great Lakes Region, Council of 1879 or Northern conservative fundamentalist Baptist, Great Lakes Region, Council of 1912?"

He replied, "Northern conservative fundamentalist Baptist, Great Lakes Region, Council of 1912."

I said, "Die, heretic!"[140]

---

139 *Gospel Herald.* Walter B. Knight. *Three Thousand Illustrations for Christian Service*, p.279.

140 From *New Republic.* Selected from *Leadership*, Fall 1992, Vol.13 #4, p.47.

Too many churches and too many relationships are split over insignificant matters! In Christ, we are brothers and sisters. We must focus on our oneness in Christ, not on our differences. We have too many things which unite us with other Christian believers to let the petty things divide us from His Body.

9-348

UNITY

Philippians 2:19-24

(POSB, note 4, point 3.)

The Benefit of Unity

In Scripture, the reason that ministers Paul and Timothy were able to work so well together was because of their friendship. This story from the classroom illustrates the importance of Christian friendships.

"Is it true," asked a student, "that all the people in the world could live in Texas?" "Yes," replied the professor, "if they were friends." And if they were not friends even the world itself is too small.[141]

Paul and Timothy's commitment of friendship advanced the cause of Christ not only to Texas, but to the entire world.

9-349

WALK

Ephesians 5: 15-21

(POSB, Introduction)

A Father's Example to His Son

The Christian believer's life is a visual sermon, whether he wants it to be or not! Whether you are walking sharply in the Spirit or failing in the flesh, you are providing an example which will be copied. Look at this short, but pointed poem:

Walk A Little Plainer Daddy

Walk a little plainer Daddy, said a little boy so frail.
I'm following in your footsteps and I don't want to fail.

Sometimes your steps are very plain.
Sometimes they are hard to see.
So walk a little plainer Daddy for you are leading me.

I know that once you walked this way many years ago
And what you did along the way I'd really like to know;
For sometimes when I am tempted I don't know what to do.
So walk a little plainer Daddy for I must follow you.

141 *The Homilope* (church envelope). Walter B. Knight. *Three Thousand Illustrations for Christian Service,* p.300.

Some day when I grow up you are like what I want to be.
Then I will have a little boy who will want to follow me.
And I would want to lead him right and help him to be true.
So walk a little plainer Daddy; for we must follow you.[142]

How the believer walks day by day throughout life is crucial to the cause of Christ and to the welfare of society. He either contributes to the building up of society or to the tearing down of society. He either carries the message of life to the world, or he carries the message of silence and death. For this reason, it is important that the believer walk carefully and strictly throughout life.

9-350

WALK

Colossians 2:1-7

A Fragrant Walk

(POSB, note 5, point 3.)

Does your walk with Christ appeal to those who are close to you? H.G. Bosch shares this story about walking in the Lord:

Dr. Charles Weigle (the composer of "No One Ever Cared For Me Like Jesus") visited Pasadena, California. Early that morning he had an opportunity to walk through some of the famous rose gardens when the full fragrance of the flowers filled the air.

Later in the day he arrived at the hotel where a Bible conference was being held. As he took his seat, a man turned to him and said, "Dr. Weigle, I know where you've been. You toured one of our lovely gardens, for I can smell the pleasing aroma on your clothing." My prayer is that I may walk so closely with the Lord that the fragrance of His grace will pervade my being. I want them to know by my words, actions, and songs that I have been with Jesus.[143]

9-351

WALK

Colossians 1:9-11

A Life Consumed by the Things of God

(POSB, note 2, point 2.)

Do the things of God consume your life? Look for a moment at this example:

Aunt Vertie, one of the godliest women I have ever heard about, was once asked the meaning of "praying without ceasing." She replied: "Well, it means what it says:

⇒ "When I put on my clothes in the morning, I thank God for clothing me in the righteousness of Christ.

142 Author Unknown.
143 Paul Lee Tan. *Encyclopedia of 7,700 Illustrations: Signs of the Times*, p.1570.

⇒ "When I wash in the morning, I ask God to cleanse me from my sin.

⇒ "When I eat breakfast, I thank Christ for being the bread of life.

⇒ "When I clean house, I ask God to be merciful and cleanse the houses of the world from sin.

⇒ "When I talk with people throughout the day, I ask God to save and grow them in Christ and to meet their particular needs.

⇒ "When I see strangers or crowds of people on the streets, I pray for the salvation of the people of the world.

On and on the list could go. Aunt Vertie prayed all day, using the events of the day to remind her of the prayer that was needed to reach the world for Christ. What a walk! A life totally lived for Christ! A life worthy of Christ! A life worthy to be called Christian!

9-352

WALK

Ephesians 4:1-6

(POSB, Introduction)

A Lost Art

It was Vance Havner who said, "Walking is a lost art. Any pedestrian along a country road these days is presumed to be either out of his head or out of gas."[144]

This philosophy is clearly seen in the language of our culture today:

1) "Life in the fast lane"
2) "I'm going to run to the store"
3) "Why walk, when we can ride?"

What is it about walking?

1) "Walking is too boring"
2) "Walking is too slow"
3) "Walking just wears me out"

Excuses, excuses, excuses. But walking is:

1) A good way to slow down the pace of life and enjoy God's creation
2) Good for your health
3) Meant to be done left...right...left...right....

Walking requires us to be consistent. When we were born, walking was not an immediate skill we performed. It was something that had to be *learned.* The same is true in the spiritual realm. Walking with God is a practical skill that takes time to learn.

And once you learn to walk as a Christian, you have a lifetime to practice and keep in top form.

---

144 Dennis J. Hester, Editor. *The Vance Havner Quote Book.* (Grand Rapids, MI: Baker Book House, 1986), p.241.

9-353

WALK

Galatians 5:13-15

(POSB, Introduction)

Drawing the Line

Have you ever received a letter in the mail that informed you of some great news: *"Congratulations! You have been pre-approved to use our credit card. We think so much of you, that we have extended your limit to $7,500.00!"* At once, your spending motor turns on as you begin to visualize all those things you cannot afford—but that does not matter—just *charge* it! All of a sudden you are tempted to cross the line between liberty and license. You are in a dilemma: Where do you draw the line? How can you control yourself?

Jesus Christ has set the believer free from having to make decisions over and over again. You face the same temptations in your Christian life day after day. But fortunately, the believer no longer has to work and work in order to secure God's approval and acceptance. The believer is accepted by God through the work of Jesus Christ.

9-354

WALK

Galatians 5:22-26

(POSB, note 2, point 2.)

Living a Crucified Life

The Christian believer belongs to Jesus. When your flesh rises up and wants to rebel against Him, remember this soldier's example:

At a dinner given by a Grand Army Post, a veteran soldier was introduced as one of the speakers. In making the introduction, the presiding officer referred to the fact that the man who was to speak had lost a leg in the war, and the veteran was greeted with loud cheering as he arose to make the address.

He began by disavowing the introduction. "No," he said, "that is a mistake. I lost nothing in the war, for, when we went into the war, we gave our country all that we had, and all we brought back was so much clear gain."[145]

The closer you walk with Jesus, the farther away you will be from fulfilling the lusts of the flesh. What have you crucified lately...or is it crucifying you?

145 Walter B. Knight. *Knight's Master Book of 4,000 Illustrations*, p.111.

9-355

WALK

Philippians 1:1-2

(POSB, Introduction)

Pressing On

When you take a picture with most cameras, it takes time for the film to develop. But if you have a camera that produces a picture instantly, you can see the picture develop right before your very eyes. At first glance, that picture looks pretty unimpressive—just a white square. But in a matter of moments, form and color begin to appear. Shapes become more distinctive and the color sharpens. In a few minutes, the subject of your attention has been captured on film, an eyewitness record of what has been seen.

In the same sense, every church needs time to develop into a healthy church. Some churches develop faster than others for a variety of reasons. As you look at your own church, do not become discouraged if it appears to be only an unimpressive white square of blank film. Christ has made an eternal commitment to the church until it becomes fully mature. Look closely, and you will begin to see Him bring shape and color—a glorious maturity—to the church.

9-356

WALK

Ephesians 4:1-6

(POSB, note 2.)

Unity and Peace: When Walls Fall Down

Simply said, division is a wall between two sides. In the 1960's the Berlin Wall was erected by the Communists of East Germany to prevent East Germans from uniting with West Germans. History tells us that this was no innocent barrier: many were killed trying to scale the wall that divided the East from the West. This wall of division separated friends from friends and family from family. The result of this division brought death and despair. At times, it seemed that the wall would stay up forever.

But God had another plan. The Communist world was turned upside down as the people in Communist countries were swept up in a global wave of nationalism and the desire for freedom. The Berlin Wall had no power against the forces of unity and freedom—and it fell, becoming prize souvenirs for collectors.

Types of Berlin Walls are built every day in churches and between believers. There is no wall worth the cost of division. The only way to keep the unity of the Spirit in the church and between believers is to remain in the Spirit.

9-357

WALK

Ephesians 4:1-6

(POSB, note 1.)

The Way to Walk Worthy

Those who decide to walk in a worthy manner have also made the choice to walk with integrity. Donald Barnhouse shares this story:

A man was going with a girl who, some of us thought, was not worthy of him. Some breathed a sigh of relief when he went into the army and was gone for...years. The girl drifted around with other fellows, and the worthy young man met a worthy girl in a distant city, fell in love with her, and married her. When the war was over, he returned to his home with his bride; one evening the first girl drove by the house and dropped in to see her old flame and to meet his wife. But the wife was not there. The first girl made no attempt to hide her affection; the man realized that he had but to reach out his hand and she would be his...There was within him something that goes with male desire, but there was something more within him also, and he began to talk about the wonderful girl he had married. He showed pictures of his wife ...and praised his wife to the skies, acting as though he did not understand the obvious advances of the girl.

It was not long before she left, saying as she went, "Yes, she must be quite a girl if she can keep you from reaching." The young man was never more joyful in his life. He said that in that moment all of the love between him and his wife was greater and more wonderful than ever...A philanderer might have scoffed at him, derided him for "sacrificing" his pleasure...There was...every sacrifice in the sense of Romans 12:1, **"I beseech you therefore, brethren, by the mercies of God, that ye present your bodies a living sacrifice, holy, acceptable unto God which is your reasonable service."**[146]

9-358

WALK

Galatians 5:22-26

(POSB, Introduction)

Walk Bearing God's Nature

When was the last time you took a bite from a beautiful orange only to be disappointed by its flavor? Instead of enjoying a sweet, juicy taste, you only tasted dry fruit. It looked like an orange, smelled like an orange, and even felt like an orange. But it did not taste like an orange should taste: sweet and juicy. Instead, it was sour and dry. The Christian life can at times be likened to an orange that is sweet and juicy, producing as expected. However, many believers are offering a life that is the exact opposite: sour and dry.

A believer is to walk bearing God's nature: a life that is marked by the Fruit of the Spirit. A life that is *sweet* and *juicy*.

Note that the fruit which is produced in the believer is the fruit of the *Spirit.* God is in the business of producing top-quality fruit which is abundant and eternal. The believer has done nothing to deserve this kind of fruit. The Fruit of the Spirit is an act of the mercy and grace of a loving God.

---

146 Donald Grey Barnhouse. *Let Me Illustrate,* p.365-366.

9-359

WALK

Ephesians 5:8-14

(POSB, Introduction)

Walk in the Light

Have you ever groped around in the dark to find a light switch? As you carefully stepped, you were fearful of what might be in your path or of some unseen danger. You felt you would never get where you were going. But what happened when you turned on the light? Your fears were erased, your heart calmed, and you got your bearings back. The same is true in our Christian walk. When we grope around in the dark, it is a scary world out there. But when we walk in God's light, He helps keep us on the right path!

Two walks through life are available to men. There is the life and walk of darkness or the life and walk of light. There is a world of difference between the two. In fact, a person's eternity is determined by which life and walk he pursues.

9-360

WALK

Ephesians 4:1-6

(POSB, note 3, point 7.)

Why to Walk Worthy - Mutual Support

When we have become one with each other, all of us who are Christian believers will become nourished and will grow.

The article "What Good Is a Tree?" in Reader's Digest explained that when the roots of trees touch, there is a substance present that reduces competition. In fact, this unknown fungus helps link roots of different trees—even of dissimilar species. A whole forest may be linked together. If one tree has access to water, another to nutrients, and a third to sunlight, the trees have the means to share with one another.

Like trees in a forest, Christians in the church need and support one another.[147]

9-361

WAR

Ephesians 6:10-20

(POSB, Introduction)

A Call to Arms

On December 7, 1941, the United States was attacked by a surprising blow from Japanese military forces. President Roosevelt called it a "Day of Infamy." The world found itself at war as nations prepared to send their armies into battle. World War II finally ended years later at a great cost to life and property. The world would never again be the same.

But has man learned from history? Learned how to prevent wars? No, history books are filled with wars and rumors of wars. The fact is, war between men is inevitable, and it will be until Jesus returns.

---

147 Craig B. Larson, Editor. *Illustrations for Preaching and Teaching,* p.32.

As bad as World War II was, there was an even greater day of infamy many years ago. Satan, in all of his deceptive cunning, convinced Adam and Eve to sin, breaking their fellowship with God. Upon their choice to sin, mankind reeled in suffering.

There are many today who act like this war is over. They do not believe that the devil is real. They do not take the time to put on the armor of God. They do not know how to be strong in the Lord and in the power of His might.

9-362

WATCHMAN

Colossians 2:8-10

(POSB, Introduction)

Let Your Light Shine

What happens to a church when the Light of the world (Jesus Christ) is hidden? Darkness in the form of false teaching seeps its way into the hearts of people. Are you doing your part to warn the world of the consequences of rejecting Christ?

Several years ago [there was] a terrible accident in which several youth were killed when their car was struck by a train. At the trial the watchman was questioned: "Were you at the crossing the night of the accident?" "Yes, your Honor." "Were you waving your lantern to warn of the danger?" "Yes, your Honor," the man told the judge.

But after the trial had ended, the watchman walked away mumbling to himself, "I'm glad they didn't ask me about the light in the lantern, because the light had gone out"[148]

God has called the Christian believer to be a watchman. The challenge is to make sure our lights do not go out but shine brightly as beacons of truth.

9-363

WILL

Ephesians 1:8-14

(POSB, note 2, point 5.b.)

Doing All of the Will of God

Is your church making a difference for the cause of Christ? Beware of the subtle trap that substitutes material wealth for God's true work.

"There is a story of an artist who was asked to paint a picture of a decaying church. To the astonishment of many, instead of putting on the canvas an old, tottering ruin, the artist painted a stately edifice of modern grandeur. Through the open portals could be seen the richly carved pulpit, the magnificent organ, and the beautiful stained glass windows. Within the grand entrance was an offering plate of elaborate design for the offerings to missions. A cobweb was over the receptacle for foreign missions!"[149]

What a tragedy! To have a beautiful, grand facility for believers to enjoy and give nothing toward the spread of the gospel to the lost of the world!

---

148 Paul Lee Tan. *Encyclopedia of 7,700 Illustrations: Signs of the Times*, p.1640.

149 *Gospel Herald.* Walter B. Knight. *Three Thousand Illustrations for Christian Service*, p.133.

9-364

Will

Ephesians 5:15-21

(POSB, note 3.)

Understanding God's Will

Are you prone to make daily decisions without knowing God's will? Bob Mumford gives the following advice:

A certain harbor in Italy can be reached only by sailing up a narrow channel between dangerous rocks and shoals. Over the years, many ships have been wrecked, and navigation is hazardous.

To guide the ships safely into port, three lights have been mounted on three huge poles in the harbor. When the three lights are perfectly lined up and seen as one, the ship can safely proceed up the narrow channel. If the pilot sees two or three lights, he knows he's off course and in danger.

God has also provided three beacons to guide us. The same rules of navigation apply—the three lights must be lined up before it is safe for us to proceed. The three lights of guidance are:

1. The Word of God (objective standard).
2. The Holy Spirit (subjective witness).
3. Circumstances (divine providence).

Together they assure us that the directions we've received are from God and will lead us safely along His way.[150]

9-365

Will of God

Galatians 6:6-10

(POSB, note 3.)

Are You Willing for His Will?

How willing are you for His will? This is a question that every believer must answer whenever opportunities to minister are made available. God has provided plenty of work to do. The key is this: be ready to serve when He opens the door. Sometimes, that open door comes at a great personal sacrifice:

"You are going out to die in a year or two. It is madness!" That is what a tutor in Oxford University, England, said to a brilliant student who was giving himself under the auspices of a missionary society for service in Africa.

It turned out that the young man did die after being on the field only a year, but he had answered his tutor in these wise and weighty words: "I think it is with African missions as with the building of a great bridge. You know how many stones have to be buried in the earth, all unseen, to be a foundation. If Christ wants me to be one of the unseen stones, lying in an African grave, I am content, certain as I am that the final result will be a Christian Africa."[151]

As the hymn reminds you, "Wherever He leads, I'll go." Is that true with you?

---

150 Craig B. Larson, Editor. *Illustrations for Preaching and Teaching,* p.108.

151 *S. S. World.* Walter B. Knight. *Knight's Master Book of 4,000 Illustrations,* p.619.

9-366

Will of God

Colossians 1:1-2

(POSB, note 1, point 2.)

Equipped to Do God's Will

When God calls you to a task, He always equips you with the abilities to accomplish His will. Do you ever worry about not having the right credentials needed to share Christ? Look at this story:

A speaker was presenting Christ to a large audience on one of the great university campuses. One of the professors in the audience was stricken by the power of the message and the calm and peaceful appearance of the speaker. Leaving the auditorium the professor said to a fellow professor walking beside him, "I suppose that preacher spends most of his time in study and preparation of sermons, away from the tension and strain of this busy world of ours."

"Would you like to meet the speaker?" the fellow professor asked. "I know him well." The professor said he would, so a meeting was scheduled for lunch the next day.

How shocked the professor was when he was taken to a snack room in one of the local factories. Sitting there at the table with the speaker, he asked the speaker about his profession. "My occupation is to do the will of God and to love people while I wait for Christ to return to earth," the speaker replied. "Meanwhile, I operate one of the machines here at the factory."[152]

The point is this: a person does not have to be a great preacher to be in the will of God. Your profession is to do the will of God and to be a strong witness for Christ no matter where God places you.

9-367

Witness

Philippians 3:17-21

(POSB, note 1.)

Being an Approachable Witness

Are people drawn to you because of your witness? Is your life like that flame which draws the moth near?

Martin was that kind of a believer. He was a medical doctor by occupation, but he was a spiritual doctor in the more important field of life. He was cut out of the same mold as two other physicians who made a significant impact on this sin-sick world—Luke the physician from the New Testament, and the Lord Jesus Himself, the Great Physician.

A gray and gentle saint, Martin's loving eyes and captivating smile would overcome the most resistant soul. Assuredly, God shared Martin with this world in order to help heal the lonely wounds in each life he crossed.

It was no surprise that children of all ages wanted to be around him. Seldom would there be an empty seat by Martin. Why? Why did people want to be near Martin? To put it very simply, he loved people. And people need to be loved above all else.

Are you approachable to others? Are there any empty seats near you?

---

152 Author unknown.

9-368

WITNESS

Colossians 1:3-8

(POSB, Introduction)

Conviction to Be a Good Witness

A Hindu student said to Billy Graham in Madras, "I would become a Christian if I could see one!" Said Graham, "And when he said that, he was looking at me! That was one of the greatest sermons ever preached to me!"[153]

When we claim to be a follower of Christ, we must assume that our lives will be closely examined by the lost. People will inspect our lives for any flaws and failures. How then can we be strong in the Lord? How can we keep from collapsing and from being a poor testimony before the world?

9-369

WITNESS

Ephesians 4:17-24

(POSB, note 1, point 7.)

Impacting Those Who Watch You

Your witness makes a big difference as you walk with Christ in this world. It is important to guard yourself from the "old man" who wants to represent you. Don't be discouraged! Your Christian life lived out makes an impact on those who are watching you. Look closely at this story and apply it to your walk:

An old man, walking the beach at dawn, noticed a young man ahead of him picking up starfish and flinging them into the sea. Catching up with the youth, he asked what he was doing. The answer was that the stranded starfish would die if left until the morning sun.

"But the beach goes on for miles, and there are millions of starfish," countered the old man. "How can your effort make a difference?"

The young man looked at the starfish in his hand and then threw it to safety in the waves. "It makes a difference to this one," he said.[154]

9-370

WITNESS

Galatians 1:1-5

(POSB, note 3, point 2.)

Making the Most of Every Moment

The Christian believer has been issued a tremendous charge to proclaim the grace and peace of God. As we all journey through life, the footing can become rather treacherous at times. Do you help others as they walk?

---

153 Walter B. Knight. *Knight's Treasury of 2,000 Illustrations,* p.34.

154 Craig B. Larson, Editor. *Illustrations for Preaching and Teaching,* p.66.

A university professor tells of being invited to speak at a military base one December and there meeting an unforgettable soldier named Ralph. Ralph had been sent to meet him at the airport, and after they had introduced themselves, they headed toward the baggage claim.

As they walked down the concourse, Ralph kept disappearing. Once to help an older woman whose suitcase had fallen open. Once to lift two toddlers up to where they could see Santa Claus. And again to give directions to someone who was lost. Each time he came back with a big smile on his face.

"Where did you learn to do that?" the professor asked.

"Do what?" Ralph said.

"Where did you learn to live like that?"

"Oh," Ralph said, "during the war, I guess." Then he told the professor about his tour of duty in Viet Nam, about how it was his job to clear mine fields, and how he watched his friends blow up before his eyes, one after another.

"I've learned to live between the steps," he said. "I never knew whether the next one would be my last, so I learned to get everything I could out of the moment between when I picked up my foot and when I put it down again. Every step I took was a whole new world, and I guess I've just been that way ever since."[155]

Do you make the most of every moment? Have you learned to show God's grace and peace every chance you get?

9-371

WITNESS

Philippians 4:20-23

(POSB, note 3.)

The Challenge to Witness

R.G. Le Tourneau, a wealthy businessman, was a great lay witness for our Lord. This was his challenge to laymen:

My challenge to laymen is [this]: when Christ said, "Go ye into all the world, and preach the Gospel," He did not mean only preachers but everyone who believed on Him as the Lord of Glory. The division between the clergy and the laity is a division of our own making...[it] was not instituted by Christ, nor was it evidenced in the early Church. They believed the word "Go" meant every man, and they obeyed the Lord's command. My challenge to you is for a return to this first century...Christianity where every believer is a witness to the grace of the Lord Jesus Christ.[156]

155 Quoted from Barbara Brown Taylor, *Leadership Journal*, Summer, 1993, Vol.XIV, #3, p.61.

156 R. G. Le Tourneau. Walter B. Knight. *Three Thousand Illustrations for Christian Service*, p.724-725.

9-372

Witness

Galatians 1:1-5

(POSB, note 2.)

The Fruit of Your Witness

Just as you can judge a tree by its fruit, the same is true for any man who claims to represent God. This point is made clear by an example from the life of John Wesley.

In one of his meetings in Spitalfields, John Wesley denounced the sins of the people. Two men, heavily under the influence of liquor, stood on the edge of the crowd. "He's saying mean things about us," they said; "let's do him in." With large rocks in their hands they crept to a vantage point from which they could hurl them at Wesley's head.

As they were about to carry out their murderous plan, Wesley's emphasis suddenly changed from sin to the Saviour, the sinner's Friend. While he lovingly and earnestly spoke of the Saviour, his face shone, and his fervent words burned their way into the hearts of his would-be murderers. The stones were dropped from their hands. They went and knelt at Wesley's feet. He put his hands on their heads and said, "God bless you, my boys! God bless you!"

As they walked away one said, "Was it God Himself?" "No, Bill, but it was a man like God!" answered the other.[157]

There is no greater way to be recognized as God's man than to proclaim the gospel in power and authority.

9-373

Witness

Philippians 1:12-19

(POSB, Introduction)

The Marks of a Mature Witness

Do you ever get a little nervous when you have to share your faith? Do you get butterflies in your stomach? You are not alone in feeling that way. How many times have you promised God that you would learn how to share your witness, only to put it off until another more opportune time? Dr. Bill Bright says:

Witnessing is an activity we frequently shrink from. To intrude in someone else's life seems not only threatening but blatantly presumptuous. We fear offending the other person, fear...being rejected, fear...doing an inadequate job of representing our Lord and even being branded a "fanatic." So we remain silent, and pray that God will use someone else to get His message to those around us who do not know Him.[158]

Sound familiar? Paul has the antidote for the fear of witnessing!

---

157 Walter B. Knight. *Knight's Treasury of 2,000 Illustrations,* p.285.

158 Dr. Bill Bright. *Witnessing Without Fear.* (San Bernadino, CA: Here's Life Publishers, 1987), p.13-14.

9-374

WITNESS

Philippians 2:12-18

(POSB, note 5.)

The Qualifications for Witnessing

It was during a recent short-term missions trip that the power of the gospel was seen in a fresh light. The businessman was seen walking into a park where he stationed himself and began to tell the story of Jesus Christ to a small group of people. The businessman was not a professional preacher by any means, but he made himself available for the Lord's work. He simply had a firm grasp on this truth: *"God does not call the qualified. He qualifies the called."*

"The people in the park just kept gathering around me as I was sharing the gospel of Jesus Christ." "Do you want me to explain the gospel to you also?" he would ask the newest members of the group as they would walk in closer. On that particular day, numbers of young people gave their hearts to Jesus; just because one unqualified man accepted the call from the God who qualifies the called.

9-375

WITNESS

Colossians 1:18-19

(POSB, note 4, point 2.)

Win the Soul—Not the Argument

There is no need for the Christian believer to get into an argument with a lost person. What good will it do if we win the argument but lose the soul?

In 1893, the World's Columbian Exposition was held in Chicago, and more than 21 million people visited the exhibits. Among the features was a "World Parliament of Religions," with representatives of the world's religions, meeting to share their "best points" and perhaps come up with a new religion for the world.

Evangelist D.L. Moody saw this as a great opportunity for evangelism. He used churches, rented theaters, and even rented a circus tent (when the show was not on) to present the Gospel of Jesus Christ. His friends wanted Moody to attack the "Parliament of Religions," but he refused. "I am going to make Jesus Christ so attractive," he said, "that men will turn to Him." Moody knew that Jesus Christ was the preeminent Saviour, not just one of many "religious leaders" of history.

The "Chicago Campaign" of 1893 was probably the greatest evangelistic endeavor in D.L. Moody's life, and thousands came to Christ.[159]

What a lesson for all generations of the world—to acknowledge and proclaim that Jesus Christ is the only Savior, the only true and living God!

---

159 Warren W. Wiersbe. *The Bible Exposition Commentary*, Vol.2, p.117.

9-376

WORD OF GOD

Galatians 3:6-14

(POSB, note 2, point 2.)

A Book That Changes the Lives of Those Who Read It

How close are you to the Word of God? Is it your desire to absorb it and infuse it into your life or do you read it and hope that something sticks?

There is a story of a missionary in Korea who had a visit from a native convert who lived a hundred miles away, and who walked four days to reach the mission station. The pilgrim recited proudly, without a single mistake, the whole of the Sermon on the Mount. The missionary was delighted, but he felt that he ought to warn the man that memorizing was not enough—that it was necessary to practice the words as well as to memorize them.

The Korean's face lit up with happy smiles. "That is the way I learned it," he said. "I tried to memorize it, but it wouldn't stick. So I hit upon this plan—I would memorize a verse and then find a heathen neighbor of mine and practice it on him. Then I found it would stick."[160]

The Bible is not just a book about people who have changed...it is a book that *changes* those who read it and live out what they read!

9-377

WORD OF GOD

Colossians 1:24-29

(POSB, note 2, point 2.)

Devotion for the Word of God

The task of the minister is to reach and nourish people, reach and nourish them by using the Word of God in order to affect every area of their lives. Here is an example of how much God's Word meant to a young girl.

In France, there once lived a poor blind girl who obtained the Gospel of Mark in raised letters and learned to read it by the tips of her fingers. By constant reading,... [her fingers] became callous, and her sense of touch diminished until she could not distinguish the characters. One day, she cut the skin from the ends of her fingers to increase their sensitivity, only to destroy it.

She felt that she must now give up her beloved Book, and weeping, pressed it to her lips, saying "Farewell, farewell, sweet word of my Heavenly Father!" To her surprise, her lips, more delicate than her fingers, discerned the form of the letters. All night she perused the form of the letters. All night she perused with her lips the Word of God and overflowed with joy at this new acquisition."[161]

160 From *Earnest Worker.* Walter B. Knight. *Knight's Master Book of 4,000 Illustrations,* p.26-27.

161 Paul Lee Tan. *Encyclopedia of 7,700 Illustrations: Sings of the Times,* p.190.

9-378

WORD OF GOD

Colossians 3:15-17

(POSB, Note 2, point 3.)

Duty: Stay Connected to God's Word

By dwelling in God's Word, we connect ourselves to "the Manufacturer's Handbook." Many car owners buy their car, get in, and drive away without taking the time to read through the owner's manual. In *Focus on the Family*, Rolf Zettersten writes:

A good friend in North Carolina bought a new car with a voice warning system...At first Edwin was amused to hear the soft female voice gently remind him that his seat belt wasn't fastened...Edwin affectionately called this voice the "little woman."

He soon discovered his little woman was programmed to warn him about his gasoline. "Your fuel level is low," she said one time in her sweet voice. Edwin nodded his head and thanked her. He figured he still had enough to go another fifty miles, so he kept on driving. But a few minutes later, her voice interrupted again with the same warning. And so it went over and over. Although he knew it was the same recording, Edwin thought her voice sounded harsher each time.

Finally, he stopped his car and crawled under the dashboard. After a quick search, he found the appropriate wires and gave them a good yank. So much for the little woman.

He was still smiling to himself a few miles later when his car began sputtering and coughing. He ran out of gas! Somewhere inside the dashboard, Edwin was sure he could hear the little woman laughing.[162]

If we attempt to live the Christian life, but unplug ourselves from God's Word, we too will find ourselves stranded on the side of the road!

9-379

WORD OF GOD

Galatians 3:6-14

(POSB, Introduction)

What Would the World Be Like If There Were No Bible?

A certain man dreamed that he went to consult his Bible and found every page blank. In amazement he rushed to his neighbor's house, aroused him from sleep, and asked to see his Bible; but they found it also blank. In great consternation they sought other Bibles, with the same result. Then they said, "We will go to the libraries and gather the quotations from books, and remake our Bible." But when they examined all the books, they found blank spaces where any Scripture quotations had been. When the man awoke, his brow was cold, yet covered with perspiration, so great had been his agony during the dream. Oh, how dark this world would be without the Bible![163]

162 Craig B. Larson, Editor. *Illustrations for Preaching and Teaching*, p.39.

163 From the *King's Business*. Walter B. Knight. *Three Thousand Illustrations for Christian Service*, p.40-41.

9-380

Work

Ephesians 6:5-9

Work As unto the Lord

(POSB, note 1, point 6.)

Is a Christian's work supposed to be below the world's standard? Of course not, but many Christians work like they believe it to be true. Our witness will have absolutely no validity if we are not good workers.

Anatoly is a Russian Christian whose greatest witness was his work ethic. He always made it a point to go beyond the expectations of his supervisors and fellow peers. Over the course of his career, God also saw his faithfulness and promoted him into positions of greater responsibility. Because of his position as a crane operator, Anatoly was able to provide a pleasant home for his family as well as send his children to quality schools.

One day an American Christian spent a typical day with Anatoly and was amazed at how hard Anatoly worked. At the end of the day, the American asked: "Anatoly, you are no longer a young man, and you have a secure position; yet you work harder than you have to work. Why?"

With a puzzled look that appeared to be searching for an English translation, Anatoly said, "I work for God—aren't Christians supposed to work harder?"

> **"And whatever you do, do it heartily, as to the Lord, and not unto men" (Col. 3:23).**

For whom and what are you working?

9-381

Work

Galatians 4:21-31

Consequences of Doing Things Man's Way

(POSB, note 2, point 2.)

We must remember that even our best efforts fall short of gaining a place in heaven. It has to be grace and grace alone. Look at this humorous story that illustrates the point well.

In his mission field, a certain missionary had to do many things for himself and his family. When the baby grew too big for the carriage he started to build a bed for the child. After he prepared the wood, he glued the mortised pieces and was ready to complete the bed. His wife thought it too cold to work in the shed so he brought the materials into the kitchen and started to work. When the bed was finished, the baby was brought to the kitchen and placed in it while his parents gazed admiringly. Suddenly the father had a disquieting thought. Suppose the bed would not go through the door! Quickly he measured bed and door and found the bed one inch too wide to pass through.

There are many people who spend their time building their lives according to the plan of this world. They take great pride in their work....The day will come when they suddenly realize the measurements will not allow [them] to pass Heaven's door.[164]

164 Donald Grey Barnhouse. *Let Me Illustrate,* p.359-360.

9-382

WORK

Colossians 3:22-4:1

Example of "Scrooge"

(POSB, note 2, point 2.)

Most of us have probably read the classic Charles Dickens short story, *A Christmas Carol.* The character, Ebenezer Scrooge, has become the standard when someone thinks about a bad employer. There has never been a more stingy man alive who treated his employees with such disdain. Poor Bob Cratchet—forced to sit in a cold office because Ebenezer refused to let him put sufficient coal in the fireplace. Scrooge paid him less than a pauper's wage, overworked him, and made every attempt to destroy his self-esteem.

As the story progresses, Bob loses his job on Christmas Eve and has to go home to a family that included a sick son, Tiny Tim. With this background, if the story ended here, we could never forgive Dickens or Scrooge. But the story did not end. Scrooge had to face his past in a dream and received a frightening glimpse of his future.

The story closes as Scrooge becomes a new man. He wakes up Christmas morning realizing that his future has been revised. The old Scrooge is gone; and in his place is a fair, giving, and just Scrooge. He brings gifts to Bob's family and rehires him at a great increase of salary.

Do you work for a Scrooge? Are *you* a Scrooge? Employers have been given a tremendous trust by God for the welfare of their employees and their families. God holds every employer accountable. Dickens' Scrooge saw the light. What will the Scrooge in your life do?

9-383

WORK

Ephesians 6:5-9

Making Christianity Practical at Work

(POSB, Summary)

Why do we work? We have learned that there is a whole lot more to work than just picking up a paycheck. God has placed each of us in a particular work place to make Christianity practical to the unchurched. Look at this challenge from J. Vernon McGee:

Don't tell me Christianity is not practical. It is practical, and it will work. A great Chinese Christian, who had attended college here in the United States and knew America pretty well said, "It is not that in America Christianity has been tried and found wanting. The problem over there is it never has been tried." That is still the problem today—we have kept [Christianity] behind stained glass windows. My friend, if Christianity cannot move out of the sanctuary and get down into the secular, there is something radically wrong. It will work if it is tried.[165]

165 J. Vernon McGee. *Thru The Bible*, Vol.5, p.276.

9-384

WORK

Colossians 3:22-4:1

(POSB, Note 1, point 4.b.)

The Reason Why We Work

Why do we work? It should certainly be for more than the prize of a paycheck. The focus to this question is sharpened by this story:

Chariots of Fire, the fact-based, Oscar-winning movie, depicts the quest of Harold Abrahams and Eric Liddell to win gold medals in the 1924 Olympics, a feat they both accomplished.

The difference between Abrahams and Liddell is transparent: Everything Abrahams did was for himself, while everything Liddell did was for the glory of God.

Eric's sister Jennie mistook her brother's love of running for rebellion against God, and pressed him to return to the mission field in China, where they both were born and their parents lived. One day his sister was upset because he had missed a mission meeting, so Eric decided to have a talk with her. They walked to a grassy spot overlooking the Scottish highlands.

Clutching her arms, trying to explain his calling to run, he said, "Jennie, Jennie. You've got to understand. I believe God made me for a purpose—for China. But He also made me fast!—and when I run, I feel His pleasure!"

That is in sharp contrast to a scene later in the movie, one hour before the final race of Harold Abrahams. While his trainer gave him a rub-down, he lamented to his best friend, "I'm twenty-four and I've never known contentment. I'm forever in pursuit, and I don't even know what it is I'm chasing."

Both men won a gold medal, but one won his medal for himself, while the other won his medal for God. Do you feel God's pleasure in what you do or, like Abrahams, does contentment elude you?"[166]

9-385

WORK

Ephesians 6:5-9

(POSB, Introduction)

The Spiritual Significance of Work

Why do you work? Have you ever taken the time to think that question through? Chuck Colson and Jack Eckerd share this story with us from their book, *Why America Doesn't Work:*

The story is told of a man who visited a stone quarry and asked three of the workers what they were doing. "Can't you see?" said the first one irritably. "I'm cutting a stone."

The second replied, "I'm earning a hundred pounds a week." But the third put down his pick and thrust out his chest proudly. "I'm building a cathedral," he said.

166 Patrick M. Morley. *The Man in the Mirror.* (Dallas, TX: Word Publishing, 1989), p.71-72.

People view work in many ways: as a necessary evil to keep bread on the table; as a means to a sizable bank account; as self-fulfillment and identity; as an economic obligation within society; as a means to a life of leisure."[167]

Why do *you* work? Is it just a routine, an unwelcome obligation? Is that all there is to life? Or is there a deeper meaning and purpose that gives your work real significance?

9-386

WORKMANSHIP, GOD'S

Ephesians 2:8-10

(POSB, note 2, point 2.)

Fashioned by the Sculptor's Hands

God not only created you physically, He also created you spiritually when you were born again. As a Christian believer, God's creative power continues as you do good works. Look closely at this story:

A sculptor had been hired to build a statue for the city square of a small eastern town. The subject of his statue was to be just an ordinary man who had no noticeable attractions. The artist had been hired because he had an eye that would bring out the details of the subject that only a master sculptor could. From the first, the artist had been determined to add the details that are unseen by the natural eye. He knew that the detail would take time but he had made a promise to himself that he would do his very best—no matter what circumstances or criticism came his way. And criticism did come, for the project had drug on and on. The city leaders had grown more and more impatient as month after month had passed without the statue being finished.

But finally, the seasoned sculptor completed his most excellent work. And now the great day of presentation had arrived. The response was just what he had planned: phenomenal.

"What a wonderful work of art!"

"Who is the subject?"

"There is no one here who looks like this statue!"

"Look at the attention given to detail."

"How do you describe something so magnificent?"

The sculptor smiled and thought to himself, "The subject, the ordinary man, is me."

The Seasoned Sculptor is also at work in our lives. Like the above illustration, we are His most excellent work that He is unveiling to the world. The Lord Jesus makes us suitable. He gives attention to the small details in our lives that need to come out, and His finished work in us leaves us speechless. Remember His promise to the believer:

> **"Being confident of this very thing, that he which hath begun a good work in you will perform it until the day of Jesus Christ." (Ph. 1:6).**

What a great blessing for the Christian—We are His workmanship!

---

167 Charles Colson and Jack Eckerd. *Why America Doesn't Work*. (Dallas, TX: Word Publishing, 1991), p.177-178.

9-387

Wrath of God

Ephesians 2:1-3

(POSB, note 4.)

The Fate of the Rebellious Sinner

Our choice of sin and rebellion smoothes the path for a nature of wrath to consume us. Children of wrath are their own worst enemy. For example:

Thomas Costain's history...describes the life of Raynald III, a fourteenth-century duke in what is now Belgium.

Grossly overweight, Raynald was commonly called by his Latin nickname, Crassus, which means "fat."

After a violent quarrel, Raynald's younger brother Edward led a successful revolt against him. Edward captured Raynald but did not kill him. Instead, he built a room around Raynald in the Nieuwkerk castle and promised him he could regain his title and property as soon as he was able to leave the room.

This would not have been difficult for most people since this room had several windows and a door of near-normal size, and none was locked or barred. The problem was Raynald's size. To regain his freedom, he needed to lose weight. But Edward knew his older brother, and each day he sent a variety of delicious foods. Instead of dieting his way out of prison, Raynald grew fatter.

When Duke Edward was accused of cruelty, he had a ready answer: "My brother is not a prisoner. He may leave when he so wills."

Raynald stayed in that room for ten years and wasn't released until after Edward died in battle. By then his health was so ruined he died within a year...a prisoner of his own appetite.[168]

168 Craig B. Larson, Editor. *Illustrations for Preaching and Teaching*, p.229.

SCRIPTURE INDEX

Galatians

Reference	Illustration			
Gal. 1	**Subject**	**Title**	**Num.**	**Page**
1-5	Christ, Jesus	Christ's work on the cross	9-126	13
1-5	Witness	Making the most of every moment	9-370	134-135
1-5	Service	The foundation of Christian service	9-324	112-113
1-5	Witness	The fruit of your witness	9-372	136
6-9	False Teaching	Beware the advances of wolves	9-185	41-42
6-9	Idolatry	A warning to those who want to save their god	9-218	58
6-9	False Teaching	Protecting the gospel	9-186	42
10-16	Changed Life	A changed life in the political arena	9-117	9-10
10-16	Cross	The cross keeps us on course	9-162	30-31
10-16	Power	The power of the gospel	9-280	91-92
17-24	Christian Example	Becoming a living example of faith	9-134	17
17-24	Reconciliation	Getting a second chance at life	9-300	101
17-24	Access to God	Practicing the presence of God	9-105	3
Gal. 2				
1-10	Evangelism	Keeping alert for "hidden people"	9-173	36
1-10	Changed Life	Only the gospel can make a difference	9-118	10
1-10	Christian Life	The christian life: Your best defense	9-137	18-19
1-10	False Teaching	Keeping your heart in tune with Christ	9-187	42-43
11-21	Justification	Justification by faith in Christ alone	9-226	62-63
11-21	Honesty	Passing the examination of honesty	9-211	54
11-21	Cross	The purpose of the cross	9-164	31-32
Gal. 3				
1-5	False Teaching	A commitment to quality	9-184	41
1-5	Salvation	An experience with Jesus Christ	9-312	107
1-5	Faith	The great benefit of struggling	9-176	37-38
1-5	Miracles	When God does the impossible	9-258	80-81
6-14	Word of God	A book that changes the lives of those who read it	9-376	138
6-14	Christ, Jesus	Christ: The curse-breaker	9-131	15-16
6-14	Word of God	What would the world be like if there were no Bible?	9-379	139
15-18	Justification	A life that affects the total person	9-225	62
15-18	Covenant	God's unchanging promise	9-158	28-29
15-18	Covenant	The integrity of a man who keeps a promise	9-159	29

GALATIANS

REFERENCE	ILLUSTRATION			
Gal. 3	**Subject**	**Title**	**Num.**	**Page**
19-22	Law	How the law reveals sin	9-230	64-65
19-22	Law	Intimidating but powerless	9-231	65
19-22	Law	The law: Lacks the power to grant eternal life	9-232	65-66
19-22	Law	No man can break the law of gravitation	9-234	66-67
23-29	Unity	Ignoring the petty things that divide believers	9-347	123-124
23-29	Faith	The meaning of being "in Christ"	9-177	38
23-29	Faith	Trust the Lord to show the way	9-178	38
23-29	Faith	What faith must be	9-179	38-39
23-29	Creation	God takes delight in His creation: The believer	9-160	29-30
Gal. 4				
1-7	Bondage	Allowing the power of the cross to set you free	9-112	7
1-7	Christ, Jesus	Christ was right on time	9-124	13
1-7	Adoption	The security of being adopted into God's family	9-107	4
1-7	Christ, Jesus	Why Christ had to come	9-133	16-17
8-11	Idolatry	Living in the midst of idolatry	9-219	58-59
8-11	Backsliding	The critical need to set up familiar spiritual landmarks	9-110	5-6
12-20	Prayer	Praying for your pastor	9-289	95-96
12-20	Integrity	Placing the greatest value on the truth	9-221	60
12-20	Ministry	Receiving the ministry of other ministers	9-255	78-79
21-31	Work	Consequences of doing things man's way	9-381	140
21-31	Security	God has a firm grip on your life	9-321	111
21-31	Light	Light overcomes darkness	9-238	68-69
Gal. 5				
1-6	Christ, Jesus	Christ has freed the believer from the law's power	9-123	12
1-6	Salvation	Man cannot add one thing to salvation	9-315	108-109
1-6	Law	The law serves as a tyrant	9-233	66
7-12	Backsliding	Freedom from worldly attachments	9-109	5
7-12	Obedience	Listening to the Umpire of your soul	9-265	84-85
7-12	Corruption	Fighting off corruption with the truth	9-156	27
13-15	Walk	Drawing the line	9-353	127
13-15	Christian Life	How to win the vicious battle within	9-136	18

GALATIANS

REFERENCE		ILLUSTRATION		
Gal. 5	**Subject**	**Title**	**Num.**	**Page**
13-15	Obedience	Is the grass *really* greener on the other side?	9-264	84
13-15	Service	The richest reward is in helping others	9-325	113
16-21	Bondage	Forced to surrender unconditionally	9-113	7
16-21	Judgment	Judgment for those who live by the flesh	9-223	61
16-21	Christian Life	Tug of war: The struggle between the flesh and the Spirit	9-141	20-21
22-26	Pride	Pride comes when the cross is forgotten	9-294	98
22-26	Walk	Living a crucified life	9-354	127
22-26	Walk	Walk bearing God's nature	9-358	129
Gal. 6				
1-5	Trust	Place your trust in Christ, not in man	9-342	121
1-5	Humility	Qualifications for spiritual service	9-215	56
1-5	Restoration	The healing results of spiritual surgery	9-304	103
1-5	Restoration	They shoot their wounded	9-305	104
6-10	Will of God	Are you willing for His will?	9-365	132
6-10	Mentoring	Ministering together	9-250	75
6-10	Mentoring	The joy of shared ministry	9-251	76
11-18	Grace	Bind your fate to the grace of God	9-201	49
11-18	Cross	All direction comes from the cross	9-163	31

EPHESIANS

REFERENCE	ILLUSTRATION			
Eph. 1	**Subject**	**Title**	**Num.**	**Page**
1-2	Call of God	"I Surrender All"	9-116	9
1-2	Ministry	Ministry to other believers	9-254	78
3-7	Adoption	Adoption by God	9-106	3-4
3-7	Redemption	Redemption is Expensive, but Christ paid it all	9-301	101-102
3-7	Spiritual Blessings	The spiritual blessings of God	9-331	116
3-7	Spiritual Blessings	Partaking of Christ's spiritual blessings	9-332	116
8-14	Holy Spirit	Holy Spirit: Given as a pledge	9-209	53
8-14	Inheritance	Joint-heirs with Jesus Christ	9-220	59-60
8-14	Holy Spirit	The great blessings of God	9-210	54
8-14	Missions	The subtle trap of materialism	9-259	81
8-14	Will	Doing all of the will of God	9-363	131
15-18	Knowledge of God	The need for the knowledge of God	9-228	63
15-18	Knowledge of God	Overcoming all distractions	9-229	64
15-18	Priorities	Doing the best things	9-296	99
19-23	Heaven	Heaven: A customized place	9-205	51
19-23	Power of God	A lack of the power of God	9-285	93-94
19-23	Power of God	The power of God concerning the resurrection	9-286	94
Eph. 2				
1-3	Sin	A lifetime of sin	9-329	115
1-3	Wrath of God	The fate of the rebellious sinner	9-387	144
1-3	Disobedience	Disobedience: The path to self-destruction	9-167	33
4-7	Mercy	Getting what you do not deserve	9-252	76-77
4-7	Purpose of God	God purposes to show off His grace	9-298	100
4-7	Postion in Christ	The believer's place	9-277	90
8-10	Workmanship, God's	Fashioned by the Sculptor's hands	9-386	143
8-10	Grace	The need for the Master Craftsman	9-203	49-50
11-18	Salvation	Lost in space	9-314	108
11-18	Access to God	Access to God: Through Christ alone	9-102	1
19-22	Church	God: The Light of the church	9-143	21
19-22	Citizenship	Citizenship in the kingdom of heaven	9-147	23-24
19-22	Cornerstone	Jesus Christ, the Sure Foundation	9-155	27
19-22	Abortion	Satan's attempt to destroy the church	9-101	1

Scripture Index

Ephesians

Reference	Illustration			
Eph. 3	**Subject**	**Title**	**Num.**	**Page**
1-13	Christ, Jesus	The great mystery of Christ	9-132	16
1-13	Access to God	The folly of false gods	9-103	2
1-13	Revelation	Understanding the mind of God with the human mind is futile	9-307	104-105
14-21	Knowledge of God	Having a passion for Christ	9-227	63
14-21	Power of God	Prayer: The source of God's power	9-287	94-95
14-21	Fullness of God	Prayer is the method for being filled	9-194	46
14-21	Maturity	The key to maturity	9-248	75
14-21	Love	The love of God	9-239	69
Eph. 4				
1-6	Walk	A lost art	9-352	126
1-6	Walk	The way to walk worthy	9-357	129
1-6	Walk	Unity and peace: when walls fall down	9-356	128
1-6	Will	Why to walk worthy - mutual support	9-360	130
7-16	Spiritual Gifts	The need to share spiritual gifts	9-333	116-117
7-16	Spiritual Gifts	The results of spiritual gifts	9-334	117-118
7-16	Spiritual Gifts	The search for significance	9-335	118
17-24	Witness	Impacting those who watch you	9-369	134
17-24	New Man	Putting on the new man	9-263	83
25-32	Anger	The consequence of anger	9-108	5
25-32	New Man	Exhortation: Don't go back to the old man	9-262	83
25-32	Christian Life	Put off the garments of the old man	9-138	19
25-32	Truth	Speak the truth	9-344	122
Eph. 5				
1-7	Morality	Example of Christian leaders in morality	9-261	82-83
1-7	Sacrifice	Sacrifice: Giving all	9-310	106
1-7	Trust	Trust: The need to follow God's orders	9-341	121
1-7	Communication	Warning: Do not tune out God's messages	9-153	26
8-14	Light (of the World)	Light awakens the sleeping	9-237	68
8-14	Light (of the World)	Light overcomes darkness	9-238	68-69
8-14	Walk	Walk in the light	9-359	130
15-21	Drunkenness	God's amazing power to deliver	9-168	34
15-21	Walk	A father's example to his son	9-349	124-125
15-21	Drunkenness	Drunkenness: Disease or desire?	9-169	34
15-21	Will	Understanding God's will	9-364	132

EPHESIANS

REFERENCE	ILLUSTRATION			
Eph. 5	**Subject**	**Title**	**Num.**	**Page**
22-33	Marriage	Sacrificial love	9-241	70
22-33	Marriage	Keeping marriage vows	9-243	71
22-33	Marriage	Protecting a marriage with hedges	9-244	72
22-33	Marriage	The need to cleave to Christ	9-246	74
Eph. 6				
1-4	Parenting	Building a relationship with children	9-269	86-87
1-4	Parenting	God's design for the world	9-270	87
1-4	Parenting	Training a child to obey willingly	9-271	88
5-9	Work	Making Christianity practical at work	9-383	141
5-9	Work	The spiritual significance of work	9-385	142-143
5-9	Work	Work as unto the Lord	9-380	140
10-20	War	A call to arms	9-361	130-131
10-20	Salvation	Helmet of salvation - staying focused	9-316	109
10-20	Satan	How to fight Satan	9-318	110
10-20	Prayer	Prayer: The Christian soldier's responsibility	9-291	97
10-20	Power of Darkness	The believer's spiritual struggle	9-284	93
10-20	Gospel	The soldier's shoes	9-200	48
21-24	Faithfulness	Being faithful where Christ puts you	9-181	39-40
21-24	Faithfulness	Christian soldiers serve eternally	9-182	40
21-24	Heaven	This world is not home to the believer	9-207	52

PHILIPPIANS

REFERENCE	ILLUSTRATION Subject	Title	Num.	Page
1-2	Church	The marks of a healthy church	9-146	23
1-2	Grace	The need for grace	9-203	49-50
1-2	Burnout	Serving for the right reasons	9-115	8
1-2	Walk	Pressing on	9-355	128
3-11	Fellowship	The benefits of Christian fellowship	9-189	44
3-11	Encouragement	Compassion: The arm of encouragement	9-170	35
3-11	Thankfulness	How to be thankful	9-337	119
3-11	Maturity	The true measure of maturity	9-249	75
12-19	Salvation	A confident assurance of salvation	9-311	106
12-19	Faith	The comfort of faith	9-175	37
12-19	Witness	The marks of a mature witness	9-373	136
20-26	Service	The challenge of service	9-323	112
20-26	Commitment	The marks of a great Christian believer	9-148	24
20-26	Heaven	Where will you spend eternity	9-208	53
27-30	Heaven	The Glorious benefits of heaven	9-206	51
27-30	Church	The marks of a great Christian believer	9-145	22
27-30	Trust	Trust in God	9-343	122

Phil. 2

REFERENCE	Subject	Title	Num.	Page
1-4	Unity	A strong church is a united church	9-345	122
1-4	Joy	Concern for one another's joy	9-222	60
1-4	Discipline	Focus on things above	9-165	32
1-4	Encouragement	Receiving signals from the Lord	9-171	35
1-4	Compassion	Need for compassion	9-154	26-27
1-4	Service	What would Jesus do?	9-326	113
5-11	Judgment	You cannot hide from God	9-224	61
5-11	Humility	Humility: The example of Christ	9-216	57
5-11	Humility	Walking in the humility of Christ	9-217	57
12-18	Christian Life	The need to persevere	9-140	20
12-18	Pure	How to be pure	9-297	99
12-18	Tongue	The need to control the tongue	9-340	120
12-18	Witness	The qualifications for witnessing	9-374	137
12-18	Christian Life	Working out your own salvation	9-142	21
19-24	Unity	The benefit of unity	9-348	124
19-24	Ministry	The requirements of ministry	9-257	79-80
19-24	Service	Learning to serve as number two	9-328	114
25-30	Courage	A man who was not a quitter	9-157	28

PHILIPPIANS

REFERENCE	ILLUSTRATION			
Phil. 2	**Subject**	**Title**	**Num.**	**Page**
25-30	Commitment	Signs of reduced commitment	9-149	24-25
25-30	Commitment	Trusting God in difficult circumstances	9-150	25
Phil. 3				
1-3	Obedience	Obedience: No negotiations with God	9-266	85
1-3	Perseverance	Pressing on: Guarding oneself	9-277	90
1-3	Rejoicing	Rejoicing keeps the right perspective	9-302	102
1-3	False Teachers	Warning: Beware of false teachers	9-183	40-41
4-16	Discipline	Focusing on the prize	9-166	33
4-16	Righteousness	Having a hunger for righteousness	9-307	104-105
4-16	Faith	Need for a relationship with Christ	9-174	37
4-16	Forgiveness	Forgiveness sets us free from the past	9-192	45
4-16	Righteousness	The blessings of having Christ's righteousness	9-309	106
17-21	Witness	Being an approachable witness	9-367	133
17-21	Return of Christ	Focus upon the return of Christ	9-306	104
17-21	Godly Examples	Your example speaks volumes	9-199	48
Phil. 4				
1-5	Peace	The value of peace	9-273	89
1-5	Gentleness	Strength under control	9-195	46
1-5	Rejoicing	Radiating joy	9-303	102-103
6-9	Peace	A step to peace: Prayer and positive thinking	9-274	89
6-9	Positive thinking	The habit of right thinking	9-278	90-91
6-9	Prayer	The result of prayer	9-293	98
10-19	Giving	Getting what only God can do	9-196	47
10-19	Giving	A spiritual checkup	9-197	47
10-19	Giving	Achieving contentment through giving	9-198	48
10-19	Money	Control of money	9-260	81-82
20-23	Thankfulness	Appreciation for God and for fellow Christians	9-336	118
20-23	Unity	Example of unity	9-346	123
20-23	Witness	The challenge to witness	9-371	135

Scripture Index

Colossians

Reference		Illustration		
Col. 1	**Subject**	**Title**	**Num.**	**Page**
1-2	Burdens	Carrying burdens in your own strength	9-114	8
1-2	Will of God	Equipped to do God's will	9-366	133
3-8	Christian Life	Being identified as a follower of Christ	9-135	18
3-8	Witness	Conviction to be a good witness	9-368	134
3-8	Hope	The believer's hope is in Christ alone, not in religion	9-213	55
3-8	Hope	Hope is focused on eternal life	9-212	54-55
9-11	Walk	A life consumed by the things of God	9-351	125-126
9-11	Prayer	The partnership of faith and prayer	9-292	97-98
9-11	Power	Warning: Do not run out of gas	9-281	92
12-14	Christ, Jesus	Count your blessings	9-120	11
12-14	Power of Darkness	Delivered from the power of darkness	9-282	92
12-14	Power of Darkness	The gospel turns on the light	9-283	93
12-14	Forgiveness	Sins are remembered no more	9-193	45
15	Communication	Do not guess about the truth—know it	9-151	25
15	Christ, Jesus	Christ, the express image of God	9-121	11
15	Christ, Jesus	Keeping our focus on Christ	9-127	14
15	Marriage	The truth was never known	9-247	74
16-17	Christ, Jesus	Christ holds everything together	9-119	10
16-17	Creation	Creation: Not an accident	9-161	30-31
16-17	Christ, Jesus	Christ's perfection is all we need	9-129	14-15
18-19	Church	Keeping Christ as the Head of the church	9-144	22
18-19	Christ, Jesus	Christ must be the Head of the Church	9-128	14
18-19	Witness	Win the soul—not the argument	9-375	137
20-23	Christ, Jesus	Christ: The Reconciler of all things	9-122	11
20-23	Reconciliation	Conditional reconciliation	9-299	100-101
20-23	Man	Unsaved man's hatred for God	9-240	70
24-29	Word of God	Devotion for the Word of God	9-377	138
24-29	Ministry	The goal of ministry: To present every man perfect in Christ	9-256	79
Col. 2				
1-7	Walk	A fragrant walk	9-350	125
1-7	False Teaching	Why is false teaching so appealing?	9-188	43
1-7	Prayer	Responsibility of prayer: To hear God's heart	9-290	96
8-10	Security	Christ is the Solid Rock	9-320	111

Colossians

Reference	Illustration			
Col. 2	**Subject**	**Title**	**Num.**	**Page**
8-10	Watchman	Let your light shine	9-362	131
8-10	Occult	Warning: Avoid attraction to horoscopes	9-268	86
11-12	Forgiveness	Christ has cleansed the believer's heart	9-190	44
11-12	Power	Resurrection power needed to live the Christian life	9-279	91
13-15	Law	No man can keep the law	9-235	67
13-15	Satan	Satan is a dangerous foe not to be ignored	9-317	109-110
16-19	Obedience	Obedience to the voice of God	9-267	85-86
16-19	Satan	Warning: Do not dabble with Satan	9-319	110
20-23	Access to God	Man has no power by himself	9-104	2-3
20-23	Christ, Jesus	Keeping our focus on Christ	9-127	15
20-23	Christ, Jesus	Christ will stand in for the believer	9-130	15
20-23	Service	The wrong motivation for service	9-327	114
20-23	Pride	Wrongly taking credit	9-295	99
Col. 3				
1-4	Christ, Jesus	Hidden with Christ	9-125	13
1-4	Christian Life	Risen with Christ	9-139	19
1-4	Communication	Know the language of heaven	9-152	25-26
5-11	Tongue	Danger of poisoned words	9-338	119
5-11	Sin	Worse for believers to sin	9-330	115
12-14	Patience	Example of patience	9-272	88
12-14	Forgiveness	Forgiveness: The power to set people free	9-191	44-45
12-14	Humility	Humility: Helps keep the focus on the gospel	9-214	56
12-14	Mercy	Putting feet on your prayers by granting mercy	9-253	77
15-17	Peace	Do you argue with peace?	9-275	89
15-17	Word of God	Duty: Stay connected to God's Word	9-378	139
15-17	Heart	The heart must be empowered by the Holy Spirit	9-204	50
18-21	Marriage	Biblical submission in marriage	9-242	70-71
18-21	Marriage	Protecting your marriage	9-245	72-73
22-4:1	Work	Example of "Scrooge"	9-382	141
22-4:1	Work	Reason why we work	9-384	142

Colossians

Reference Col. 4	Illustration Subject	Title	Num.	Page
2-6	Evangelism	Staying sensitive to the needs of the lost	9-172	35-36
2-6	Tongue	Have a ready witness on your tongue	9-339	120
2-6	Prayer	Prayer: A strategic operation	9-288	95
7-18	Faithfulness	Faithful even unto death	9-180	39
7-18	Service	Qualifications of a servant	9-322	112
7-18	Salvation	Salvation: From a religion to a relationship	9-313	107
7-18	Backsliding	Warning: Backsliding does not happen suddenly	9-111	6

TOPICAL INDEX

Topical Index

Subject		Scripture	Page
Abortion			
9-101	Satan's attempt to destroy the church	Eph.2:19-22	1
Absolution (See Forgiveness)			
Access to God			
9-102	Access to God: Through Christ alone	Eph.2:11-18	1
9-103	The folly of false gods	Eph.3:1-13	2
9-104	Man has no power by himself	Col.2:20-23	2-3
9-105	Practicing the presence of God	Gal.1:17-24	3
Accounting (See Justification)			
Adoption into God's Family (See Assurance)			
9-106	Adoption by God	Eph.1:3-7	3-4
9-107	The security of being adopted into God's family	Gal.4:1-7	4
Adult (See Maturity)			
Adversary (See Satan)			
Advocate (See Christ, Jesus)			
Agreement (See Covenant; Peace; Reconciliation; Unity)			
Alcoholism (See Drunkenness)			
Allegiance (See Faithfulness)			
Almighty (See Christ, Jesus)			
Alpha and Omega (See Christ, Jesus)			
Altar (See Sacrifice)			
Amen (See Christ, Jesus)			
Ancestors (See Parenting)			
Angel of Light (See Satan)			
Anger			
9-108	Consequence of anger	Eph.4:25-32	5
Anointed One (See Christ, Jesus)			
Apocalypse (See Revelation)			
Apostasy (See Backsliding; Faithfulness)			
Appreciation (See Thankfulness)			
Arrogance (See Pride)			

SUBJECT		SCRIPTURE	PAGE
Ascension (See Christ, Jesus)			
Assembly (See Church)			
Assurance (See Faith; Heaven; Hope; Security)			
Astrology (See Occult)			
Atoning Blood - Atonement (See Christ, Jesus; Justification; Redemption; Sacrifice; Salvation; Sin)			
Attitude (See Rejoicing)			
Authority (See Power)			
Backbiting (See Tongue)			
Backsliding (See Faithfulness)			
9-109	Freedom from worldly attachments	Gal.5:7-12	5
9-110	The critical need to set up familiar spiritual landmarks	Gal.4:8-11	5-6
9-111	Warning: Backsliding does not happen suddenly	Col.4:7-18	6
Battle (See War)			
Bearing Testimony (See Witness)			
Beelzebub (See Satan)			
Beginning (See Creation)			
Behavior (See Walk)			
Belief (See Faith; Trust)			
Beloved Son (See Christ, Jesus)			
Benediction (See Prayer)			
Benevolence (See Giving; Mercy)			
Bible (See Access to God; Law; Word of God)			
Birth (See Creation)			
Birthright (See Inheritance)			
Blood of Christ (See Cross; Redemption)			
Blots Out (See Forgiveness)			
Body of Christ (See Church)			
Bond (See Covenant)			

Subject		Scripture	Page
Bondage			
9-112	Allowing the power of the cross to set you free	Gal.4:1-7	7
9-113	Forced to surrender unconditionally	Gal.5:16-21	7
Book of Law (See Word of God)			
Born Again (See New Man)			
Bought (See Redemption)			
Branch (See Christ, Jesus)			
Bravery (See Courage)			
Bread of Life (See Christ, Jesus)			
Bride (See Church; Marriage)			
Brotherly Love (See Mercy; Unity)			
Burdens			
9-114	Carrying burdens in your own strength	Col.1:1-2	8
Burnout (See Service)			
9-115	Serving for the right reasons	Phil.1:1-2	8
Call of God			
9-116	"I Surrender All"	Eph.1:1-2	9
Calmness (See Anger; Peace)			
Captivity (See Bondage)			
Celebration (See Rejoicing)			
Certainty (See Trust)			
Chains (See Bondage)			
Changed Life			
9-117	A changed life in the political arena	Gal.1:10-16	9-10
9-118	Only the gospel can make a difference	Gal.2:1-10	10
Charity (See Giving; Mercy)			
Chastity (See Pure)			
Chief Shepherd (See Christ, Jesus)			
Childish (See Maturity)			
Choice (See Will)			

	SUBJECT	SCRIPTURE	PAGE
Christ, Jesus			
9-119	Christ holds everything together	Col.1:16-17	10
9-120	Count your blessings	Col.1:12-14	11
9-121	Christ, the express image of God	Col.1:15	11
9-122	Christ: The Reconciler of all things	Col.1:20-23	12
9-123	Christ has freed the believer from the law's power	Gal.5:1-6	12
9-124	Christ was right on time	Gal.4:1-7	13
9-125	Hidden with Christ	Col.3:1-4	13
9-126	Christ's work on the cross	Gal.1:1-5	13
9-127	Keeping our focus on Christ	Col.1:15	14
9-128	Christ must be the Head of the church	Col.1:18-19	14
9-129	Christ's perfection is all we need	Col.1:16-17	14-15
9-130	Christ will stand in for the believer	Col.2:20-23	15
9-131	Christ: The curse-breaker	Gal.3:6-14	15-16
9-132	The great mystery of Christ	Eph.3:1-13	16
9-133	Why Christ had to come	Gal.4:1-7	16-17
Christian Calling (See Call)			
Christian Example (See Witness - Witnessing)			
9-134	Becoming a living example of faith	Gal.1:17-24	17
Christian Life (See Salvation; Walk)			
9-135	Being identified as a follower of Christ	Col.1:3-8	18
9-136	How to win the vicious battle within	Gal.5:13-15	18
9-137	The Christian life: Your best defense	Gal .2:1-10	18-19
9-138	Put off the garments of the old man	Eph.4:25-32	19
9-139	Risen with Christ	Col.3:1-4	19
9-140	The need to persevere	Phil.2:12-18	20
9-141	Tug of war: The struggle between the flesh and the Spirit	Gal.5:16-21	20-21
9-142	Working out your own salvation	Phil.2:12-18	21
Church (See Missions)			
9-143	God: The Light of the church	Eph.2:19-22	21
9-144	Keeping Christ as the Head of the church	Col.1:18-19	22
9-145	The marks of a great Christian church	Phil.1:27-30	22
9-146	The marks of a healthy church	Phil.1:1-2	23
Citizenship (See Heaven)			
9-147	Citizenship in the kingdom of heaven	Eph.2:19-22	23-24
Clean - Cleanliness (See Pure)			
Clergy (See Ministry)			
Commandments (See Word of God)			
Commit (See Trust)			
Commitment (See Service)			
9-148	The marks of a great Christian believer	Phil.1:20-26	24
9-149	Signs of reduced commitment	Phil.2:25-30	24-25
9-150	Trusting God in difficult circumstances	Phil.2:25-30	25

Subject		Scripture	Page
Communication			
9-151	Duty: Do not guess about the truth—know it	Col.1:15	25
9-152	Duty: Know the language of heaven	Col.3:1-4	25-26
9-153	Warning: Do not tune out God's messages	Eph.5:1-7	26
Communion (See Fellowship)			
Compassion (See Mercy)			
9-154	Need for compassion	Phil.2:1-4	26-27
Complete (See Maturity)			
Conceit (See Pride)			
Condemnation (See Salvation)			
Confidence (See Trust)			
Conformity (See Obedience)			
Congregation (See Church)			
Consecration (See Service)			
Considerate (See Gentleness)			
Consistency (See Walk)			
Conviction (See Faith; Security)			
Cornerstone (See Christ, Jesus)			
9-155	Jesus Christ, the Sure Foundation	Eph.2:19-22	27
Corruption (See Integrity; Sin)			
9-156	Fighting off corruption with the truth	Gal.5:7-12	27
Counselor (See Christ, Jesus; Mentoring)			
Courage (See Patience; Trust)			
9-157	Man who was not a quitter	Phil.2:25-30	28
Courtesy (See Gentleness)			
Covenant			
9-158	God's unchanging promise	Gal.3:15-18	28-29
9-159	The integrity of keeping a promise	Gal.3:15-18	29
Cowardice (See Courage)			
Creation			
9-160	God takes delight in His creation: The believer	Gal.3:23-29	29-30
9-161	Creation: Not an accident	Col.1:16-17	30

SUBJECT		SCRIPTURE	PAGE
Creator (See Christ, Jesus)			
Cross (See Christ, Jesus; Pride; Redemption)			
9-162	The cross keeps us on course	Gal.1:10-16	30-31
9-163	All direction comes from the cross	Gal.6:11-18	31
9-164	The purpose of the cross	Gal.2:11-21	31-32
Cruelty (See Compassion; Mercy)			
Debauchery (See Drunkenness)			
Decalogue (See Law; Word of God)			
Deceit (See Tongue; Truth)			
Deceiver (See Satan)			
Decision (See Will)			
Defense (See Security)			
Delight (See Joy)			
Deliverance (See Bondage; Redemption; Salvation)			
Deliverer (See Christ, Jesus)			
Demon(s) (See Satan)			
Design of God (See Purpose of God)			
Desire (See Hope)			
Despair (See Hope; Joy)			
Determination (See Perseverance)			
Devil (See Satan)			
Devotion(s) (See Faithfulness; Love; Prayer)			
Discipleship (See Mentoring)			
Discipline			
9-165	Focus on things above	Phil.2:1-4	32
9-166	Focusing on the prize	Phil.3:4-16	33
Disclosure (See Revelation)			
Discord (See Unity)			
Dishonesty (See Honesty)			

Subject		Scripture	Page
Disobedience (See Morality; Obedience; Sin)			
9-167	Disobedience: The path to self-destruction	Eph.2:1-3	33
Disorder (See Peace)			
Disruption (See Peace)			
Distrust (See Faith)			
Divination (See Occult)			
Divinely Inspired (See Word Of God)			
Divorce (See Marriage)			
Doubt (See Faith)			
Drunkenness			
9-168	God's amazing power to deliver	Eph.5:15-21	34
9-169	Drunkenness: Disease or desire?	Eph.5:15-21	34
Duty (See Service; Work)			
Emotions (See Heart)			
Encouragement (See Joy)			
9-170	Compassion: The arm of encouragement	Phil.1:3-11	35
9-171	Receiving signals from the Lord	Phil.2:1-4	35
Endurance (See Patience)			
Enslavement (See Bondage)			
Estate (See Inheritance)			
Eternal Life (See Salvation)			
Eternity (See Heaven)			
Ethics (See Righteousness)			
Evangelism (See Witness - Witnessing)			
9-172	Staying sensitive to the needs of the lost	Col.4:2-6	35-36
9-173	Keeping alert for "hidden people"	Gal.2:1-10	36
Everlasting Father (See Christ, Jesus)			
Evil One (Spirit) (See Satan; Sin)			
Exhortation (See Ministry)			
Expect (See Hope)			
Expiation (See Redemption; Sacrifice)			

SUBJECT		SCRIPTURE	PAGE
Exultation (See Joy; Rejoicing)			
Fairness (See Honesty)			
Faith (See Hope; Justification; Obedience; Salvation; Trust)			
9-174	Need for a relationship with Christ	Phil.3:4-16	37
9-175	The comfort of faith	Phil.1:12-19	37
9-176	The great benefit of struggling	Gal.3:1-5	37-38
9-177	The meaning of being "in Christ"	Gal.3:23-29	38
9-178	Trust the Lord to show the way	Gal.3:23-29	38
9-179	What faith must be	Gal.3:23-29	38-39
Faithfulness (See Truth)			
9-180	Faithful even unto death	Col.4:7-18	39
9-181	Being faithful where Christ puts you	Eph.6:21-24	39-40
9-182	Christian soldiers serve eternally	Eph.6:21-24	40
False Teachers			
9-183	Warning: Beware of false teachers!	Phil.3:1-3	40-41
False Teaching			
9-184	A commitment to quality	Gal.3:1-5	41
9-185	Beware the advances of wolves	Gal.1:6-9	41-42
9-186	Protecting the gospel	Gal.1:6-9	42
9-187	Keeping your heart in tune with Christ	Gal.2:1-10	42-43
9-188	Why is false teaching so appealing?	Col.2:1-7	43
Father (See Parenting)			
Father of Lies (See Satan)			
Favor (See Grace)			
Fear - Fearlessness (See Courage)			
Feelings (See Heart)			
Fellowship (See Unity)			
9-189	The benefits of Christian fellowship	Phil.1:3-11	44
Fetters (See Bondage)			
Fight (See War)			
First Adam (See Christ, Jesus)			
Flock (God's) (See Church)			
Focus (See Discipline; Humility)			
Forbearance (See Anger; Patience)			

Subject		Scripture	Page
Force (See Power)			
Forgiveness (See Compassion; Grace; Mercy; Redemption; Restoration; Salvation; Sin)			
9-190	Christ has cleansed the believer's heart	Col.2:11-12	44
9-191	Forgiveness: The power to set people free	Col.3:12-14	44-45
9-192	Forgiveness sets us free from the past	Phil.3:4-16	45
9-193	Sins are remembered no more	Col.1:12-14	45
Forsaking God (See Fellowship)			
Foundation (See Christ, Jesus; Cornerstone)			
Freedom (See Bondage)			
Fretfulness (See Patience)			
Friendship (See Fellowship; Unity)			
Fullness of God			
9-194	Prayer is the method for being filled	Eph.3:14-21	46
Gate, The (See Christ, Jesus)			
Generosity (See Giving; Mercy)			
Gentleness			
9-195	Strength under control	Phil.4:1-5	46
Genuine (See Truth)			
Giving (See Money)			
9-196	Examine the strength of your giving	Phil.4:10-19	47
9-197	A spiritual checkup	Phil.4:10-19	47
9-198	Achieving contentment through giving	Phil.4:10-19	48
Gladness (See Joy)			
Gnashing of Teeth (See Wrath of God)			
God (See Christ, Jesus)			
Godliness (See Righteousness)			
Godly Examples			
9-199	Your example speaks volumes	Phil.3:17-21	48
God's Anger (See Wrath of God)			
God's People (See Church)			
Good News (See Gospel)			

SUBJECT		SCRIPTURE	PAGE
Good Shepherd (See Christ, Jesus)			
Goodness (See Integrity; Righteousness)			
Gospel (See Evangelism; False Teaching; Missions; Power; Salvation; Word of God)			
9-200	The soldier's shoes	Eph.6:10-20	48
Gossip (See Tongue)			
Grace (See Justification; Salvation)			
9-201	Bind your fate to the grace of God	Gal.6:11-18	49
9-202	The need for grace	Phil.1:1-2	49
9-203	The need for the Master Craftsman	Eph.2:8-10	49-50
Gratefulness (See Thankfulness)			
Great High Priest (See Christ, Jesus)			
Grief (See Joy)			
Groom (See Marriage)			
Guidance (See Light)			
Guiltless (See Pure)			
Happiness (See Joy; Rejoicing)			
Harmony (See Peace; Unity)			
Hatred (See Compassion)			
Head of the Church (See Christ, Jesus)			
Healed (See Forgiveness)			
Heart (See Mercy; Prayer; Sin)			
9-204	Must be empowered by the Holy Spirit	Col.3:15-17	50
Heaven (See Communication)			
9-205	Heaven: A customized place	Eph.1:19-23	51
9-206	The glorious benefits of heaven	Phil.1:27-30	51
9-207	This world is not home to the believer	Eph.6:21-24	52
9-208	Where will you spend eternity?	Phil.1:20-26	53
Heir of All Things (See Christ, Jesus)			
Helpfulness (See Encouragement; Service)			
Holiness (See Righteousness)			
Holy Ghost (See Holy Spirit)			

SUBJECT		SCRIPTURE	PAGE
Holy Scriptures (See Word of God)			
Holy Spirit			
9-209	Holy Spirit given as a pledge	Eph.1:8-14	53
9-210	The great blessings of God	Eph.1:8-14	54
Honesty			
9-211	Passing the examination of honesty	Gal.2:11-21	54
Honor (See Bondage; Honesty; Integrity; Righteousness)			
Hope (See Faith; Trust)			
9-212	Focused upon eternal life	Col.1:3-8	54-55
9-213	The believer's hope is in Christ alone, not in religion	Col.1:3-8	55
Hostility (See Anger)			
Humanity (See Man)			
Humbleness (See Humility)			
Humility (See Gentleness)			
9-214	Humility: Helps keep the focus on the gospel	Col.3:12-14	56
9-215	Qualifications for spiritual service	Gal.6:1-5	56
9-216	The example of Christ	Phil.2:5-11	57
9-217	Walking in the humility of Christ	Phil.2:5-11	57
I AM (See Christ, Jesus)			
Idolatry			
9-218	A warning to those who want to save their god	Gal.1:6-9	58
9-219	Living in the midst of idolatry	Gal.4:8-11	58-59
Ignorance (See Witness)			
Image of God (See Christ, Jesus)			
Immaculate (See Pure)			
Immanuel (See Christ, Jesus)			
Impatience (See Patience)			
Impiety (See Backsliding)			
Importance (See Priorities)			
Impure (See Pure)			
Imprisonment (See Bondage)			
Inheritance (See Redemption)			
9-220	Joint-heirs with Jesus Christ	Eph.1:8-14	59-60

SUBJECT		SCRIPTURE	PAGE
Iniquity (See Sin)			
Inner Strength (See Patience)			
Innocent (See Pure)			
Insecurity (See Security)			
Insight (See Judgment)			
Inspiration (See Encouragement)			
Instruction (See Discipline; Law; Mentoring)			
Integrity (See Honesty; Truth)			
9-221	Placing the greatest value on the truth	Gal.4:12-20	60
Invocation (See Prayer)			
Jehovah (See Christ, Jesus)			
Jesus Christ (See Christ, Jesus)			
Job (See Work)			
Joy (See Encouragement; Rejoicing)			
9-222	Concern for one another's joy	Phil.2:1-4	60
Judgment (See Mercy)			
9-223	Judgment for those who live by the flesh	Gal.5:16-21	61
9-224	You can not hide from God	Phil.2:5-11	61
Justice (See Judgment)			
Justification (See Salvation)			
9-225	A life that affects the total person	Gal.3:15-18	62
9-226	Justification by faith in Christ alone	Gal.2:11-21	62-63
Keeper (See Watchman)			
Kindness (See Compassion; Mercy)			
King, The (See Christ, Jesus)			
Kingdom (See Church)			
Knowledge (See Assurance)			
Knowledge of God			
9-227	Having a passion for Christ	Eph.3:14-21	63
9-228	The need for the knowledge of God	Eph.1:15-18	63
9-229	Overcoming all distractions	Eph.1:15-18	64

Subject		Scripture	Page
Labor (See Work)			
Lamb (Of God) (See Christ, Jesus)			
Lamp (See Word of God)			
Language (See Tongue)			
Law (See Word of God)			
9-230	How the law reveals sin	Gal.3:19-22	64-65
9-231	The law: Intimidating but powerless	Gal.3:19-22	65
9-232	The law: Lacks the power to grant eternal life	Gal.3:19-22	65-66
9-233	The law serves as a tyrant	Gal.5:1-6	66
9-234	No man can break the law of gravitation	Gal.3:19-22	66-67
9-235	No man can keep the Law	Col.2:13-15	67
Laziness (See Perseverance)			
Legacy (See Inheritance)			
Legalism			
9-236	Legalism stunts your growth	Gal.4:21-31	68
Liar(s) (See Truth)			
Liberate (See Redemption)			
Lie (See Truth)			
Life (See Man)			
Light (of the Word) (See Christ, Jesus)			
9-237	Light awakens the sleeping	Eph.5:8-14	68
9-238	Light overcomes darkness	Eph.5:8-14	68-69
Lion of the Tribe of Judah (See Christ, Jesus)			
Litany (See Prayer)			
Lord (of All; of Glory; of Lords) (See Christ, Jesus)			
Love (See Sacrifice)			
9-239	The love of God	Eph.3:14-21	69
Lowliness (See Humility; Pride)			
Loyalty (See Faithfulness)			
Lucifer (See Satan)			
Lying (See Tongue)			
Magic (See Occult)			

SUBJECT		SCRIPTURE	PAGE
Man - Mankind			
9-240	Unsaved man's hatred for God	Col.1:20-23	70
Man of Sorrows (See Christ, Jesus)			
Manliness (See Courage)			
Marriage			
9-241	Sacrificial love	Eph.5:22-33	70
9-242	Biblical submission in marriage	Col.3:18-21	70-71
9-243	Keeping marriage vows	Eph.5:22-33	71
9-244	Protecting a marriage with hedges	Eph.5:22-33	72
9-245	Protecting your marriage	Col.3:18-21	72-73
9-246	The need to cleave to Christ	Eph.5:22-33	74
9-247	The truth was never known	Col.1:15	74
Master (See Christ, Jesus)			
Maturity			
9-248	The key to maturity	Eph.3:14-21	75
9-249	The true measure of maturity	Phil.1:3-11	75
Meekness (See Gentleness; Humility; Patience; Pride)			
Mentoring			
9-250	Ministering together	Gal.6:6-10	75
9-251	The joy of shared ministry	Gal.6:6-10	76
Mercy - Mercifulness (See Compassion; Forgiveness; Grace; Prayer; Restoration; Salvation; Sin)			
9-252	Getting what you do not deserve	Eph.2:4-7	76-77
9-253	Putting feet on your prayers by granting mercy	Col.3:12-14	77
Message (See Word of God)			
Messiah (See Christ, Jesus)			
Might (See Power)			
Mildness (See Gentleness)			
Mind of God (See Will of God)			
Ministry (See Service; Spiritual Gifts)			
9-254	Ministry to other believers	Eph.1:1-2	78
9-255	Receiving the ministry of other ministers	Gal.4:12-20	78-79
9-256	The goal: To present every man perfect in Christ	Col.1:24-29	79
9-257	The requirements of ministry	Phil.2:19-24	79-80
Miracle(s)			
9-258	When God does the impossible	Gal.3:1-5	80-81

Subject	Scripture	Page
Misbehave (See Sin)		
Missions (See Will)		
9-259 The subtle trap of materialism	Eph.1:8-14	81
Modesty (See Humility; Pride; Pure)		
Money (See Stewardship)		
9-260 Control of money	Ph.4:10-19	81-82
Morality (See Sin; Disobedience; Pure)		
9-261 Example of Christian leaders	Eph.5:1-7	82-83
Morning Star (See Christ, Jesus)		
Mortality (See Man)		
Mother (See Parenting)		
Mourning (See Joy)		
Nerve (See Courage)		
New Man		
9-262 Exhortation: Don't go back to the old	Eph.4:25-32	83
9-263 Putting on the new man	Eph.4:17-24	83
Obedience (See Gentleness; Prayer; Righteousness; Trust; Work)		
9-264 Is the grass really greener on the other side?	Gal.5:13-15	84
9-265 Listening to the Umpire of your soul	Gal.5:7-12	84-85
9-266 Obedience: No negotiations with God	Phil.3:1-3	85
9-267 To the voice of God	Col.2:16-19	85-86
Observance (See Obedience)		
Occult (See Satan)		
9-268 Warning: Avoid attraction to horoscopes	Col.2:8-10	86
Offend (See Sin)		
Offering (See Sacrifice)		
Old Testament (See Law)		
Omnipotence (See Power)		
Oneness (See Unity)		
Only Begotten Son (See Christ, Jesus)		
Oppress (See Burdens)		

Subject		Scripture	Page
Oracles (See Word of God)			
Order (See Discipline; Peace)			
Pardon (See Forgiveness; Grace; Mercy; Restoration; Salvation)			
Parenting			
9-269	Building a relationship with children	Eph.6:1-4	86-87
9-270	God's design for the world	Eph.6:1-4	87
9-271	Training a child to obey willingly	Eph.6:1-4	88
Pastoral Care (See Ministry)			
Patience (See Anger; Courage)			
9-272	Example of patience	Col.3:12-14	88
Peace (See Rejoicing; War)			
9-273	The value of peace	Phil.4:1-5	89
9-274	Holding on to the peace of God	Phil.4:6-9	89
9-275	Do you argue with peace?	Col.3:15-17	89
Peace of Mind (See Security)			
Penance (See Sacrifice)			
Pentateuch (See Law)			
People (See Man)			
People of God (See Church)			
Perfection (See Righteousness)			
Perseverance (See Faith; Patience)			
9-276	Pressing on: Guarding oneself	Phil.3:1-3	90
Petition (See Prayer)			
Piety (See Righteousness)			
Pity (See Compassion; Mercy)			
Pleasure (See Will)			
Pledge (See Covenant)			
Portion (See Inheritance)			
Position in Christ			
9-277	The believer's place	Eph.2:4-7	90
Positive Thinking			
9-278	The habit of right thinking	Phil.4:6-9	90-91

SUBJECT		SCRIPTURE	PAGE
Power			
9-279	Resurrection power needed to live the Christian life	Col.2:11-12	91
9-280	The power of the gospel	Gal.1:10-16	91-92
9-281	Warning: Do not run out of gas	Col.1:9-11	92
Power of Darkness			
9-282	Delivered from the power of darkness	Col.1:12-14	92
9-283	The gospel turns on the light	Col.1:12-14	93
9-284	The believer's spiritual struggle	Eph.6:10-20	93
Power of God			
9-285	A lack of the power of God	Eph.1:19-23	93-94
9-286	Concerning the resurrection	Eph.1:19-23	94
9-287	Prayer: The source of God's power	Eph.3:14-21	94-95
Prayer - Prayerfulness (See Heart; Mercy; Obedience; Patience)			
9-288	A strategic operation	Col.4:2-6	95
9-289	Praying for your pastor	Gal.4:12-20	95-96
9-290	Responsibility: To hear God's heart	Col.2:1-7	96
9-291	The Christian soldier's responsibility	Eph.6:10-20	97
9-292	The partnership of faith and prayer	Col.1:9-11	97-98
9-293	Getting what only God can do	Ph.4:6-9	98
Preaching (See Ministry)			
Precepts (See Word of God)			
Pregnancy (See Abortion)			
Pride			
9-294	Pride comes when the cross is forgotten	Gal.5:22-26	98
9-295	Wrongly taking credit	Col.2:20-23	99
Prince of Darkness (See Satan)			
Prince of Peace (See Christ, Jesus)			
Prince of This World (See Satan)			
Priorities (See Discipline)			
9-296	Doing the best things	Eph.1:15-18	99
Promise(s) (See Commitment; Covenant; Security; Word of God)			
Prophecy (See Revelation)			
Protection (See Security; Security)			
Provoke (See Anger)			
Psychic (See Occult)			

SUBJECT		SCRIPTURE	PAGE
Purchase (See Redemption)			
Pure - Purity (See Morality)			
9-297	How to be pure	Phil.2:12-18	99
Purpose of God			
9-298	God wants to show believers His grace	Eph.2:4-7	100
Rage (See Anger; Wrath of God)			
Ransomed (See Redemption - Redeemed; Forgiveness)			
Reality (See Truth)			
Rebellion (See Disobedience)			
Reconciliation (See Peace; Salvation)			
9-299	Conditional reconciliation	Col.1:20-23	100-101
9-300	Getting a second chance at life	Gal.1:17-24	101
Redemption - Redeemed - Redeemer (See Christ, Jesus; Forgiveness; Sacrifice; Salvation; Sin)			
9-301	Redemption is expensive, but Christ paid it all	Eph.1:3-7	101-102
Refuge (See Security)			
Regeneration (See New Man; Pure; Salvation)			
Regression (See Backsliding)			
Rejoicing (See Peace)			
9-302	Rejoicing keeps the right perspective	Phil.3:1-3	102
9-303	Radiating joy	Phil.4:1-5	102-103
Release (See Redemption)			
Reliance (See Faith)			
Religion (See Faith; Salvation)			
Remembered No More (See Forgiveness)			
Remission (See Forgiveness)			
Renewal (See Restoration)			
Repentance (See Salvation)			
Request (See Prayer)			
Rest (See Work)			
Restitution (See Restoration)			

Subject	Scripture	Page
Restoration (See Reconciliation)		
9-304 The healing results of spiritual surgery	Gal.6:1-5	103
9-305 They shoot their wounded	Gal.6:1-5	104
Resurrection (See Power)		
Resurrection, The (See Christ, Jesus)		
Return of Christ		
9-306 Focus upon the return of Christ	Phil.3:17-21	104
Revelation (See Law)		
9-307 Understanding the mind of God with the human mind is futile	Eph.3:1-13	104-105
Righteous One (See Christ, Jesus)		
Righteousness (See Integrity; Justification; Morality)		
9-308 Having a hunger for righteousness	Phil.3:4-16	105
9-309 The blessings of having Christ's righteousness	Phil.3:4-16	106
Rock (See Christ, Jesus)		
Ruler of the Kingdom of the Air (See Satan)		
Sacrifice		
9-310 Giving all	Eph.5:1-7	106
Saints (See Church)		
Salvation (See Christian Life; Grace; Missions; Redemption; Security; Will of God)		
9-311 A confident assurance of salvation	Phil 1:12-19	106
9-312 An experience with Jesus Christ	Gal.3:1-5	107
9-313 Salvation: From a religion to a relationship	Col.4:7-18	107
9-314 Lost in space	Eph.2:11-18	108
9-315 Man cannot add one thing to salvation	Gal.5:1-6	108-109
9-316 The helmet of salvation - staying focused	Eph.6:10-20	109
Satan (See Occult)		
9-317 A dangerous foe not to be ignored	Col.2:13-15	109-110
9-318 How to fight Satan	Eph.6:10-20	110
9-319 Warning: Do not dabble with Satan	Col.2:16-19	110
Satisfaction (See Redemption; Restoration)		
Savior (See Christ, Jesus; Sin)		
Scripture(s) (See Law; Word of God)		
Seated in the Heavenlies (See Position in Christ)		

SUBJECT		SCRIPTURE	PAGE
Security			
9-320	Christ is the Solid Rock	Col.2:8-10	111
9-321	God has a firm grip on your life	Gal.4:21-31	111
Seek God (See Prayer)			
Self-love (See Pride)			
Separation (See Fellowship)			
Serpent (See Satan)			
Service - Servitude (See Bondage; Burnout; Commitment; Ministry; Spiritual Gifts; Work)			
9-322	Qualifications of a servant	Col.4:7-18	112
9-323	The challenge of service	Phil 1:20-26	112
9-324	The foundation of Christian service	Gal.1:1-5	112-113
9-325	The richest reward is in helping others	Gal.5:13-15	113
9-326	What would Jesus do?	Phil.2:1-4	113
9-327	The wrong motivation	Col.2:20-23	114
9-328	Learning to serve as number two	Phil.2:19-24	114
Setting Free (See Redemption)			
Severance (See Unity)			
Sharing (See Fellowship)			
Sign from Heaven (See Revelation)			
Signs (See Miracle)			
Sin (See Disobedience; Morality; Salvation)			
9-329	A lifetime of sin	Eph.2:1-3	115
9-330	Worse for believers to sin	Col.3:5-11	115
Sincerity (See Truth)			
Sinless (See Pure)			
Sojourners (See Walk)			
Son (of David; of God; of the Most High; of Man) (See Christ, Jesus)			
Sonship (See Adoption)			
Sorcery (See Occult)			
Spiritism (See Occult)			
Spiritual Adultery (See Corruption)			

SUBJECT		SCRIPTURE	PAGE
Spiritual Blessings			
9-331	The spiritual blessings of God	Eph.1:3-7	116
9-332	Partaking of Christ's spiritual blessings	Eph.1:3-7	116

Spiritual Death (See Sin)

Spiritual Food (See Word of God)

Spiritual Gifts (See Ministry)			
9-333	The need to share	Eph.4:7-16	116-117
9-334	The results of spiritual gifts	Eph.4:7-16	117-118
9-335	The search for significance	Eph.4:7-16	118

Spiritual Ignorance (See Word of God)

Spotless (See Pure)

Steadfastness (See Faithfulness; Patience; Perseverance)

Stewardship (See Money)

Strength (See Power)

Strife (See Unity)

Subject To (See Bondage)

Submission (See Humility; Marriage)

Substitution (See Christ, Jesus)

Sufferings (See Christ, Jesus)

Supernatural (See Occult)

Support (See Encouragement)

Sword of the Spirit (See Word of God)

Teaching (See Mentoring)

Tempter (See Satan)

Ten Commandments (See Law)

Tenderness (See Compassion; Gentleness)

Terror (See Courage)

Testimony (See Witness)

SUBJECT		SCRIPTURE	PAGE
Thankfulness			
9-336	Appreciation for God and for fellow Christians	Phil.4:20-23	118
9-337	How to be thankful	Phil.1:3-11	119
Timidity (See Courage)			
Tongue, The (See Witness - Witnessing)			
9-338	Danger of poisoned words	Col.3:5-11	119
9-339	Have a ready witness on your tongue	Col.4:2-6	120
9-340	The need to control the tongue	Phil.2:12-18	120
Transfiguration (See Christ, Jesus)			
Transgression (See Sin)			
Trespass (See Sin)			
Trust (See Courage; Faith; Hope; Security)			
9-341	Need to follow God's order	Eph.5:1-7	121
9-342	Place your trust in Christ, not in man	Gal.6:1-5	121
9-343	Trust In God	Ph.1:27-30	122
Truth (See Integrity; Word of God)			
9-344	Speak the truth	Eph.4:25-32	122
Turning Away (or Back) (See Backsliding)			
Uncontaminated (See Pure)			
Uncovering (See Revelation)			
Undefiled (See Pure)			
Understanding (See Judgment)			
Unfaithfulness (See Faithfulness)			
Unity (See Fellowship)			
9-345	A strong church is a united church	Phil.2:1-4	122
9-346	Example of unity	Ph.4:20-23	123
9-347	Ignoring the petty things that divide believers	Gal.3:23-29	123-124
9-348	The benefit of unity	Ph.2:19-24	124
Uprightness (See Obedience; Righteousness)			
Vengeance (See Wrath of God)			
Virgin (See Pure)			
Virtue (See Honesty; Integrity; Morality)			
Vocation (See Call of God)			
Volition (See Will)			

SUBJECT		SCRIPTURE	PAGE
Vows (See Covenant)			
Walk - Walking (See Witness - Witnessing)			
9-349	Father's example to son	Eph.5:15-21	124-125
9-350	A fragrant walk	Col.2:1-7	125
9-351	A life consumed by the things of God	Col.1:9-11	125-126
9-352	A lost art	Eph.4:1-6	126
9-353	Drawing the line	Gal.5:13-15	127
9-354	Living a crucified life	Gal.5:22-26	127
9-355	Pressing on	Phil.1:1-2	128
9-356	Unity and peace: When walls fall down	Eph.4:1-6	128
9-357	The way to walk worthy	Eph.4:1-6	129
9-358	Walk bearing God's nature	Gal.5:22-26	129
9-359	Walk in the light	Eph.5:8-14	130
9-360	Why to walk worthy - mutual support	Eph.4:1-6	130
War			
9-361	A call to arms	Eph.6:10-20	130-131
Watchman (See Witness - Witnessing)			
9-362	Let your light shine	Col.2:8-10	131
Wedding (See Marriage)			
Weeping (See Joy)			
Wicked (See Righteousness; Sin)			
Will (See Missions)			
9-363	Doing all of the will of God	Eph.1:8-14	131
9-364	Understanding God's will	Eph.5:15-21	132
Will of God			
9-365	Are you willing for His will?	Gal.6:6-10	132
9-366	Equipped to do God's will	Col.1:1-2	133
Wisdom (See Judgment; Light; Tongue; Truth; Word of God)			
Witchcraft (See Occult)			
Witness - Witnessing (See Christian Example; Evangelism; Tongue; Walk - Walking; Watchman; Work)			
9-367	Being an approachable witness	Phil.3:17-21	133
9-368	Conviction to be a good witness	Col.1:3-8	134
9-369	Impacting those who watch you	Eph.4:17-24	134
9-370	Making the most of every moment	Gal.1:1-5	134-135
9-371	The challenge to witness	Phil.4:20-23	135
9-372	The fruit of your witness	Gal.1:1-5	136
9-373	The marks of a mature witness	Phil.1:12-19	136
9-374	The qualifications for witness	Phil.2:12-18	137
9-375	Win the soul-not the argument	Col.1:18-19	137
Wonders (See Miracle)			

SUBJECT		SCRIPTURE	PAGE
Word of God (See Christ, Jesus; Law)			
9-376	A book that changes the lives of those who read it	Gal.3:6-14	138
9-377	Devotion for the Word of God	Col.1:24-29	138
9-378	Stay connected to God's Word	Col.3:15-17	139
9-379	What would the world be like if there were no Bible?	Gal.3:6-14	139
Word, The (See Christ, Jesus)			
Words of Christ (See Word of God)			
Work (See Walk - Walking; Witness - Witnessing)			
9-380	As unto the Lord	Eph.6:5-9	140
9-381	Consequences of doing things man's way	Gal.4:21-31	140
9-382	Example of "Scrooge"	Col.3:22-4:1	141
9-383	Making Christianity practical at work	Eph.6:5-9	141
9-384	Reason why we work	Col.3:22-4:1	142
9-385	Spiritual significance of work	Eph.6:5-9	142-143
Workmanship, God's			
9-386	Fashioned by the Sculptor's hands	Eph.2:8-10	143
Worship (See Service)			
Worship of Idols (See Idolatry)			
Wrath (See Anger)			
Wrath of God (See Disobedience; Salvation; Sin)			
9-387	The fate of the rebellious sinner	Eph.2:1-3	144
Wrongdoing (See Sin)			

Acknowledgments

Every child of God is precious to the Lord and deeply loved. And every child as a servant of the Lord touches the lives of those who come in contact with him or his ministry. The writing ministries of the following servants have touched this work, and we are grateful that God brought their writings our way. We hereby acknowledge their ministry to us, being fully aware that there are so many others down through the years whose writings have touched our lives and who deserve mention, but the weaknesses of our minds have caused them to fade from memory. May our wonderful Lord continue to bless the ministries of these dear servants and the ministries of us all as we diligently labor to reach the world for Christ and to meet the desperate needs of those who suffer so much.

Acknowledgments and Bibliography

Arterburn, Stephen and Jack Felton. *Toxic Faith: Understanding & Overcoming Religious Addiction.* Nashville, TN: Oliver-Nelson Books, 1991.

Barclay, William. *The Letters to the Galatians and Ephesians.* Philadelphia, PA: Westminster Press, n.d.

Barna, George. *The Frog In The Kettle.* Venture, CA: Regal Books, 1990.

Barnhouse, Donald Grey. *Let Me Illustrate.* Grand Rapids, MI: Fleming H. Revell Company, 1967.

Bright, Dr. Bill. *Witnessing Without Fear.* San Bernadino, CA, Here's Life Publishers, 1987.

Briscoe, Stuart. *Everyday Discipleship for Ordinary People.* Wheaton, IL: Harold Shaw Publishers, 1988.

Bryant, David. *In the Gap.* Madison, WI: Inter-Varsity Missions, 1981.

Buckingham, Jamie. *Into the Glory.* Plainfield, NJ: Logos International, 1974.

Card, Michael. *That's What Faith Must Be.* Birdwing Music (a division of The Sparrow Corporation) and BMG Songs, Inc./Mole End Music (ASCAP), 1988.

Christianity Today. Carol Stream, IL: Christianity Today, Inc., 1991, 1993.

Colson, Charles and Jack Eckerd. *Why America Doesn't Work.* Dallas, TX: Word Publishing, 1991.

Cornwall, Judson. *Leaders Eat What You Serve.* Shippensburg, PA: Destiny Image Publishers, 1988.

Crabb, Dr. Lawrence J., Jr. *The Marriage Builder.* Grand Rapids, MI: Zondervan Publishing House, 1982.

Cymbala, Jim. From the article *"How To Light The Fire"* in *Leadership Journal.* Carol Stream, IL, Fall 1994.

Doan, Eleanor. *The Speaker's Sourcebook.* Grand Rapids, MI: Zondervan Publishing House, 1971.

Graham, Billy. *Peace With God.* Garden City, NY: Doubleday & Co., 1953.

Hester, Dennis J., Editor. *The Vance Havner Quote Book.* Grand Rapids, MI: Baker Book House, 1986.

Hughes, R. Kent. *Disciplines of a Godly Man.* Wheaton, IL: Crossway Books, 1991.

Hybles, Bill. *Honest to God?* Grand Rapids, MI: Zondervan Publishing House, 1990.

Jenkins, Jerry B. *Hedges - Loving Your Marriage Enough To Protect It.* Chicago, IL: Moody Press, 1989.

Knight, Walter B. *Knight's Master Book of 4,000 Illustrations.* Grand Rapids, MI: Eerdmans Publishing Company, 1956.

________. *Knight's Treasury of 2,000 Illustrations.* Grand Rapids, MI: Eerdmans Publishing Company, 1963.

________. *Three Thousand Illustrations for Christian Service.* Grand Rapids, MI: Eerdmans Publishing Company, 1971.

Larson, Craig B., Editor. *Illustrations for Preaching and Teaching.* Grand Rapids, MI: Baker Book House, 1993.

Leadership Journal. Carol Stream, IL: Christianity Today, Inc., 1994.

Lee, Robert. *Sourcebook of 500 Illustrations.* Grand Rapids, MI: Zondervan Publishing House, 1970.

Lehman, F. M. Nazarene Publishing House, 1945.

Logan, Robert. *Beyond Church Growth.* Grand Rapids, MI: Fleming H. Revell Company, 1989.

MacDonald, Gordon. *Rebuilding Your Broken World.* Nashville, TN: Oliver-Nelson Books, 1988.

Marshall, Peter and David Manuel. *The Light and the Glory.* Old Tappan, NJ: Fleming H. Revell Company, 1977.

McGee, J. Vernon. *Thru The Bible,* Vol.5. Nashville, TN: Thomas Nelson Publishers, 1983.

Morley, Pat. *The Rest Of Your Life.* Nashville, TN: Thomas Nelson Publishers, 1992.

________. *The Man in the Mirror.* Dallas, TX: Word Publishing, 1989.

Rice, John R. *Prayer: Asking and Receiving.* Murfreesboro, TN: Sword of the Lord Publishers, 1970.

Smalley, Gary and Dr. John Trent. *Giving The Blessing: Daily Thoughts On The Joy Of Giving.* Nashville, TN: Thomas Nelson Publishers, 1993.

Stanley, Charles. *How to Listen to God.* Nashville, TN: Oliver-Nelson Books, 1985.

Stott, John R. W. *Men Made New: An Exposition of Romans 5-8.* Grand Rapids, MI: Baker Book House, 1978.

Strauss, Lehman. *Devotional Studies in Philippians.* Neptune, NJ: Loizeaux Brothers, n.d.

________. *Galatians and Ephesians.* Neptune, NJ: Loizeaux Brothers, n.d.

Tan, Paul Lee. *Encyclopedia of 7,700 Illustrations: Signs of the Times.* Rockville, MD: Assurance Publishers, 1985.

White, William R. *Stories for the Journey.* Minneapolis, MN: Augsburg Publishing House, 1988.

Wiersbe, Warren W. *The Bible Exposition Commentary,* Vol.2. Wheaton, IL: Victor Books, 1989.

Wuest, Kenneth S. *Ephesians and Colossians.* "Word Studies in the Greek New Testament, " Vol.1. Grand Rapids, MI: Eerdmans Publishing Company, 1966.

Zettersten, Rolf. *Dr. Dobson: Turning Hearts Toward Home.* Dallas, TX: Word Publishing, 1989.

LEADERSHIP MINISTRIES WORLDWIDE

PURPOSE STATEMENT

LEADERSHIP MINISTRIES WORLDWIDE

exists to equip ministers, teachers, and laymen in their understanding, preaching and teaching of God's Word by publishing and distributing worldwide *The Preacher's Outline & Sermon Bible*™ and related ***Outline Bible*** materials, to reach & disciple men, women, boys and girls for Jesus Christ.

MISSION STATEMENT

1. To make the Bible so understandable - its truth so clear and plain - that men and women everywhere, whether teacher or student, preacher or hearer, can grasp its message and receive Jesus Christ as Savior, and . . .

2. To place the Bible in the hands of all who will preach and teach God's Holy Word, verse by verse, precept by precept, regardless of the individual's ability to purchase it.

THE GOSPEL IS FREE, BUT THE COST OF TAKING IT IS NOT

The ***Outline Bible*** materials have been given to LMW for printing and especially distribution worldwide at/below cost, by those who remain anonymous. One fact, however, is as true today as it was in the time of Christ:

LMW depends on the generous gift of believers with a heart for Him and a love for the lost. They help pay for printing, translating and distributing of ***Outline Bible*** materials into the hands of God's servants worldwide, who will present the Gospel message with clarity, authority and understanding beyond their own.

LMW was incorporated in the state of Tennessee in July 1992 and received IRS 501(c)(3) nonprofit status in March 1994. LMW is an international, nondenominational mission organization. All proceeds from USA sales, along with donations from donor partners, go 100% into underwriting our translation and distribution projects of ***Outline Bible*** materials to preachers, church and lay leaders, and Bible students around the world.

Leadership Ministries Worldwide

Publisher & Distributor of OUTLINE Bible *Materials*

Currently Available Materials, with New Volumes Releasing Regularly

- **The Preacher's Outline & Sermon Bible® — DELUXE EDITION** 3-Ring, looseleaf binder

Volume 1 . .St. Matthew I (chapters 1-15)
Volume 2 . .St. Matthew II (chapters 16-28)
Volume 3 . .St. Mark
Volume 4 . .St. Luke
Volume 5 . .St. John
Volume 6 . .Acts
Volume 7 . .Romans
Volume 8 . .1 & 2 Corinthians (1 volume)
Volume 9 . .Galatians, Ephesians, Philippians, Colossians (1 volume)
Volume 10 . .1 & 2 Thessalonians, 1 & 2 Timothy, Titus, Philemon (1 volume)
Volume 11 . . Hebrews -James (1 volume)
Volume 12 . . 1 & 2 Peter, 1,2 & 3 John, Jude (1 volume)
Volume 13 . . Revelation
Volume 14 . . Master Outline & Subject Index

FULL SET — 14 Volumes

- **The Preacher's Outline & Sermon Bible® — OLD TESTAMENT**

Volume 1 . . . Genesis I (chapters 1-11)
Volume 2 . . . Genesis II (chapters 12-50)
Volume 3 . . . Exodus I (chapters 1-18)
Volume 4 . . . Exodus II (chapters 19-40)
Volume 5 . . . Leviticus
Volume 6 . . . .Numbers
Volume 7 . . . .Deuteronomy
Volume 8 . . . .Joshua
Volume 9 . . . .Judges/Ruth

New volumes release periodically

- **The Preacher's Outline & Sermon Bible® — SOFTBOUND EDITION**
  Identical content as Deluxe. Lightweight, compact, and affordable for overseas & traveling
- **The Preacher's Outline & Sermon Bible® — 3 VOL HARDCOVER w/CD**
- **The Preacher's Outline & Sermon Bible® — NIV SOFTBOUND EDITION**
- **Practical Word Studies In the New Testament — 2 VOL HARDCOVER SET**
- **The Minister's Personal Handbook - *What the Bible Says . . . to the Minister***
  12 Chapters - 127 Subjects - 400 Verses OUTLINED - Paperback, Leatherette Deluxe
- **The Teacher's Outline & Study Bible™ • New Testament Books •**
  Complete 45 minute lessons - 4 months of studies/book - 200± pages; Student Journal
- **OUTLINE Bible Studies series: 10 Commandments - The Tabernacle**
- **CD-ROM: Preacher, Teacher, and Handbook- (Windows/STEP) - WORDSearch**
- **Translations of Preacher, Teacher, and Minister's Handbook: Limited Quantities**
  Russian - Spanish - Korean - Hindi - Telugu - Tamil - Chinese - German • *Future: French, Portuguese*

— Contact us for Specific Language Availability and Prices —

For quantity orders and information, please contact either:

Leadership Ministries Worldwide **or** *Your OUTLINE Bible Bookseller*
PO Box 21310 • Chattanooga, TN 37424-0310
(423) 855-2181 (9am - 5pm Eastern) • FAX (423) 855-8616 (24 hours)
E•Mail - info@outlinebible.org **FREE** Download Samples & 24 hr Orders: **www.outlinebible.org**

Equipping God's Servants Worldwide with OUTLINE Bible Materials
LMW is a nonprofit, international, nondenominational mission agency

Outline Bible Resources

This material, like similar works, has come from imperfect man and is thus susceptible to human error. We are nevertheless grateful to God for both calling us and empowering us through His Holy Spirit to undertake this task. Because of His goodness and grace, ***The Preacher's Outline & Sermon Bible*** ® New Testament is complete in 14 volumes, and the Old Testament volumes are releasing periodically.

The Minister's Handbook is available and OUTLINE Bible materials are releasing electronically on **POSB-CD** and our **Website**.

God has given the strength and stamina to bring us this far. Our confidence is that, as we keep our eyes on Him and grounded in the undeniable truths of the Word, we will continue working through the Old Testament volumes and the second series known as *The Teacher's Outline & Study Bible*™. The future includes helpful OUTLINE Bible books and **Handbook** materials for God's dear servants.

To everyone everywhere who preaches and teaches the Word, we offer this material first of all to Him in whose name we labor and serve, and for whose glory it has been produced.

Our daily prayer is that each volume will lead thousands, millions, yes even billions, into a better understanding of the Holy Scriptures and a fuller knowledge of Jesus Christ the incarnate Word, of whom the Scriptures so faithfully testify.

You will be pleased to know that a small portion of the purchase price has gone to underwrite and provide similar volumes in other languages (Russian, Korean, Spanish, and others yet to come). A preacher, pastor, teacher, layleader, or Bible student somewhere around the world will be more able to present God's message with clarity, authority, and understanding beyond his or her own power. *Amen.*

LEADERSHIP MINISTRIES WORLDWIDE

P.O. Box 21310 • Chattanooga, TN 37424-0310
(423) 855-2181 FAX (423) 855-8616
Email – info@outlinebible.org
www.outlinebible.org – ***FREE*** download materials